The Naked Truth About Men

(And Romance)

By

Kathryn Foster, Ph.D

Men, by and large, did not fair well in the evolutionary machine, as they cut off from their relational and emotional selves through centuries of killing animals, the silent stalking of prey, and combat. But when a woman is asked to make a man her primary source of love, affection, and emotional intimacy, she has to figure out what to do.

Rivercreek Publishing
Texas
2013

Kathryn Foster, Ph.D., is a psychologist in private practice in Fort Worth, Texas. With a masters degree in marriage and family counseling and a Ph.D. in psychology, she has practiced psychotherapy for 26 years. Especially for men, she has also written *What Women Want...Really!* Contact her through her website at www.kathrynfosterphd.com.

~~~~~~~

Other Books by Kathryn Foster:

Non-fiction:
*When Your Relationship Changes
(companion book to The Naked Truth About Men)*

Fiction:
Sessions: Memoirs of a Psychotherapist (a novel)
Finding My Way (a novel)
Mystery at the Secret River (for girls, 10-14 years)

The author of this book does not dispense medical or
psychological advice for any physical, emotional, relational,
or spiritual problems, either directly or indirectly. It is
recommended readers seek the more personal advice
of a physician or psychotherapist. The intent of the book is
only to offer information of a broad nature to assist readers in
their quest for well-being. In the event that the reader applies
information from this book personally, which is always one's
constitutional right, the author and publisher assume no
liability for these choices or outcomes.

Acknowledgements

My greatest gratitude goes to the hundreds of clients who were at their most genuine and vulnerable during sessions with me over the last 26 years. As they relinquished facades and pretenses, I learned.

The role of the psychologist is to provide a permissive space wherein a client can deeply explore her or his feelings, motivations, and thoughts. Each person enters therapy with attunement to certain emotions, a unique vocabulary by which to express her or his experience, and special awarenesses, all of which enrich the therapist's ability to do the same. I've been privileged to witness the courage and fortitude as clients grapple with their relationships. I've been with some through the ambiguity and pain that led to the hard decision to break up, and with others as they decided to live in greater tolerance, while still others turned their relationship around, often by revamping their expectations. My encounters with both genders as they tried to understand their romances will hopefully deepen this book.

Dawn Maybeck, MA, LPC, psychotherapist in Charlotte, North Carolina, lent her candor, sassiness, and emotional acuity as a critiquer of the manuscript. For her affirmations, I am indebted. As Dawn was reviewing the book, she saw a couple where the woman was dissatisfied with her guy. Dawn used the concepts in chapters 2–4 to explain men, which led to her female client changing her expectations. They were later seen kissing in the parking lot. The shift helped her accept him. I wish more couples more kissing. I sought Dawn's help because of her fundamental grasp on people and no-holds-barred frankness.

Barb Borschette, acupuncturist in Ft Worth, Texas, adamantly said two things: the book needed to be "out there" as soon as possible, and it needed to be shorter. To this, I decided to put the original into two books, the second called *When Your Relationship Ends*. The second book includes perspective and coping mechanisms for people whose relationships either end or change in another way.

Thank you to Kim Perrone, herbalist and acupuncturist who has healed me many times and supported my quest for what's true. We used muscle testing to find the veracity of some of the concepts in this book. If that idea interests you, you may want to read *Power vs. Force* by David Hawkins, M.D., Ph.D. He explains how to use kinesiology to measure truth.

Becky Login Ramirez meticulously edited the book, word by word. Life would have it that she was going through a divorce at the start of the editing and beginning a new relationship at the end. She says the book validated her feelings about what had gone on in her marriage. Later she said that knowing gender differences helped her approach her new relationship differently and to communicate more clearly because she'd become more adept at identifying her own feelings. I wish this for every reader.

Robyn O'Brien, the "book doctor," both edited and helped me with the hundred questions a person has when writing and publishing. She is a gentle and kind soul from whom it is easy to receive help. Robby Janitz answered the rest of my technical/computer questions and laughingly calls me "techno girl."

My daughter, Jessica Foster, sketched the front cover. Her acumen for knowing people led to the perfect portrayal. My life, beginning when she was age three, has always been enriched by her candid sketches of people.

Rich Abanes, Broadway actor and dancer/author/graphic designer, worked his magic on the cover picture.

I am also in debt to the men I've known throughout life. They have given me, as they do any woman, the greatest gift: the ability to define myself by comparison.

Table of Contents

Introduction

My intended audience for this book is the relationally adept, nuanced, mind-reading type of woman (composing 40-50% of the population of women) who is also frustrated in her romantic relationships. I outline her traits in Chapter 2, as contrasted to male "systemizers." The book is also for men who ask, alongside Sigmund Freud and Mel Gibson, "What do women want?" as well as those who wonder, "Why is the divorce rate so high?" Mainly, though, the book is aimed at revamping expectations of—and giving understanding to— romantic relationships.

So, my caveat is that this book won't relate much to women with masculinized brains who may not expect the same things from a relationship. Likewise, women in relationship with a man with a feminized brain may feel quite content in their unions. Even these situations can get complex, though. For instance, a woman who's conditioned herself to the male work world may still bring out her feminine brain when in a romance. Also, the guy with the feminized brain still has testosterone running through his veins, and as you'll see in Chapter III, testosterone affects how men relate.

You may identify with some of the stories presented throughout this book. In hopes of adding fresh truth, I've composited the experiences of hundreds of clients I've known over 26 years of doing psychotherapy. Names and identities have been changed and synthesized to protect their confidentiality.

Surprised

I think I've been surprised by men my whole life. And that's ok. I had a grad school professor who always said, "The human organism learns insofar as it is surprised." That is, the surprises have taught me, among other things, what's in this book.

Throughout my life, I've almost always been lucky enough to have a best girl friend. I could say anything to her and she would understand; she "got" me. Marriage, touted as the most intimate of relationships, was one of my biggest surprises. I married the right person, I believe, and know he's one of the more empathic kinds of guys, but the closeness was nothing like what I'd experienced with girl friends. I had dated a lot before marriage, but dating, I found, did little to prepare me for a long term relationship, which we'll discuss in Chapter I.

I was surprised, having been brought up by a father who held high expectations for me, by the limitations put on women when I entered the ministry. This was in the 70s and 80s, so no surprise there. While a father may revel in the high achievements of his daughter because she's "his," other men may find it a threat.

A sort of flower child from the Pacific Northwest, I vowed to adopt orphans rather than have my own children, since my generation grew up watching the overpopulation of our world with unease. Besides, I was passionate about my career. So when the doctor surprised me, saying I did not have the flu, but was instead three months pregnant, I was consternated. (Yes, I know.) Yet, six months later, on the delivery table, I was utterly amazed at the welling up of commitment, focus, and unqualified love streaming from me as I gave birth and how those motivating feelings capture me still.

I was surprised, as a marital therapist and psychotherapist, at how many women reflected my own experience of marriage and how men came from such a different set of motivations. There is nothing like the deep-listening of therapy to let you in on the true reality of the genders. This is, after all, the setting where men don't just mimic the politically correct postures of the day, but say what's actually true for them. It's also where women speak openly and candidly, no matter how their feelings may scare them. I have combined composite stories from clients along with the research, hoping to bring a depth to this book.

After a 22 year marriage and my divorce in 1996, I was again surprised at how good it felt to be free from the limitations of marriage. I tuned into myself in a way not possible since my single days in college. I still had three teenagers at home, but they didn't hinder my need to get inside myself in the way a husband did. I had automatically synced myself to his needs instead of my own.

Surprised again, I discovered through the pursuit of an attorney–rancher how satisfying it was to date, but still, to live alone. Taken back by how easy it was to find dates as a woman in her forties and then in her fifties, (what was that quote from *Sleepless in Seattle*? "It's easier to be killed by a terrorist than get married over the age of 40") I slowly came to understand that I wasn't really seeking marriage after all. I treasured my blossoming exploration of life in every way—spiritually, financially, and in terms of taking risks. Though I learned so much each time I entered the life of a new dating partner, I still treasured my doing-it-on-my-own-terms. Yet without those dating experiences, I would never have ridden a donkey, gone sky diving, chosen a jury, reconnected with the university setting, traveled around the United States, and learned to love swing dancing. Additionally, I gained an insider's view of the professions of each man I dated—quite an education—and learned the male perspective in a way not possible without close relationships.

And, in the spirit of full disclosure, I think I've always been boy crazy. It began with David, age 5. We held hands and shared our secrets walking to and from kindergarten. We loved each other. When it was time for him to leave me at my house each day, we would gently, softly kiss. And so, no doubt, my interests for the topics in this book began.

Simple Observations

I'm sitting in an Italian restaurant next to a male friend and we're both observing. At one table, there's a couple in their mid 30s. He's obviously come from work and she from caretaking their eight-year-old daughter, who's on spring break. He's aloof, wanting to be somewhere else, maybe drinking a beer and watching basketball with guy friends. She leans toward him, trying to engage him. With each attempt, we see a wave of pain washing over her. She's dressed up with makeup and jewelry, making herself beautiful for him.

At another table is a group of seven ladies—ranging from 30–45 years old—who appear to be taking a lunch break. Perhaps they meet monthly for lunch. At times, they laugh uproariously and at other times, they are silent, leaning in to hear a friend's disclosure, some tearing, making profound, empathic eye contact. As they reluctantly leave the restaurant and one another's company, they spontaneously hug. They are joyful.

I am surmising here, granted, as I observe, so I question my male friend about his observations. He sees what I see at the first table. He hates men, he tells me with a snarl.

"Me thinks thou doth protest too much," I tease.

"I know. I was like him, once," he laments, his eyes still glaring at the married guy. My friend is older now; his testosterone has gone down a bit. He feels sorry for the woman. He loves girls, he says.

Having practiced psychotherapy, including a lot of relationship therapy for almost three decades, I have had a lot of time to observe people in their relationships.

Language

Let's begin with language. The English language does not even give me a way to write this book. I squirm every time I come to using the word "he" when I really mean "human" or "person" and don't want to indicate gender or when I want to include both genders. What is that? We haven't even resolved that fundamental problem. We are forced to use fully patriarchal language. That biases us constantly. Until we change language, we cannot hope to overcome patriarchy. I considered using s/he, his/her, fe/male, and saying if someone has a better suggestion, let him/her speak up! Then I decided to, more often than not, just use feminine terms as an attempt to balance things out, though that leaves me apologetic to male readers. May the males, however, remember that, for centuries, women have had to transpose language addressed to men, so that the term "brothers" or "statesmen" referred to her, too.

Gender Differences

Our souls are wrapped in gender. How different does that make a woman from a man?

Consider this. We share most of our genes (95-98.4%) with the chimpanzee, or, if you look only at the active genes, 99.6 percent. That powerful .4% left over boosted humans from banana eaters to writers of prose, builders of skyscrapers, and organizers of the Red Cross.[1] So when someone says females and males share most the same genes, you can imagine there's still room for quite a difference. Both sexes have toes, noses, thyroid glands, and kidneys. Both paint, sing, think, laugh, and relate. Both can be lazy, energetic, ambitious, creative, and meditative. But something very different has shaped one sex compared to the other: killing. There is a transformative experience one gender goes through that the other cannot: childbirth.

The female–male genetic difference, however small, shows up in long—term romances. Having different vision cells (i.e., rods and cones), we actually see the world differently. We hear differently, are fundamentally motivated by different things, and even use our brains in different ways—especially when it comes to the use of feeling–language. Way back when, the differences between the genders were exacerbated by role division: men hunted and killed, women nurtured. But even if women had been given the role of animal killing, they still would have been more relational than men. The act of giving birth so changes a woman that her essential nature is to be relational.

For a long time, universities dared not explore the intriguing topic of male/female differences because it was politically incorrect. After all, feminism was fighting hard to prove that women and men were no different so that women would be given greater opportunity in the work world. We sometimes forget to pay homage to those on whose shoulders we now stand. Because progress was made, it is ok now to look at the differences. A myriad of books have come out on this topic. But this book turns to the question, "What perspective is most adaptive given what we now know?"

Divorce as a Sign

If it were just a cantankerous Susie and Johnny down the street who were breaking up, we could toss it off as personality problems. If it were men and women divorcing equally, we could think of it differently. But that isn't the case. Most divorces—a little over two-thirds—are brought about by women, many of whom are in the middle of raising children, and the divorce will mean going it alone and with less money. Almost all (90%) of divorces among college-educated couples are initiated by women.[2]

If the divorce rate were 10–20 percent, we could call divorces personal tragedies. But when it's 50–60 percent in the United States, we have to call it a cultural phenomenon. Divorces aren't anomalies; they've become a normal part of human life.

The Rise of Femininity

Women are having a problem with men in romantic relationships. Women wonder if they're alone in their frustrations with men. Perhaps the most striking statistic saying women are unhappy in relationships with men has to do with the high divorce rate among women with children. Of all categories, a mother, you would think, would make sacrifices to keep a live-in, committed partner, and legally bound at that. Though these women face the stigma of no other man wanting to take on their kids, facing, perhaps, no sex ever again, knowing they'll do the mounds of homework, cleaning, shopping, and breaking up sibling fights alone, not to mention maintaining their own work hours, they are, nevertheless, divorcing. They're that clear about how little the relationship gives them or how disempowering it feels.

The heterosexual drive rivets our attention to that sexy, sweet, strong guy and glues it into a heart-bond. A smart woman will still keep her wits about her enough to face basic facts about men. Because testosterone drives a guy toward activity and making him feel efficacious, he fears a woman will be a distraction in this feel-good pursuit. Because he loves to zero in on the function of things and various systems, he cultivates objectivity and distance. He keeps his distance, only allowing himself to get so close, allotting the relationship a limited amount of time, so that his real drive in life, his own accomplishments, can be fulfilled. Testosterone does not cause him to put a relationship ahead of everything in the way that oxytocin does for a woman. This is the bottom-line truth women must face. When a man beams his attention on you, it is wonderful, but it is temporary, or, at best, off and on.

In truth, today's woman doesn't need Cinderella's prince to change her life; she can change it herself. But our nervous systems are still primed to seek a one-and-only to lean on. A potent hormonal cocktail (more on that later) tantalizes us for the first 12–18 months of a new romance, keeping the imagination and hope of women percolating. But something new is on the horizon.

One age is dying and a new age is birthing. The old is patriarchy, the new is egalitarianism. It has been a long labor. It is about the emergence of the feminine spirit. Long squelched, she is rising, but only insofar as she recreates her expectations of men and romantic relationships.

Part I: The Truth about Men

Chapter 1:
Expectations

...Laila learned that boys differed from girls in this regard. They didn't make a show of friendship. They felt no urge, no need, for this sort of talk. Laila imagined it had been this way for her brothers too. Boys, Laila came to see, treated friendship the way they treated the sun: its existence undisputed; its radiance best enjoyed, not beheld directly."

—*A Thousand Splendid Suns*[3]

Susan, nine, ambles up to her grandmother's back porch, taking the steps by twos, and eagerly embraces her grandmother who meets her at the door. Then she runs through the kitchen and down the hallway, calling, "Kendra! I'm here!" Her cousin, just seven months older, emerges from the back bedroom and they smile brightly and hug. They shut the door and, for hours, share memories and feelings and stories. Thus begins a girl's summer vacation.

The closeness the two girls share, filled with disclosures and intimate talk, brings meaning and satisfaction to their young lives. They share everything—from the details of their relationship with their parents to how they feel about their classes. They dream about their future careers and romances. Nothing is held back. They are fully genuine with one another. They hide out from their male cousins, seeing their rough-housing, slapstick humor, and loudness as immature.

Once puberty hits, their urgency to share grows and Susan and Kendra feel the exciting warmth of, together, figuring boys out. They giggle into the night, analyzing the mysterious, frustrating, and tantalizing opposite gender.

And then, years later, it happened. Susan noticed Josh staring at her in class in their third year of law school. He was handsome, well-liked, and smart. They both played tennis in the evenings with other partners on separate courts. One night was particularly filled with flirtations as they sustained eye contact from across the way, and he hit his ball into her court, sauntered over to retrieve it, apologizing, and smiling broadly despite himself.

After the game, Susan told her friend, "You go on. I'm gonna sit here on the bench and recover. You kicked my butt."

"Sure," her friend uttered coyly. "Just tell me everything that happens with you and Josh." Her friend winked and walked off.

Josh's friends playfully punched his shoulder and rammed into him, eyeing Susan, but then left, and Josh found his way to Susan's bench. He put his foot up on the bench and began leaning in, stretching and flexing his calf muscles.

"I got slaughtered tonight," Susan admitted, looking down.

"Well, your partner is….shall we say, powerful." Josh cupped his hand over his muscles, demonstrating that Susan's partner was strong and big, unlike Susan's petite frame. He scanned her body and gave her an endearing look. They lingered, and then sauntered toward the school apartments, beginning the magic moments of talking and brushing up against each other.

Susan saw Josh melt when he spotted her in the cafeteria the next day, and felt her stomach flip-flop as he sheepishly walked toward her. "Dinner tomorrow night? I can cook," Josh asked, smiling.

The relationship blossomed and the urgency to merge heated up. His ardent pursuit made Susan so confident in the relationship that she gradually opened herself to most everything two people can do between the sheets. They felt high when together and slightly blue when apart. They felt open to new experiences, needed less sleep than usual, felt powerful and energized, and absolutely obsessed with each other.

Six months later, they began talking about marriage and then children. The excitement pounded in Susan. It was everything she wanted. She'd never felt more alive.

Let's step back and look at what's happening.

Experiencing a tornado or an out of control fire or even a booming thunderstorm with torrential rain can cause you to pay respect to Mother Nature. But she strikes inside our bodies as well, and never so powerfully as when she intends for humans to couple.

Mother Nature causes humans to merge
both physically and emotionally.

Helen Fisher, in *Why We Love*, says romantic love includes the desire to fuse physically with the other and to merge emotionally. Lovers, she found, aggrandize, focus on, and become dependent on one another. They rearrange their priorities; feeling empathic, hopeful, sexual, loving, tender, and jealous, they desire exclusivity.

The lovers drink from Mother Nature's brew, a potion of hormones resulting in "romantic love." The brew's first ingredient is dopamine, which rivets the lovers' attention to one another, fires their motivation to please each other, and causes ecstasy about being together. Dopamine is the hormone behind the craving and dependency found in addicts. That is, dopamine causes the lovers to cling to one another, crave and depend on one another. The second ingredient is testosterone, which drives the pursuit: "I will make her mine!" The man, who is particularly endowed with the hormone, says, "Whatever it takes." This can result in promises that won't be kept, but it is such a kick to hear them! The third component of the soup is upped norepinephrine, causing lovers to be energetic, exhilarated, less needful of sleep and food, and able to remember small details about one another. The romantics are on a high together and may be surprised to find one another less motivated and a little lazier later on. A fourth part of the recipe particularly influences the female. Oxytocin, the soft, generous hormone, causes benevolent behaviors and the seeking of a loving attachment. This makes her very open to giving and giving to her guy.

Increased oxytocin causes a woman
to give and give to her guy.

An odd feature of Mother Nature's brew is that one vital hormone is actually *lowered*. Decreased serotonin (caused by elevated dopamine and norepinephrine) causes more addict-like thinking: obsessiveness. Fisher found that many lovers say they think of the other 90 percent of their waking hours.[4] It also causes them to feel blue and a little anxious if they can't be together. Now you know the impetus behind love songs.

Returning to our story, Susan was flattered when Josh pulled her close when they were out; he knew other men were ogling her, so he would clarify for them that she was his. He took on her battle with her apartment manager over the poor air conditioning and she felt safe. He intensely sought her company, starving to look at her and touch her, and she thought that meant he wanted to build a relationship with her mental and emotional self. She enjoyed his intense and possessive courting behaviors but had no idea how the testosterone behind them would effect the relationship later.

Finally, their wedding day arrived and the church Susan had grown up in was crackling with excited well-wishers, people she'd known since she was a child. Their presence brought further legitimacy and foundation to the marriage, and the swell of confidence took her off-guard as she walked down the aisle. All the people who had formed her roots in life seemed to be saying, "We approve." She was amazed at how right stepping toward him felt. Her new life. Her prince.

Josh fought back tears when he saw her in the Theia Chantilly lace gown. The sheer sleeves made him think of having sex with her forever. The three-foot train reminded him of how traditional Susan was and how she'd never leave him. His life, at least on this front, was now secured. Her bridesmaids had loved the silver crystals and seed pearl trimming of the ivory dress and had gathered around her in the dressing room in a circle of history and love. To top it off, it seemed like Susan's parents liked Josh's.

Little seeds of doubt sprouted during the honeymoon. Susan quickly shooed them away. *Wasn't everything wonderful?* Snapshots of the wedding played in her mind. He was on the phone a lot. *He's just trying to impress his new boss.* He wanted to watch three hours of sports during one of their four days away. *Well, he's a guy and guys do that.* They had hardly talked on the flight home. *Talking isn't everything.*

When girls find a significant other of the opposite sex, they will carry the expectation of intimate dialogue and open sharing into that relationship. Susan expected the long conversations and in-depth sharing that led to a strong emotional connection with Kendra and other girl friends to be repeated in this relationship.

"Could we talk tonight?" Susan asked Josh, trying hard to stifle her overwhelming need.

"Sure. What about?" Josh asked without eye contact.

"I don't know, just talk."

"Oh, that again. I don't know what you want from me," Josh said, impatience in his voice.

At about three years into the marriage, despite her best efforts, Susan found herself submerged in disappointment. Josh would talk on and on about work, but not about their relationship. She had a job with a law firm, too, but she hoped their emphasis would be on something more than work. Since they both worked, she'd expected him to help around the house out of respect. She hadn't expected him to leave his stuff everywhere. She thought the romantic behaviors of their courtship would continue, but month by month, it seemed to be dropping off.

> When girls find a significant other of the opposite sex,
> they will carry the expectation of intimate dialogue
> and open sharing into that relationship.

Her cousin, Kendra, had been calling her and Susan, between work, housework and her sadness, hadn't gotten around to returning the calls. Finally, feeling desperate, Susan called her.

"What's wrong, Honey?" Kendra said warmly, able to pick up the sadness immediately.

"I am so sorry I haven't called you. I've felt too...deadened and embarrassed."

"Deadened? Are you okay? And don't you dare ever be embarrassed around me! I've known your secrets since you were old enough to tell them."

"I didn't know how to talk about this, though," Susan confessed.

"I'm always here for you, Susan. Has something happened?"

"Yes. No. Something's been sneaking into my relationship with Josh, overtime. It's a sense of loss that I'm uncomfortable mentioning. I mean, I'm supposed to be loyal to him, right?"

"Not at the expense of yourself. It's okay. Tell me more," Kendra encouraged.

"We don't talk. Not like you and I do. Maybe something's wrong. I think he loves me, I guess. I don't think he sees the sense in chit chat, but then we don't speak of our dreams either. It's blank. I can't draw him out. Something's terribly missing in this relationship and yet it's what I rely on for...everything. With work and related social events, I hardly have time to pursue friendships."

Now, having finally opened up, Susan's words tumbled forth. "I've asked, 'Am I doing something wrong?' So I clean better—I mean, the house is immaculate, though it's constant work. I wonder why I would get a law degree just to end up the chief cook and bottle washer. I like my job—it's meaningful. I think it's saving me. I've stopped asking him for help around the house. Asking is too exhausting and just makes it all too clear we don't really have a partnership.

"This is the deal. I believed any sacrifice would be worth getting the magic back. But I think he's just fine the way things are." There was a pause.

Kendra, worried, probed. "Your voice sounds tight."

"I know," Susan managed. "It's me squelching a scream. I am so stifled.

I need to ask him about his withdrawal, his lack of emotion. I guess.
I don't know. I've had a few 'come to Jesus meetings' with him, but I
think he just feels criticized. Honestly, Kendra, when I'm in the shower,
alone, I shake and cry." And she did cry, then.

"Oh, Sweetie. Come to my house, okay? Can you get away? We'll figure it out together. Take a few days." Kendra paused, wanting to help,
and groping for words. "I love you, you know."

Later, she asks Josh, "Do you mind if I get away for a few days? Go
see my cousin Kendra?"

"That sounds fun. Go ahead," he says a little too enthusiastically and
Susan imagines him playing a few extra rounds of golf and drinking
beer with buddies, relieved to be away from her sadness.

Once at Kendra's home, Susan responds to her empathy and describes
her loneliness and the feeling that Josh doesn't *see* her. "Why doesn't
he want to continue the romance we started? I'd give anything for the
connection I felt with him then." She'd been dreaming of such a romance most of her life. It seems to her that, if he tried or if he loved her
enough, he would simply put his focus on those behaviors again and
make her so happy. After all, he was capable of it once. She is tempted
to conclude his love has faded.

Disappointment, often teetering on depression,
occurs because females,coming into marriage with such
different expectations, are caught off-guard.

Disappointment, often teetering on depression, occurs because females,
coming into marriage with such different expectations, are caught
off-guard. They try to make changes in the relationship, but it doesn't
work. There are fundamental things you can't change about a man, but
most women don't know or accept that. They explain, they plead, they
withdraw, and they go to therapy. Because the woman doesn't know the
problem is coming, she enters into commitment high on the hormonal
cocktails he's also imbibing; she doesn't see her fate coming. She is like
psychologist Martin Seligman's depressed dogs.

In 1964, Martin Seligman was a graduate student performing experiments on 150 dogs. In a two-sided cage, one with an electrified floor, the dogs frantically tried to escape and learned to move quickly to the safe side. But when the door between the sides was shut and the dogs couldn't escape the shocks, they eventually laid down, hopeless and passive.[5]

Likewise, women entering long-term romantic relationships try at first to change a man. They are confounded by some of his limitations and suspect he just hasn't received good parenting, needs more love, needs direction on how to relate, or needs to work through something from his past. After a while, though, her frustration turns to hopelessness. Helpless to change the most important relationship of her life, she experiences a great sadness.

Neuroscientists have found that Mother Nature's romantic love cocktail lasts between 12–18 months.[6] Then the specific behaviors and attitudes brought on by the potion decline, and "normal" returns for each. For Susan, that will mean being her highly relational, giving, empathic self—the stuff brought on by the oxytocin in her body. For Josh, that will mean testosterone will motivate him to propensities described in Chapter 2.

Mother Nature's emotional high that comes along with
a new relationship only lasts 12–18 months.

After being breast fed, coddled, loved, and nurtured by women, it seems odd that boys don't go on to imitate the values and relational skill of women. The answer is *hormones*, as explained by Louann Brizendine, M.D., in her book *The Male Brain*.

At eight weeks, Josh's baby brain was saturated and defeminized by testosterone, giving him the propensity for male behaviors and attitudes, which we'll talk about in Chapter 2. His testosterone ran high from 1–12 months, making sure his "maleness" was in place. Then it lowered till age 11, causing him to prefer boys, not girls, as playmates. That is, through childhood a boy's testosterone isn't high enough to put his sex drive in gear, but he is still different enough from girls to seek male buddies to spend his time with. And even during this time, the hormone responsible for defeminizing him (MIS) remains securely in place, and to further lock in his masculinity, his estrogen runs low.

At puberty—bang! Testosterone zooms up 20-fold, making Josh turned on by female body parts—not necessarily women's character or personality, but breasts, butts, faces. His hearing becomes less acute, so he finds less meaning in dialoguing. He prefers action. His tendency is to perceive male faces as antagonistic, so he is suspicious of other males, and though he shares activities with them, he rarely seeks closeness.

Meanwhile, at puberty, Susan, saturated with oxytocin and estrogen, became closer to the females in her life, creating strong bonds. She would work hard to avoid any antagonism with female friends. Her hormones cried out for emotional closeness and primed her to use dialogue to find it.[7]

At puberty, a guy's hearing becomes less acute,
so he finds less meaning in dialoguing.

The hormones pumping day and night through Josh's veins would incline him toward building social hierarchies, so sports, the military, and power corporations intrigued him. He loved testing his own powers, be they physical or mental, and this, rather than relationships, would become his major life motivation. For him to take on a modicum of Susan's relational abilities, his hormones would have to be lowered, something nature does in males, only on special occasions, temporarily during courtship and the birth of his child.

Every cell in Josh's body is male; he has a Y chromosome, and his genes are mega fuel–injected by hormones. Males use different brain circuits than women. Intuitively, women have always known this, but now, not much is hidden from our eyes. The use of the PET, the fMRI, hormonal and genetic mappers venture inside the brain making male–female differences undisputable.

Studies show that married women are more
prone to unhappiness and illnesses, including
depression, than single women.

Defeated Expectations and Depression

In *Backlash*, Susan Faludi cites several research studies showing how
married women are prone to unhappiness and illness. Quoting from the
1990 Mills Longitudinal Study that followed women for 30 years, she
elucidates how married women are at greater risk than single ones for
depression and illnesses like migraines, colitis, and high blood pressure. She references a *Cosmopolitan* review of 106,000 women that
found singles not only have better health, they make more money and
have more sex to boot! Further, Gerald Klerman and Myrna Weiss-
man, researchers, scoped all studies on depression in women, ruling out
causes like PMS, genes, and the birth control pill, and found only two
causes that stood: marriage and low social status. In reviewing studies of women from the last few decades, Faludi found that, compared
to singles, wives suffer 20% more depression and an astonishing *triple*
the rate of mental illness. This is odd considering society's approval
for women marrying and the shunning of the single lifestyle in past
decades. She also cites a long study (twenty-five years) of college-educated females reporting that married females had more loneliness, and
lower self esteem, and felt unattractive and incompetent (even at child
care) when compared with singles.[8] We'll look at the "whys" of this in
Chapter 2.

Once inside a relationship, a woman runs into the facts about men I'll
describe in the next three chapters. Hitting the wall, the woman goes
through the grieving cycle. At first, she's in shock. Then she tries to
bargain with him, trying to change him, making him realize what an
intimate relationship should be about. Then she becomes angry, but,
because women are not supposed to show anger, this is a quiet thing,
often turned inward against herself. *If I were just prettier or thinner or
wittier*, she surmises. Then she enters into a long depression, sometimes
actual clinical depression but, more often, some version of "the blues."
A woman is twice as likely to be depressed as a man. It's been assumed
this is because of hormones, but researchers haven't been able to sub-

stantiate the claim. One male family doctor told me he believes there are so many women depressed because of the lousy relationships they're in. This may be true because women put so much stock in intimate relationships, valuing them so highly. Finally, she moves either into divorce or resignation (which usually carries with it more depression), or she accepts the way he is, dividing her attention to other fulfillments.

A woman tries to bargain with her guy,
trying to change him, making him
realize what an intimate relationship should be about.

In *The Development of Emotional Competence*, Carolyn Saarni says boys inhibit feelings like sadness, vulnerability, and worry and look stoic in situations that should provoke emotion.[9] (Again, boys may inhibit to some extent, but their brain structure and hormones make it likely they just aren't feeling that much.) Consequently, later in life, a woman doesn't know what her guy is feeling. You can't readily read whether he likes something or doesn't; whether something makes him sad; why he's disturbed about a movie he's walking out of. *You don't know*. So, what do you do? You guess. You try to pull it out of him. You read articles like "How to get your guy to communicate," "Seven Ways to Promote Dialogue in your Marriage," etc., etc., ad nauseum.

But you want to know him. In fact, you want the "in-to-me-see" of intimacy. But there's no seeing inside, unless someone expresses himself verbally or facially.

Relationships depend on Person A picking up on the emotional cues given by Person B, who then validates the cues by expressing his or her feelings. This creates a tremendous surge of intimacy because the two are able to tune into each other. In short, a guy leaves few cues to respond to, leaving a vacuum in the exchange, leaving it flat. Saarni claims that not only does the ability to communicate one's feelings lie at the center of one's relationships, *but it defines how far a relationship can go*.

She goes on to show how establishing emotional intimacy depends on the emotional immediacy one is able to display. First, there must be genuineness about one's expression. Then, a person must give back, creating a back-and-forth exchange of feelings. Intimacy involves the dovetailing of three things: facial expressions that reveal ones feelings, benevolent intentions toward the other that are communicated silently, and disclosing information about oneself that is increasingly *personal and emotional*. The trouble is that men simply feel emotionally neutral much of the time and, if they have a feeling, often inhibit its expression. How, then, can men be read? And if not read, how can women feel intimate with them?

Reading non-verbal communication makes us smart in relationships, giving us insight into someone else and awareness about how our own behaviors affect that person. If we say something and the listener smirks or gasps or cringes, we figure out how to change our approach. Women feel unknown by the men they live with because men tend not to read these cues. He doesn't pick up on her cringes, so he doesn't know what she doesn't like. Likewise, he doesn't pick up on her sighs, so he doesn't know what she likes.

Saarni studied 113 children ages 6 to 12. She wanted to see if kids could discern how much genuineness would be experienced between two made-up story characters. Most, or 67%, of the kids knew that *less genuineness* would be expressed if two of the following were present: (1) low-intensity emotion, (2) a difference in status between the main characters, and (3) low connection between the characters—i.e., if they weren't close friends, related, or in love. That is, these three qualities contribute to less honesty and openness. However, the majority of both older children and adults would agree that if there were high-intensity feelings, the characters were equal in power, and if they were strongly affiliated, then genuine expression of feelings would be expected.

So then, women expect more genuineness—more disclosures, more openness, more display of one's humanness, less sticking with factual information—when people are close to them and most certainly with the guy she's devoted her life to! Hello. When a woman considers a romantic partner her equal, when she believes they have strong feelings for each other, and when their connection is strong, she expects emotional genuineness.

During courtship, men are, temporarily,
more like women.

Unfortunately, though, men's inhibited or not-there-in-the-first-place expression of feelings causes them to signal to loved ones that they don't really want to be close. However, during the initial forming of a romance, men's oxytocin is up, inhibiting their testosterone, so they do express more emotion because, in fact, *they are temporarily more like women.*

Consider that, when a person enters another culture, she may feel lost and misunderstanding the tiniest of social cues, not being able to find the cues she is used to. The lack of validation gradually leads to feeling discouraged and misunderstood, or suffering from culture shock. I contend that this happens in marriages; women come into the relationship with such a different experience of life, especially in the area of emotional communication. She feels hopelessly unable to find the intimacy she expected.

There's an abiding denial in our culture about the limited capacity of males to meet female's relational needs. After the 12–to 18–month high burns off, reality creeps into her fantasy. Because society is bound together, worshipping at the idol of romantic love, wanting to believe it is the ultimate hope, she has no one to turn to. More often than not, a woman grapples with society's unrealistic expectations of long term romantic relationships—and men's inabilities—all alone.

When people's expectations go unmet, they feel lonely, theorizes J.E. Young in his study of depression. He also offers a key for assuaging loneliness—that is, changing our expectations.[10]

When people's expectations go unmet, they feel lonely.

A woman expects, above all, a rich emotional quality in her committed relationship. She makes sure there are shared activities and intimate dialogues. She tries to find reasons why he seems emotionally cut off, or is unable to intuit people and circumstances as she does. He hasn't invested time in analyzing his parents' psychologically, she realizes, so he's doomed to unthinkingly repeating his past. Especially because he once courted her, she can't figure out what happened to "Hello, Gorgeous," and "You mean the world to me."

He is surprised by her, too. He thought marriage would provide a structure for their lives. They would support each other (or, she would motivate him to climb the work ladder) and they would have sex. *She wants an elusive closeness he wouldn't have the energy for or interest in.* He feels deficient and criticized because he can't supply what she wants. He backs away, seeking appreciation from the workplace where the expectations are clear and he can meet them. As we'll see, success brings him upped testosterone and that feels good.

Her defeat turns into a plan to escape the marriage. She's explained it to him, she's cried, she's threatened, but to no avail. There's nothing left for her to try. Raising the children becomes her focus, though she didn't enter marriage with that intent. She wants to do what's best for them. She goes silent and he hears "peace at last—she must be happy." The resentment grows as she handles most of the childcare, shopping, cleaning, and home organization, usually while holding an outside job. Once in awhile, she confronts him again, but, basically, she's just biding her time. He's somewhat put off by attitudes that seep through. But if she's willing to have sex, he figures everything's pretty much okay. He doesn't expect a lot from relationships anyway. If she won't have sex, then it's sex, not emotional closeness that becomes his focus.

He feels deficient and criticized because he can't
supply what she wants.

He has, all along, had little ability to read her, so when she announces she's filed, he's truly shocked and off-balanced. Sometimes men, at this point, reflect and admit their selfishness. Sometimes they're angry, reminding the woman of her commitment and how she'll hurt the kids by leaving. He may claim he will suddenly change. Some want to enter marital therapy.

Here is where it gets odd for marital therapists. Ellen Maccoby documented how the sexes develop alone, not seeking each other as playmates, preferring to engage with their own sex. Until, suddenly, after puberty hits, the sex drive engages and the sexes are suddenly thrown together, without much knowledge of each other. Then they marry, still with little understanding.[11] Across cultures, studies find that twice the number of females sink into depression, when compared with men. It happens in the early to mid-20s, about when females enter their first serious relationship with a guy. At this age, women get a bubble-bursting taste of the limits of romance.[12]

The sexes develop separately and marry
with little understanding of the other.

Therapists are up against the tremendous difference between women and men as they try to help the couple. The man is often unaware he says thoughtless things and she is so beyond that now. She began working on making close relationships work, seeking one-on-one time, very early in life. Her relational skills surpass his.

Women want men to be empathetic, yet men's brains don't
hold near the empathy capability that women's do.

Every marital therapist knows that what the female really wants from him is empathy. Yet his brain doesn't hold near the empathy capability hers does. The therapist valiantly teaches the man the kinds of things to say, hoping he'll be motivated at this point to memorize them.

In many cases, the men willing to enter therapy also begin a pursuit of their wives, much like courtship. This time, the behaviors don't fool her. She's seen this before and it makes her even more suspicious. The flowers, the new ring, the cards with handwritten promises, the surprise trip to Hawaii—to her, these mean he's trying to get back what he wants: sex and a clean house with a smile on her face. Not interested. Now she can see through courtship behaviors; she already knows what's on the other side. Many author–therapists recognize and can articulate the problem long–term romances face.

John Gray, Ph.D., Is the author of *Men are from Mars, Women are from Venus*.[13] He advises women to encourage a man to make baby steps and then praise him for doing so. This can feel so insufficient to a woman compared with what she really needs from him that it seems laughable to the point of tears. She's already tired from using that technique on her kids. Gray advises women to be pragmatic, giving her man a heads up on how long she will need to talk. In my experience, this makes women mad, though I think Gray offers the most workable advice on the market.

John Gottman, Ph.D., author of *The Seven Principles of Making Marriage Work*,[14] advises couples to learn about each other, respect each other's differences, acknowledge your partner's important events, yield to your partner, empathize, and share values through rituals or traditions. Basically, he is telling women what they already do naturally at the beginning of a marriage before they lose hope. But when their man won't cooperate and shows little interest, she realizes she's carrying all the weight to no avail and she feels defeated. She's happy to hear a therapist reinforce her ideas, but what next? It's back to the original question: how do you motivate the guy long term?

Terrrence Real, M.S., author of *The New Rules of Marriage*,[15] advises women to put their foot down with the guy, being truly ready to leave the relationship if he doesn't change, and then stop hiding their ugly attitudes behind his bad behavior. Going to the bottom line, though—that is, threatening to leave—can only be used so many times in a relationship before it has to be carried to completion and the relationship ends.

Michele Weiner-Davis, MSW, author of *Divorce Busting*,[16] believes the real solution is marital education, that knowing the male–female differences will help.

Other author–therapists—realizing men typically don't contribute much skill or effort—rely on women to make the changes in a relationship. They teach women to help men become what they need: better listeners, more emotionally sensitive, more able to apologize. In the end, this gives already overwhelmed women more "to dos" and the sense that a relationship is more trouble than it's worth. Authors instruct her to carefully word her requests, don't do it too often, and be consistent. What these authors don't see is that by the time a woman begins her quest for help, she's already terribly hurt and tired. Trying to assist a man who isn't motivated is too much when she's drawing from her own dry well.

It's time to consider something new.

The problem is that men can't give, except temporarily, what women really want in a love relationship. Only when we stop denying that can we get to workable solutions.

For too long, women in marriages have been like Seligman's dogs. But we have entered the end of the Age of Women Sacrificing for Romance and it's time to consider something new.

Chapter 2:

Men Are Fuel Injected With A Win-Kill-Self-Sex Potion

"I'd rather be mad with the truth than sane with lies."
—Bertrand Russell

Two-thirds of divorces in the US are initiated by women, and some say 90% of college-educated women who divorce are the initiators.[17] Since 1973, the National Opinion Research Center has repeatedly found, in interviewing couples, that women are not as happy with their marriages as are the men.[18] Women aren't finding what they want from men and haven't been for a long time. If my private practice is any indicator, I suspect many of the one-third of divorces initiated by men are because the men realize they are unable to please their female partners. That is, it's still about women being disappointed.

Women leave despite their being a lot more patient than men. An international Gallup Poll asking people in twenty-two cultures whether men or women are more patient voted overwhelmingly that females are. The reason lies in females' having more receptors sites for serotonin.[19]

Among 40–69 year olds, women seek splits 66% of the time, probably because baby boomers were the first generation entering marriage with a higher expectation of self-fulfillment.[20] But the problem may be even greater. Research shows that while half of relationships end in divorce, half of those in stable marriages wish they were not married. As one client lamented, "I think my parents died of marriage."

Though relationship problems seem personal and unique to the couple, the divorce rate proves the sociological nature of the problem. It is not just about your relationship: it is, in fact, about *the nature of heterosexual relationships.*

It's normal to project oneself onto a significant other,
believing he shares the same needs and priorities
and, in fact, the same nature.

Raised on Cinderella, Snow White, Beauty and the Beast, (or the newer versions of these), girls are led to believe if they are beautiful, a man will lavish all the romantic attention on them they desire. Movies rarely show the difficulties of a real relationship, but focus on the courtship only, when a man is intent on securing a bond. Women's magazines fuel the obsession for the perfect, but unrealistic romance. Bridal magazines complete the fantasy in lace and white. It's normal to project oneself onto a significant other, believing he shares the same needs and priorities, and, in fact, the same nature. The bad news is it's not true: men have different natures. Most would prefer to catch an action movie than a chick flick. They don't sit around reading about how to make a relationship work and they don't dream of weddings. The media inserts the guy lovingly gazing at the woman, but except during the courtship period, it's not natural for males to value relationships like females do.

It's not natural for males to value relationships like females do.

I'm a psychologist, so I like the idea that humans can change. After all, I sit in a chair over 40 hours each week trying to facilitate change in people. But I think Steven Pinker, author of *The Blank Slate: The Modern Denial of Human Nature*, has something important to tell us. Rather than being born as blank slates (thank you, Mr. John Locke), humans enter with rather unmalleable predispositions gifted to us to meet the demands of survival.[21] Yes, there's room for individual differences and for culture to stamp its mark on each of us. But just as the giraffe keeps his evolved long neck so he can reach the tender leaves at the tops of the trees, so humans come with gender-specific hormones and brain structures. Cultural relativism, or the belief that nurture triumphs over nature, has a special allure because we all want to believe we can shape humanity into something wonderful. But relativism has led women astray, particularly when it comes to their relationships with men. It's time for somebody to tell the truth. Further, the psychological genius Sigmund

Freud admonished us to seek understanding about the primal influences that have shaped us, or, he warned, we will function in ignorance.

We all want to believe it's possible
to shape humanity into something wonderful.

As James Dabbs explains in *Heroes, Rogues, and Lovers: Testosterone and Behavior*, masculinity is more about physiology than a boy's being shaped through parenting. After all, General Douglas McArthur's overly-involved mother moved with him to West Point to coddle him, yet eons of evolution assured his vibrant manliness.[22] Furthermore, boys raised in dad-absent homes show that boys do not imitate their mothers; they still show masculine behaviors, say psychologists Stevenson and Black after analyzing 67 studies.[23]

For 99.9% of our human (hominid) history, men hunted and women gathered. Not enough time has passed to shape the genders differently.[24] The brain structures and hormones unique to each gender are still in place and these differences affect our relationships. Men hardened themselves to kill; women softened themselves to tend infants. Many deplore how gamey female–male relationships are, how disingenuous. It is the innate differences, though, including the different values and motivations, that make for the shenanigans.

Having information about men can
help you realistically set your expectations.

Yet, we enter romance without knowledge of one another. As Eleanor Maccoby documents, the genders play separately—rather repelled by each other's ways—until sexual urges compel them, without much introduction, to be intimates.[25] It is unfair for women to enter romantic relationships with nothing more than butterflies.

After the high of a new romance has burned off, women need to limit the amount of emotional fulfillment they expect from their relationships with men and here's why.

Men and Testosterone

"Hormones play our lives like instruments."[26]
—D. Lindsey Berkson, *Hormonal Deception*

Men average 10–20 times the testosterone women have.

And as we speak of the effects of testosterone on men, consider the argument of George Gilder, activist and creator of a think tank, who said he opposed feminism because single men are naturally barbarians and without women and marriage, they would go uncivilized. Consider the burden this places on young women, who, ironically, are expecting sensitivity and closeness from marriage.[27]

The effects of testosterone can be studied in an embryo, in the lab, by injecting females with it, and by studying how it affects men across cultures and across generations. When the AARP asked women why they leave their marriages, 23% said it was because of abuse (verbal, physical, or emotional), and 17% said it was because of marital cheating.[28] Thus, we see that the kill–conquer–fuck reputation of testosterone lives on. Though women get mad at each other, they have never, in human history, shown the violence men have. Researchers Daly and Wilson scrutinized murder records for the last 700 years from various cultures, finding that men killing men happened *thirty to forty times* more often than did females killing each other.[29] Almost all (90%) murderers in North America are men, the FBI's Most Wanted List usually features *all* men, and criminal CEOs and CFOs from Enron to Bernie Madoff are typically men, with Martha Stewart a lone exception.[30] Today, almost all persons in prison are male. It has taken laws, law enforcement and law suits—not just kindly suggestions—to get men to change their chauvinistic behaviors toward women at work and home.

Murder records for the last 700 years
from various cultures show that men killing men
happened *thirty to forty times* more often than did
females killing each other.

Males aged fifteen to twenty-four commit the majority of crimes, according to Anthony Synnott, Ph.D., sociology professor at Concordia. A young man doesn't yet possess the wisdom to balance testosterone's aggressive, impulsive, and defiant inclinations. It is this fact that explains the sharp rise in crime from the late 1960s to the 1980s: twelve million young men invaded society, a huge increase from former times.[31]

Conversely, women are loaded with the relationship hormone, Oxytocin, noted for inducing nurturance—emotional and physical—and bonding. This love drug causes her to *prioritize* relationships, to value connection and to sacrifice for it. Far from fucking it or killing it, she wants to take care of it.

In terms of relationship skills, men got the raw end
the evolutionary deal.

In terms of relationship skills, men got the raw end of the evolutionary deal. Hunting animals, they learned to be silent as they stalked their prey and used language in staccato, factual ways. Going to battle against other men, they zeroed in on being tough and hardened emotionally. Men's testosterone grew as they needed it for survival—beating off vultures, being ready to meet goring animals, and coming up against beasts thousands of pounds heavier than they. Cruel and bold, men took dominion over the animal kingdom. A man couldn't succumb to loving a little Thumper or beginning a caring relationship with Bambi's mother in the forest. He had to wound and butcher Wilbur the Pig without an iota of empathy.

Recently, researchers scoped our current world, finding 179 remaining hunter–gatherer societies. Hunting is the purview of men only in 166 of those societies; in a mere thirteen, both genders hunt, yet they couldn't locate even one society where women hunted alone.[32]

On the other end of the spectrum, women, living in groups, used language to build connection, teach and succor children. While men shut down their empathy in order to kill animals and enemies, women tuned into their empathy and intuition and used it daily to care for infants and toddlers who could not speak, along with the sick and elderly. With compassion, they searched the plant world for ways to heal tribe members. Further extending their communication skills, they educated children. What evolution taught women—nurturance and communication—works well to establish and keep emotional connection now. What men learned does not. The paradoxical male identity of lover and killer has never worked out really well, as Shlain in *Sex, Time and Power* points out.[33]

While men shut down their empathy in order to kill animals and enemies, women tuned into their empathy and intuition.

While men grew courage and the raw nerve to take risks that go with hunting or war, women learned to apologize, disclose, be genuine with others, express feelings, and read non-verbal communications. For 99.9% of human history, these were the lessons experienced by the genders, repeated and drilled into our genetic makeup. We each adapted to the roles we were given.

It is this history that leaves the modern woman in a bind. Her skills for relationship far surpass that of her male counterpart, but it is to him that she looks for connection. Let's examine more traits of the male hormone.

Men Don't Prioritize Relationships

"Marriage is where a woman exchanges the attention of many men for the inattention of one."
—Helen Rowland

Sara, 43, and married 21 years, says "I get the impression my husband isn't capable of offering more in a relationship. I see flickers of potential, but it never comes into fruition."

How testosterone affects social skill and interest

Since we are never without the profound influence of hormones, it starts early. In an attempt to understand the early effects of testosterone, a hospital in Cambridge analyzed amniotic fluid coming from pregnant women. Later, they studied the toddlers who were born to those mothers, and found that those with low fetal testosterone (i.e., mostly girls) made better eye contact and had larger vocabularies. Making eye contact translates to having interest in people and a good vocabulary shows interest in communicating, *both early signs of empathy*. When the children were four, their social skills were measured again. Those children who had had *high* pre-birth testosterone (i.e., mostly boys) now had *lower* social skills. Conversely, the low levels of testosterone found in toddler girls resulted in higher language skills, more eye contact, and better social skills.[34]

Exposure to high testosterone in the womb,
as occurs with boys, results in low
social skill in preschoolers.

Men value side-by-side activities rather than the one-on-one empathic sharing women crave. Sally Wheelwright and Simon Baron-Cohen created the Friendship and Relationship Questionnaire to test this sex difference. When men were asked if they liked focusing on a friend's feelings or preferred just sharing an activity, they answered, on average, that the latter was their preference. Women answered the other way around.[35]

Jason, in a marital session, asked his wife point–blank, "What do you want from me?" She replied, "Friendship." Her answer was clear in her mind: she wanted emotional support through dialogue and a sense of closeness. I asked him, "How would you define friendship, Jason?" He replied, "A friend is someone who will get out of bed and help you change a tire at 2 AM." His view of amity was utilitarian and about survival, not emotional connection.

A common problem in marital therapy is men believing their partners are trying to control them. Men's testosterone makes them alert to turf issues. Testosterone also causes them to read male facial expressions as hostile. This keeps them from getting close to other males and developing relationship skill. Many wives feel their partners assume negative intent in them—that she wants to control him—even though what she really wants is understanding. A study of violent men showed they translate neutral actions into hostile ones. They are threatened by perceived slights.[36]   In normal men, the suspiciousness and assumptions they make hinders them from being as relational as women.

It is not possible for most men to be as consistently nurturing as women. The emotional sensitivity necessary for infant care lies at the heart of femininity, and spills over into the rest of life. Girls are born with it, and women are doused with it again when they give birth and more so as they continually attach and care for a child. For most women, once they have received these large doses, they will never be the same again. Their tender and gentle sensitivities will far surpass men's.

Many women notice that relational interest shows up in how one watches TV or a movie. Cynthia, 44, is bothered that her husband talks over the dialogue on TV or during movies because he doesn't care about the relational aspects of the show that she loves picking up on. He seeks only the general plot and details of the action scenes. She wants the character development, the subtleties shown by the people, the nuances of their relationships. The intricacies of relational closeness are lost on the testosterone-driven gender.

Men are More Self Oriented

The research

Psychologists Cross and Madson (1997) studied how the genders arrange their self-concepts, finding that while women are connected and mutually supporting of others, men look to their *own* successes, aptitudes, principles, and individuality to define themselves.[37]

While women find self esteem in having strong personal relationships, men find self esteem in their accomplishments, finds Josephs, Markus, and Tafarodi (1992) in a survey of college students.[38]

Paul Zak, a neuroeconomist at Claremont Graduate University, runs a lab that tests testosterone's effects and says it orients the brain toward the self, rather than toward the needs of others. High testosterone males divorce more often and spend less time with their offspring.[39]

Men's testosterone orients their brains toward the self,
rather than toward the needs of others.

The Ventral Tegmental Area is more active in men than women. It manufactures dopamine, the feel-good drug, and drives men toward seeking rewards. Dopamine is a selfish hormone, about *your* own fun, finding what interests *you*, pumping up for *your* next goal. Thus, compared to women, men are more about their own activities and goals and less about relationships. This tendency also contributes to addictiveness.

A defeminizing substance in men called Mullerian Inhibiting Substance (MIS) predisposes men to exploratory behavior. This, too, draws male interest away from the relational world. The more testosterone, the more likely an animal will roam away from home and challenge or dominate a rival. These are self-involved, non-relational activities.[40]

If women were loaded with testosterone, the results would be similar. Mona Lisa Schulz, M.D., Ph.D., cites research finding that females born with excess testosterone place less importance on getting married or being mothers.[41] They are more about themselves.

High testosterone creates a push to get your own way, Alan Booth, Ph.D., a Penn State sociologist, states. He juxtaposed the relationship histories with the testosterone levels of 4,462 males. High testosterone males had trouble getting along with or being close to their spouses, had difficult relationships with their children, and were more likely to be unfaithful and to divorce.[42]

Another research study has to do with flirtations. John Lydon, Ph.D., of McGill University in Montreal worked with 724 college students and found that men, after interacting with a sexy, available female, thought of their own romantic partners more negatively than before. Females, however, after interacting with a sexy, available guy, worked to shore up their current relationship. After his initial findings with 724 college students, Dr. Lydon then gave men a chance to come up with a plan to protect their *current* relationships and this helped. However, he found, the women didn't need training; protecting their romance came naturally.[43]

The great anthropologist Margaret Mead said, "Men have to learn to want to provide for others, and this behavior, being learned, is fragile and can disappear rather easily under social conditions that no longer teach it effectively."[44] So what does all this research mean and how does it affect people in real life?

The way his self-orientation plays out

For men, winning holds the rush of increased testosterone and happy dopamine. Avoiding defeat at all costs rallies men's interest to The Challenge (work, sports) or The Battle Cry (war). Feeling one's power and testing one's limits, rather than investing in relationships, becomes the primary focus. How fast, how high, and how many become themes, even if it's who can fart the loudest. Proving himself and feeling invincible revs his brain circuit. Where do you think we got the word "cocksure"?

Because testosterone encourages enterprising and stimulates the pursuing of goals, it causes a man to feel gratified living in his own plans more than in relationship. Men can give only a limited part of themselves to a relationship for fear it will drain them of the energy and focus they need to succeed outside it. That is, they can only devote so much time and concern to a wife, children, and home. If too much is asked, he may feel resentful or angry.

Yes, he treasures his wife, but he must limit the amount of attention he gives her or he will be depleted from his true aspirations. Besides, he had no clue she'd want so much from him. Whereas most brides enter marriage with boundless love to give, he uses the relationship as a footing from which to build his career. Whereas she would rearrange herself and give up a lot for the sake of love, he doesn't anticipate that, and remains clearly in himself, bent on his goals. The relationship is his place to rest and rejuvenate for the next day.

Men have a strong sense of "I."

Women work and work trying to get men to be more thoughtful and caring, but truth be known, he's wired in a certain way and is essentially less relational. He may change some during midlife when testosterone recedes. *In the meantime, she spends years believing and hoping that her investment in the relationship may change him.*

Karen, 46, says, "We've been married eighteen years, had three kids, but he has never *decided* to be a father or a husband for that matter. He lives his life just as he did as a single guy. He doesn't think like a 'we'; he remains an 'I.' He doesn't think in terms of helping with the kids or house. If he does, it's a favor to me."

An insightful male client in his mid 30's said in a marital session, "Bless her heart, I don't help her. She just wants my support. I'm this huge hunk of clay and she's trying to shape me. I get selfish, and want to watch hockey or my police shows, to lie around. I agree two weeks in advance to plans with our kids, but when it comes right down to it, and if I don't want to do it, I won't, and I make her justify why she wants to. I accuse her of overcompensating with the kids or being overextended, but all she wants is a little cooperation and help from me."

"I'm always pulling him along," his wife says in tears. "It's a struggle. Yes, I'm exhausted from taking care of the kids and from my job, but the real stress is having to argue with him, to figure out ways to manipulate him. I don't like having to do that. Can't we just be partners?" He won't hold up his end of the stick, despite his insight.

We get down to where the rubber meets the road. I ask him, "What have you expected of your wife regarding meals?"

"That she'll fix them."

"What did you expect?" I ask the wife.

"That we'd be 50/50 partners and chop lettuce side by side."

Men don't value relationships as much
as they do fulfilling their goals.

Another woman reports her boyfriend forgets the appointments they make with each other or gets them slightly wrong. He doesn't make these mistakes at work. She, rightfully so, feels slighted. Truly, he doesn't value the relationship as he does his work or believe it requires the commitment work does. But few women need to be told to keep appointments with a romantic partner; they are primed early for relationship.

Men see a woman as motivation to succeed at work

"The greatest living experience for every man is his adventure into the woman. The man embraces in the woman all that is not himself, and from that one resultant, from that embrace, comes every new action."
—D. H. Lawrence.

So, if not for emotional connection, why do men seek a relationship with a woman? First, for sex--and sex, for him, *is* the emotional connection. Another primary reason, though, is that women provide incentive for men to work, circling back to what men want to do anyway. Testosterone gives men a sense of agency, the drive to get things done, to make things happen. Having a woman in his life fuels him to fulfill his need to achieve.

Men seek a relationship with a woman for sex and because women provide incentive for them to succeed at work.

Kahlil Gibran, a male Lebanese painter and writer who impacted Americans greatly, wrote in 1901, "I am indebted for all that I call 'I' to women, ever since I was an infant. Women opened the windows of my eyes and the doors of my spirit. Had it not been for the woman-mother, the woman-sister, and the woman-friend, I would have been sleeping among those who seek the tranquility of the world and their snoring." There's something about femininity that awakened his energy and set him on fire to achieve, potentiating his gifts. "A woman is to a nation what light is to a lamp. She illumines the world, responsible for man's genius and achievement." Gibran believed women were the developers of men.

Gibran's story is not unlike that of Franklin Delano Roosevelt, who received inspiration for The New Deal from his female Secretary of Labor. We credit him, but she was the guiding light. And who knows how much his wife, Eleanor, lit his greatness — she who said, "You gain strength, courage, and confidence by every experience in which you really stop to look fear in the face. You must do the thing which you think you cannot do."

In the movie *Cross Creek*, Mary Steenburgen plays the author of the book *The Yearling* and compliments her lover, saying he's something of a poet. He replied, "With you, I think I'm everything." The testosterone surge that goes with winning (in this case, her) causes him to realize she empowers him to achieve. A woman may feel flattered by such a statement, but remain unaware of what he's really saying.

Sex fuels his testosterone. Testosterone pushes men to achieve. Achievement raises testosterone. Testosterone makes a man want sex. Sex fuels testosterone. Herein is the feedback loop men seek from women.

Men rely on women, not primarily for emotional support, social connection, to give them children, to keep them connected to their children, or to provide the physical support of clothing, food, and a stocked home, but to motivate them to reach their potential at work. This is why men say they prove their love by working. A woman can be quite taken back by this orientation. *She thought his primary motivation would be to keep an ongoing emotional connection with her.*

Paul Zak, neuroeconomist, found testosterone leans one to the self rather than to the needs of others. It causes a high focus and drivenness and desire for social status — in other words, to succeed at work.[45]

Men Seek Social Dominance

Political correctness demands we couch male dominance in terms like "taking responsibility" or "exercising leadership skill." But, in close relationships, many women experience it as nothing less than men having to have their own way.

The research

"I think it fair to say that no matter the century the pattern has not changed: if you made a list of the most despicable one thousand characters of the twentieth century, they would all be men. It was men who robbed, raped, pillaged, plundered, burned, and bombed their way through history, ancient as well as modern."
—Leonard Schlain[46]

Studies show that testosterone makes men self-assured with a desire for group or public control. When we say a man has been emasculated, we mean he has no control. Seventy three percent (73%) of men score higher on social dominance than the average woman does, according to Lippa and Arad.[47]   Using force (or withdrawal) to make a woman do what they want is one form of dominance. The Center for Disease Control reports that, due to domestic violence, one fourth of American women are debilitated physically and emotionally. Each year, they say, 1,200 females are killed and two million injured by their partners.[48]

The extreme example of social dominance is murder,
where empathy is cut off altogether in order
to have one's own way.

The most extreme form of social dominance is taking what you want by murdering. Killing someone is the epitome of being non-relational because the killer must disregard all empathy for the other and become fixated on his own wants. After surveying studies across time, D. M. Buss, author of *The Murderer Next Door*, says almost all murders are committed by men.[49]

About 32% of all female murder victims in the US die at the hands of spouses, ex-spouses, boyfriends, and ex-boyfriends, but experts believe the true numbers may be as high as 50 percent to 70 percent instead. Over 50 percent of these murderers stalk their lover first. Men commit the vast majority of spousal homicide in all other countries, too. The most common cause of wife battering everywhere in the world is male possessiveness. In contrast, in 1998, only 4% of male homicide victims were killed by a former or current female partner. There's a big difference between men's and women's need for dominance.

Historically many societies have actually *fostered* this male predilection to guard a mate from poachers or desertion. For instance, English common law regarded the slaughter of an adulterous wife as understandable, even *justified*—if done in the heat of passion. Legal traditions in Europe, Asia, Africa, Melanesia, and among American Indians also condoned or overlooked murder by a jealous husband. And until the 1970s, in several American states it was ok (i.e., lawful) to kill an adulterous wife.[50]

There's a big difference between men's
and women's need for dominance.

If we look beyond romantic relationships, the subject of this book, for just a moment, we immediately see the international consequences of the testosterone-driven sex leading nations. Tsutomu Yamaguchi said, "The only people who should be allowed to govern countries with nuclear weapons are mothers, those who are still breast-feeding their babies."[51]   Most violence has been committed by men who began fantasizing about it as boys. Taking aggressive risks and seeking revenge, men bring their tendencies into world politics *and* into their intimate relationships. Creating a more equal female-male mix in all arenas of life will tip society to less violence and more nurturance. Now, we return to our real topic.

Women rarely injure or murder someone, and, if jealous, they try seduction first.[52]   But then, the structure of a man's brain is different from hers. His amygdala, an almond-shaped mass deep inside the brain, is particularly sensitive to danger and tends toward impulsivity. Furthermore, it is fueled by cortisol, the stress hormone causing bursts of energy; vasopressin, the hormone released after intercourse causing men to be jealous; and testosterone, the hormone associated with aggression and dominance. Not only is the amygdala larger in men than in women, but women's greater oxytocin calms their amygdalas.

The second most extreme form of social dominance is rape. The old picture of the cave man clubbing a woman and dragging her back to his cave is like the current trend toward date rape. The guy uses drugs to subdue a woman for his own means.

Studies show that 83% of women are
more "tender-minded" than your average guy.

Meta-analysis are particularly interesting because it averages the results of *many* studies. Psychologists Eagly and Steffen meta-analyzed 64 studies on aggression and found 61% of men to be more aggressive than women.[53]   Feingold meta-analyzed personality traits and found that the greatest gender difference was in levels of assertiveness: Sixty-nine percent of men were more assertive than women. He also found that a whopping 83% of women were more "tender-minded" than your average guy.[54]

How social dominance plays out

In our times, few men murder or rape, so how does male dominance that stems from testosterone impact current relationships? Susan, 50, says, "I was fighting his dominance every day. I felt overrun. I was always asking myself, 'If I don't give in, what will the consequences be?' It was exhausting. Eventually, I had to get out or die."

Joan, 62, was raised in a small town, in a Baptist church, where she was taught that a woman accommodates her man. Her marriage has been difficult, and she just kept thinking, "If I can just be perfect...". Over the years, she's lost herself and remains chronically depressed. Women with these beliefs are usually older, carry their mother's perspective, or have religious influences. On the other end of the spectrum is a younger woman like Jennifer, 29, who will not put up with being controlled and goes toe-to-toe with her husband. She and her husband blow up in direct power struggles and stay hurt or angry with each other.

"I had to leave the relationship," Christine, 48, said, "in order to find my autonomy outside his disapproval."

Valerie, married 24 years, says, "He's squashing me. I have an idea and he minimizes it. I'm criticized for every move I make. I've become a semblance of myself, ineffective because I'm playing out potential conversations and replaying old ones."

Sylvia, a hospital administrator, 43, says, "Robert suppresses me. Everything has to conform to his way, so I lose my self-expression—at least at home."

Jill, 28, says, "When I ask him to slow down because he's clearly driving dangerously, he speeds up." Trying to maintain a love relationship with him is difficult when "he's willing to risk my life so he can be in control."

Because it is males who have held societal power, men feel the need to prove themselves to other men above wanting to please their female partners. Again, we reflect on how important work is to men in that it provides a proving ground other men can see.

You may be surprised at a man's insensitivity
when he wants his own way.

"His way, his needs first—that's how my relationships with men have been. I feel selfish or like I'm not being empathic if I try to get my own needs met," Sara begins. Notice that, oddly, *she's* the one who feels selfish and unempathic.

Sara, 43, continues, "I did everything he didn't care to do, from housework to errands to child care. He did what he wanted to do: just as much childcare as was fun for him. He started arguments to get his way late at night when I was dead tired, in order to assure I'd give in. It was about winning. If I expressed emotion, he would say I was overly sensitive."

Margaret, 28 and newly married, says, "My husband's bravado, posturing, defensiveness all seem alien to the relational world I've known. My relationships—at least with female family members and girlfriends and boys in the throws of an early relationship—have been filled with

49

emotional closeness. With him, I don't have that and it's empty. The reasons I want to be in a relationship aren't there. I guess he wants me to be afraid of him."

A man mistakes a woman's attempts at collaboration
for her not having her own goals.

Men don't understand when women are ego-less, unselfish, giving. They don't come from that place. They assume a woman will fight on her own behalf, like he would, and speak up and defend herself if she has a problem. A man gets the impression that a woman wants to sacrifice or that she doesn't have her own goals or that those goals can be easily set aside for his. He doesn't reach out to explore what's happening inside her.

Men don't understand women's deferential language (i.e., "Honey, would you like to have the Johnsons over for dinner tomorrow?") The guy, being hierarchical, thinks she feels incompetent to make up her mind, so it's time for him to step into leadership. She's trying to collaborate, but he misses that.

Because males' feelings are bound to their decision-making, they feel invested in, even defensive if their decisions are questioned. They would like, therefore, a woman to go along with them, freeing them to make decisions unilaterally. One reason men like women as friends, business partners, or life partners is because of women's willingness to be corroborative. Women show deference naturally—oxytocin makes them generous. He'll turn some decisions over to you, not wanting to be involved in something—say, the purchase of a refrigerator—but still doesn't actually collaborate. His tendency is to be dominant or be uninvolved. Her tendency is to partner.

Being collaborative begins with caring enough to listen. Alli, 28, feels frustrated by her husband's lack of attunement with her and says, "Until I get real angry, he doesn't listen." When she gets angry though, it makes him feel justified to call her a bitch or point out how unreasonable she's getting. She feels she can't win.

But females, not coming from a power base, want empathy. Jenny says, "I want him to *know* what I feel. I want him to *care* about my feelings," she says. He misinterprets and thinks her need for an apology is her trying to dominate him. "I just want him to *know* and *see* me."

Women seek understanding from men and are rarely
interested in having power over them.

Sometimes the male need for power affects small things in a relationship. Tom was almost falling asleep at the wheel and driving so slowly they were hardly making headway. But he can't let his wife who has a perfect driving record drive because he must continually be in charge.

Andrew, 54, confided, "It was really important I control her." He told his physician-wife to do things yet "the things I insisted she do weren't really important to me." Suddenly, his wife had had enough. She's not sure why she was so passive for two decades, when family and friends kept telling her he was emotionally abusive. Was it because of their son? Was it because all her energies were going toward keeping him satisfied? Andrew said, "I wanted to assert *something* because I'm like a househusband." He made a third the money she did and was the one to take their son to and from school. Controlling her made him feel "like a man." She left abruptly and he felt he couldn't live without her, yet he said he wasn't aware his controlling was "such a big deal."

Commitment phobias are often just
a spinoff of social dominance.

Many self help books address men's commitment phobia, which is often just a spinoff of social dominance. When a man turns over his sexual needs to a woman, he realizes the tremendous power she has over him. He steps back to ponder if giving up his autonomy is worth it.

Many religions have promoted the subservice of wives to husband's leadership, as does a prominent writer of the New Testament, the Apostle Paul. He goes so far as to group the instruction to women alongside children obeying parents and slaves obeying masters. Perhaps this was Paul's own way of creating peace among families, as opposed to an actual edict coming from the Loving Supreme. One thing is clear: Paul wasn't setting out to further the development of females. Nonetheless, society has moved in the direction of subduing men's social dominance through laws while affording women greater earning power. Despite Paul, where she makes more money, she has a greater say in a marriage.[55]   Some believe the impetus behind evolution is actually God. If that is true, God is moving society toward the development of females.

It seems obvious that what's happened in relationships, as illustrated above, is what's always happened in classrooms. Boys take over the leadership spots making girls spectators. If put in all girls' schools, girls lead, do better in math and science, and sustain their self-belief, according to professors Davis and Myra Sadker.[56]   These professors, having studied sexism in the classroom for over ten years, said girls' schools were "where girls are the players, not the audience." They assert that girls maintain their confidence in single-sex schools. In co-ed environments, not only do boys take over class discussions, they are five times more likely to seize a teacher's attention and eight times more apt to impulsively interject remarks, skipping the protocol the girls observe: raising your hand and waiting to be called on.[57]

Men's social dominance explains why women have *pretended* to be less competent, less assertive, less prideful of their accomplishments, and more willing to sacrifice their identities and needs in a relationship. What's the use of being aware of your preferences if you know he'll plow over them? In her love and empathy, she gave him the role he wanted in the relationship, while she, unfortunately, lost herself, and, no doubt, her genuine ability to respond to him. When dominance extends into romances, it damages the very heart of what made the relationship desirable in the first place, at least for women.

Men's social dominance explains
why women have *pretended* to be less competent and more
willing to sacrifice their needs in a relationship.

Making money makes men feel dominate

When men "win," and work is filled with ways to do so, they have a testosterone surge.

Cynthia, 34, married a fellow social worker, and they worked together in a disadvantaged foreign country. Back in the states, his new career in commercial real estate blossomed and they had two children. He's up at 5 AM, home at 6, plays with the kids for 45 minutes while on his iphone, and then spends the rest of the night emailing. They have lost communication, but they find some comradery sharing a little too much alcohol late in the evening. She shops because she's bored and they now have a lot of money. In fact, if he retired now, they'd be ok. When she tells him how unhappy she is, he calls her an ungrateful bitch. He has an insatiable, addictive drive to work. He loves the rush of making money. He's happy living in his systemized brain, with little thought for the possible relationships available to him at home. He says he'll work hard for 5-10 years and then they will be able to do whatever they want. But what she wants is emotional closeness with him. She has allowed him to invalidate her feelings. She has allowed her mother to tell her how lucky she is that he's such a good provider. She is empty, lost, disappointed, and starting to have emotional and physical problems.

Men who experience a drop in social status
experience four times the depression.

Cathleen, having been married 30 years, says matter-of-factly, "I don't think my husband has a soul. He's selfish and shut down. All he cares about is making money."

It is unclear what will happen in romances as women continue to soar in their current sequence of getting better educated, leading to finding better careers, leading to making more money. Certainly, the earning power of females, where nearly 40% are now the primary earner, challenges a man's sense of dominance. What we do know is that men whose social status drops, experience four times the depression, when compared with women who move down the job ladder.[58] As we move deeper into the

21st century, men's depression is bound to increase. Most jobs (75%) lost due to the recession beginning in 2007 belonged to men. But even with an economic recovery, it is unlikely men's time-honored careers will return.[59]

Yikes—how'd we get here?
Our deep past

To answer that, we ask, what were our ancestors doing? How did men's dominance grow so much greater than women's? Laura Betzig believes our forefathers from Mesopotamia, China, Egypt, the Incas and Aztecs were controllers, too. She believes that the kind of men who prevailed mated with hundreds of women and killed other men to get their way.[60] These men were all about themselves.

That is, aggressive, dominant men—those low enough in empathy and non-relational enough to kill—are the ones who spread their seed. *Our genetic pool is swimming with these genes.* Today, following the same masculine hierarchical style, America's male CEOs wield inordinate control, shaping our lives and often the lives of the world's citizens. It's doubtful these male decisions come anywhere close to the kinds of decisions female leaders would make. (Of the Fortune 500 corporations, twelve are topped by females, with no increase in the year 2010 to 2011.[61] But I digress.)

Dominance and a self orientation in males
existed for thousands of years.

Going even further back, male mammals' displays of social dominance resulted in higher testosterone. This translated into more and better sex and higher volumes of ejaculated sperm, note Ogas and Gaddam, *A Billion Wicked Thoughts.*[62] That is, taking control has held big benefits for the male of the species, both human and animal.

Furthermore, we ask, "How have we viewed leadership in the past?" Primitive peoples and the military looked for a firm hand, someone with a single-minded focus who could nail down the minimum number of steps needed to efficiently achieve the goal. Leadership was about cutting to the chase. The object wasn't to get others to think or to inspire their best creative efforts. It was about obedience. Who could inspire obedience? Someone you wouldn't question—someone dominant. A leader whom people feared? Well, that was a plus.

Taking control has held big benefits
for the male species, both human and animal.

These leaders tended to have lower amounts of empathy, so they could view people as machines, considering only what others could contribute or how they could be used. Leaders didn't worry about each member individually or what anybody felt. The *function* of the individual was important, but the *person* was dispensable. Someone's feelings were the last consideration. Firing low achievers hasn't been a problem for low-empathy leaders who don't consider the consequences for the individual.

Our male leaders have lacked empathy
and been rewarded for it.

And being in leadership paid off for our male ancestors! Paul Zak's lab found that high testosterone males are ambitious and highly focused. Testosterone climbs in a man when he attains high status.[63] Remember seeing apes on a National Geographic show fighting to defeat other males so they can "have" the best mate? Well, it's still going on. Studies of *current* pre-industrial societies in Brazil and Venezuela find that aggression wins men economic gain, slaves, additional wives, and revenge and leads to higher social status, making him more desirable as a husband and father to their children, according to David Geary. While some men had no children, another had *forty-three*. One man had 401 more great-grandchildren than his neighbor![64] Aggression was the key. Those who murdered (that is, who weren't very empathic or relational) doubled their number of spouses and tripled their number of kids, compared to non-killing men. All this to say that dominance reaped desirable rewards for our forbearers.

Think Castro, Che, Mao, Lenin, Stalin and contemporary leaders ordering genocide. Looking closer to home, the authors of *Snakes in Suits* consider the penetration of psychopaths into US corporations. Charming, confident, lacking empathy, and manipulative, they exploit an organization's practices and structures.[65]

Psychopathy is an extreme lack of empathy. In the male work hierarchy, a psychopath can rise to the top because ruthlessly getting to the bottom line is more valued by him than showing empathy to employees, Mother Nature, or consumers. He makes tomato sauce with corn syrup despite health consequences because it's cheaper. He makes Styrofoam cups rather than paper, despite the gathering of such cups in our oceans. He makes sodas that kids consume that are about as good for you as drinking motor oil. Psychopathic CEOs show up *four times more* than in the general population. Other top dogs show psychopathic traits but don't fully fit the full diagnosis of "psychopathic." Psychologist Jon Ronson believes that not only are many CEOs and politicians are psychopaths, but that dog-eat-dog capitalism is itself a manifestation of psychopathy.[66] As women rise, will they change this? They certainly possess the empathy to do so.

The link between the rise to leadership and
sexual improprieties is high testosterone.

Ever wonder why so many powerful men commit egregious sexual sin? Dominique Strauss-Kahn headed the International Monetary Fund and was a lead candidate for the French presidency for 2012. On May 14, 2011, he was charged with sexual assault and attempted rape of an American hotel housekeeper. (Couldn't he hold off till after the election?) Before this incident, a young journalist reported he'd tried tearing her clothes off, a lawmaker vowed she'd avoid being alone with him again after being groped, and his second wife's goddaughter kicked and slapped him as he tried undressing her. Those French men![67]

But wait. America has its own share of risk-taking leaders who believe the rules don't apply to them. And they get away with it. Reports have it that our third president, Thomas Jefferson, fathered six kids with his slave. Governor Arnold Schwarzenegger fathered a child with a household helper. Newt Gingrich was carrying on an affair with a staff member while trying to impeach Clinton. Clarence Thomas ascended to the Supreme Court despite accusations of sexual harassment from his former employee. Woody Allen photographed his partner's adopted daughter and then married her. Bill Clinton was acquitted despite having sexual relations with a staffer. John F. Kennedy was known for his affairs. Tiger Woods joined those who didn't really get in trouble.

Other powerbrokers do get in trouble—well, okay; they get a slap on the wrist. Mike Tyson was jailed for rape, but only for three years. Roman Polanski, filmmaker, sexually assaulted a 13-year-old, served 42 prison-days, and then successfully fled the country. Eliot Spitzer frequented prostitutes while simultaneously arraigning prostitute rings. John Ensign, US Congressman and religious fundamentalist, broke laws concealing an affair and Ted Haggard, evangelical minister, articulated opposition to same-sex marriage while seeking a massage from a male prostitute.[68] John Edwards' using campaign funds to hide his mistress and baby didn't escape the judge's notice.

The link between the rise to leadership and sexual improprieties is high testosterone, which rises both when men ascend in status and when men cheat, according to Dr. Paul Zak, senior researcher for UCLA and testosterone expert.

A woman's natural tendency is to give of herself freely, but it is necessary that she guard herself and set boundaries with men.

Has much changed? Women still identify with Mary Chapin Carpenter as she sings, "He Thinks He'll Keep Her," (speaking of a woman who marries, sacrifices herself to make her guy's life easy and then, at 36, meets him at the door and says I don't love you anymore) and Faith Hill as she sings "I Can't do that Anymore," about a woman who sacrifices to run his castle but has no personal fulfillment. Despite anti-discrimination laws and movies with female heroines, the basic nature of men doesn't change, so women still fight men's insensitivity to them.

Collaboration—the opposite of dominance

The opposite of social dominance is collaboration and it's what women believe a relationship is all about. Girls rank "building intimate relationships" and "enjoy working with other students" above "being dominant," found researchers Willingham and Cole. Boys gave preference to enjoying "doing *better than* friends" and would choose "social status" over "intimacy."[69]

Perhaps primologist De Waal would say it comes down to differing values. Across time and culture, men value the same thing: struggling to win, determining who gets what, and having control or greater strength.[70]

Men value winning and showing strength
over the feminine trait of being collaborative.

A woman's natural tendency is to give herself freely to a relationship, but it is necessary that she *guard* herself, *keep in touch* with herself, and *set boundaries* to protect herself. She has to get alone, get quiet, or talk things through with a confidant to know what *she* wants. She has to stand up for herself. More on this later. Evolution did not equip men with a propensity toward collaboration. If he gives in to you or your perspective he may see it as "kissing ass." You're now "one up" and his "status" in the "relationship hierarchy" has been jeopardized. He remembers this and suddenly you feel you're boxing shadows. He argues over weird things. He has an agenda you can't see. The conflict is all about his need to be *at the top*. He is, in effect, showing you your place. This is odd to a woman because she's not hierarchical. This is why our foremothers connived to let a man think her ideas were actually his and she then applauded him for his brilliance.

If a guy gives in to his female partner,
he then sees her as "one up" and his "status" in the
"relationship hierarchy" has been
jeopardized.

Men are Sexually Driven

"Sex is the reason for marriage. If that's broken, the relationship is broken," says one well-educated husband, 36.

The Medial Preoptic Area, located in the brain's hypothalamus and having to do with the sexual hunt, is 2.5 times greater in men. Thus self-help books tell women to let the guy, at the beginning of a relationship, pursue her; she will turn him off if he doesn't *feel* the hunt. Men's Periaqueductal Gray brain circuit, located in the mid-brain, is more active in males during sex, contributing to *intense* pleasure.[71] So, even if a woman is a multiple-orgasmer, she may value sex less than her guy does.

Sexual preoccupation is common to males.

Between ages nine and fifteen, a boy's daily quotient of *one cup* of circulating testosterone per day *soars to two gallons a day*, livening his hypothalamus to grow over twice that of a girl's, pushing sexual conquest to the front of his thinking.[72] I have found that teen boys and grown men entering therapy often want to understand if they are sexual perverts when, actually, they have the normal preoccupation with sex common to males.

"Boy crazy" girls aren't dreaming of intercourse, but enjoy studying boys' psychological makeup and how the male–female dynamics work. In the end, she would be disappointed to learn boys are so shallowly penis-driven, while she is so heart-driven. Women complain, "All he wants is to get me in bed," but men rarely if ever say that of a woman. She finds his orientation disingenuous. Being part of a "meat market" feels minimizing.

When a woman starts explaining her emotional needs in a marital session and inquires about his, I have heard many men say something like, "I'm not that complicated. I just want sex and a happy wife. That's it." She's left baffled. She always thought there was more there. But a happy wife means he's been successful at his husband-job and thus, his testosterone and dopamine rise.

A summary of 177 studies found that, when compared to the average female, 71% of men affirmed casual sex and 83% masturbate more than women do.[73] Feingold found that males deemed liking a woman's body significantly more important than did women, who valued other traits in men.[74] International researchers also found that 69% of men regard physical attractiveness as more important than does the average female, which holds true across cultures, meaning it has to do with how men are, not what they're taught.[75] Women seek committed, emotionally close affiliations, with sex as a part of the whole, while, compared with women, men are more interested in sex for sex's sake, according to Roscoe, Diana, & Brooks.[76]

Across cultures, men are more likely to seek multiple mates, sexual stimulation through porn, and/or sex from prostitutes.[77] This makes sense since testosterone promotes sexual bustle. Men fancy having about fourteen sexual partners—some one night stands—in a lifetime, while women want one or two.[78]

Women find the physical parts of a
relationship unusually important to a man.

Unknowingly, a woman may come into the relationship already "indebted" to him or needing to prove that *his* commitment to her is "worth it." After all, he's relinquished free access to sexual variety *for her*. From there, men may feel justified having an affair because she offers less sex. She may be avoiding sex because he's a poor lover, won't offer enough emotional connection to justify sex, or because she's pregnant or has recently had a baby, making her exhausted or in temporary hormonal chaos. Nevertheless, he may feel justified treating her poorly or going behind her back for sex. "All marriage is legalized prostitution," a man tells me. That's the bottom line: he pays for her things and she gives him sex. So if she's not sexual, he counters by being stingy.

"Sex is the most wonderful thing in the world," John, 42, tells me, "and I can't figure out why, though my wife orgasms, she doesn't want it more. Why not all the time?" For men, sex is love, and for a lot of men, if the sex in a relationship is good, then they'd be happy with the relationship no matter what else was going on. Well, as long as he doesn't feel too put down by her criticisms.

John's wife says, "When my husband was, at the beginning of our relationship, so crazy about my body, I found it mildly flattering. He commented on it all the time. 'It.' That's what I call my body. I mean, I take care of 'it,' but 'it' is not 'me.' I kept wondering when the relationship was going to go deeper. Because we have good sex, he feels like we have a soul connection. But a soul connection means something else to me. You know that movie, *Carmen*, where, after she's dead, her lover kisses her whole body and he feels like it's finally his? Well, even though we've been together for so long, I feel kinda like I'm Carmen and my husband's having a relationship primarily with my body."

Rachel, 47, had been caretaking her sick mother-in-law for months. After calls to the insurance companies, arranging health care, emptying bed pans, holding down her part-time job, and managing her three teenagers, she was often worn out at the end of the day.

But one night her husband leveled with her, saying, "I only ask one thing from you."

"What's that?" she asked, her mind scanning her many activities.

"Sex."

She was shocked. What about how she kept the house or brought comfort to his mother or made his life easy?

"I need physical intimacy like I need air and food," another man says. Women are often stumped by how sexuality composes such a major part of a man's life. Consider the song sung by Joe Cocker, "You Give Me Reason to Live," where he describes a woman stripping. Few women would see a man stripping as giving her that kind of fulfillment.

While a woman seeks a man she can be attracted to mentally, meaning that she likes the way he thinks or is attracted to his character, a man's first priority is physical attraction. Sometimes emotional, mental, physical and spiritual attractions eventually follow, but many women find that men's acumen toward the physical prevents them from seeing them in deeper ways.

His sexual desire can be stronger than his desire to relate.

His physical attraction to her doesn't mean a whole lot because a stranger giving cat calls is attracted to her and wants her body, too. It feels shallow; she wants something deeper, more meaningful. She wants him to seek to truly know her and then love her for who she is beyond her physical body.

Ted, 36, admits he was not looking for wit, intelligence or charm; he just wanted to make sure her butt wouldn't get too big after having a baby.

A woman can't always tell if a man is using her for sex or really loves her. She knows that her body isn't the essence of her and that it will age and change. Her character and her thoughts seem more important.

In his classic book, *His Needs, Her Needs*, Willard Harley, Jr. outlined the top five needs men expect to have met in a marriage. The first three for men were sexual fulfillment, recreational companionship, and an attractive spouse. The first three for women were affection, conversation, and honesty and openness.[79] Two physical expectations for men; two emotional expectations for women.

At the start of a relationship, he doesn't notice that she's never talked with him about her parents or her work or what college she graduated from. He doesn't know about her nearly as much as she knows about him. She's asked questions, drawing him out, wanting to know the true person, the inner self, what he feels and wants and dreams. He seems to believe he "knows" her because they've had sex. She, in fact, remains unknown to him, so she wonders what he means when he says he loves her.

A male college student whose girlfriend wants to wait for marriage to have sex, says, "What I've always done with my male ego about our not having sex, since I couldn't blame myself, is to make up stories about why she wasn't willing."

I ask, "Didn't that keep you from talking to her in a genuine way and really getting information about her true feelings and reasons?" He shrugged.

Men and women have evolved differently. When male hunters killed or pursued animals, their testosterone rose sharply as did their sex drives. When female gatherers nurtured children, their testosterone remained less developed and their estrogen and oxytocin rose. In fact, it was important her sex drive wasn't too high because she needed a nonsexual relationship with her children.

For men, sex *is* emotional closeness.

Consequently, most couples face a sexual dilemma: his sex drive is much higher than hers. The high-desire person in a relationship feels deprived, like his spouse is withholding from him, perhaps purposely making him miserable. The low-desire person feels pressured, consumed by his needs, overwhelmed. He comes to her with the weighty expectation of sex, sex, sex and she feels no matter how much she gives, it's never enough. He says, "My wife and I have a two-hour conversation and I feel close to her, but I am still disappointed and hurt if it doesn't lead to sex. That is the main validation I want from her." Another man reports, "I can't feel special without sex." Many men think a relationship is sex, love is sex, and marriage is sex. He feels that no matter what else they share—family, a home, hobbies—the only thing that *counts* is sex. Even at middle age when his testosterone begins going down, and men and women are more alike hormonally, his testosterone level is still about ten times what hers is.

Why do fathers warn their daughters about boys, but moms don't warn boys about girls, generally speaking? Isn't it because boys can engage a girl emotionally through touch or charm, leading her to believe it's reasonable for her to expect an ongoing relationship with him, only to find he detaches and breaks her heart? He was just experimenting sexually, which had little to do with her as a person. Have you ever heard a man say, "I'm worried she's just using me for sex?"

Even though a man shares a home and children with a woman, even though he's experienced a wedding, childbirth, childrearing, career building, and many shared relationships—from friends to in-laws—with a woman, he may prefer and trade her for a sexually hot woman if the opportunity presents.

Growing access to pornography is disturbing to women, partly because in some men it can replace the need for actual contact or create impotence without the hyper stimulation porn gives. (True male fulfillment can only come from direct contact with a woman, however. More later.)

A male client, 32, explains his ongoing use of porn, after his girlfriend objects to it. "I use porn to cope. It's emotional, not physical. It gives me a high. It's what I use for emotional connection."

"Well, Mona's wondering," I say, and glance at her, "if you limited your porn use, would you be more available for a sexual relationship with her?"

"No," he says, "it doesn't have anything to do with that."

I ask, "What would increase your being sexual with her?"

"If she didn't criticize me," he responds.

"It's hard not to criticize you, though," I suggest, "when you keep using porn."

His girlfriend, Mona, speaks, "I'm very careful, though, about what I say. I'm gentle."

"That's true," he admits. "But I can't stand *any* criticism. It reminds me of when I was a child."

"Do you see how she's in a bind?" I ask.

He thinks. "Yes, my using porn hurts her, so she's on my back about it."

"I think you may be unaware that your porn use does make it less likely you'll be sexual with her. And instead of using porn, what would you think about finding true, healthy ways to cope?" The problem is that he may prefer porn to working directly with his feelings.

Sexual talk and sexual jokes make a man happy, so if his significant other is down, he might use this kind of talk to try cheering her up. It doesn't go over; she wants dialogue and empathy.

The real problem is this: For men, sex *is* the relationship. Researchers find that males are about four times more likely than women to see sex and emotional closeness as the same thing.[80]   Men can stretch to give a woman romance and dialogue before sex, but he doesn't need it himself to feel close.

Males are about four times more likely than women
to see sex and emotional closeness as the same thing.

And, then, just when a woman hopes for talking and cuddling, a man falls asleep after sex. This postcoital narcolepsy is caused by oxytocin, the hormone women have more of dawn to dusk, that makes a man, finally, feel safe and warm. He sleeps, but the woman feels neglected.

Joseph Campbell speaks for most men (but not women) when he says that it is the purely physical experiences that give us life's meaning. For Mr. Campbell and other men, this statement seems true, and sex represents one of those ultimate physical experiences. For women, though, it is emotional and relational experiences that make them feel alive.

Sexual attraction is so important that a man may withdraw from the relationship if his female partner gains weight. She wonders why he can't just love her soul.

For women, emotional and relational
experiences, rather than physical ones, are
what make them feel alive.

Men Have Relied on Women to Make Their Relationships Work

About ten thousand years ago, a societal ladder rose that excluded women from property ownership and education. In a strait jacket financially, she finessed her way in relationships with wage-earning men. She supported and encouraged his success, and made life easy for him, from providing clothes and food to emotional sustenance. She listened, cheered him up, and worked to understand him. She was unequivocally supportive of him. The responsibility to make the relationship work fell to her. He was the one meant to benefit relationally from their union. Women gave. And because she relied on his good graces for her children's and her own support, making sure her primary relationship was in good repair felt imperative to her. This was not easy because her marriage, most likely, was an arranged alliance.[81]

Males have never experienced a long period
of history where their very existence depended
on the quality of relationship they created
with a person of the opposite sex.

Her need added another ring to her relationship acumen. Not only, then, did she gain empathy through the hormonal flood at childbirth, doing the highly relational work of teaching children, healing the sick, and working in groups with other women, but a long period of financial dependency demanded she become a relationship expert. Men, on the other hand, have not experienced a long period of history where their very existence depended on the quality of relationship they created with another person. *Men, therefore, still think of relationships as a soft place to land, not as something requiring effort.* Men still cling to the old relationship format: a relationship with a woman is supposed to be good for *them.*

Prior to this, women had autonomously provided most of the daily food, using their own initiation to find it, traveling as far as they needed. Men hunted, but women separately provided 60% to 80% of the community's sustenance.[82]

66

Mary, 28 and well educated, couldn't stand the smell of her husband's breath when he wanted sex first thing in the morning. "Could you ask him to pop a lifesaver?" I asked.

"I can't tell him! I don't want to hurt his feelings," she said. Yet the smell made her nauseous and turned off her sexual arousal.

The long history of financial dependence caused women to be more submissive than assertive in relationships.

Other Testosterone-Caused Factors that Hinder Closeness with Males

Snoring

One of the joys of a relationship is cuddling up with another warm body all night long, but when a guy snores, a woman is randomly awakened and sleeps nervously. He, not aware of his snoring, may feel offended when she moves to another room. Her empathy alerts her to how important the physical relationship is to him, including sleeping together. Yet she has to face that her disjointed sleep can contribute to illness and fatigue. About twice as many men snore as women and snoring increases with age, says Duran, Esnaola, and Iztueta.[83]

Marie's husband snores, keeping her awake, so that she never really gets a night's sleep. "He's defensive when I tell him I'm exhausted. And he won't wear a dental device—it bugs him. He doesn't want to go to the doctor. All he wants is for me to stay in bed with him."

Abuse of substances

Dopamine is the hormone that, when released, makes us happy. One study found that, following imbibing alcohol, men experience their dopamine to a greater degree than do women. Researchers believe that the greater dopamine release in men leads them to associate alcohol with pleasure and positive rewards, thus prompting men's drinking more. Nationally, the risk of men developing alcohol abuse or dependency is nearly *twice* as high as in women.[84]

Remember the AARP study showing 23% of women divorce because of verbal, physical or emotional abuse and 17% because of marital cheating? Another 18% divorce because of men's alcoholism or drug abuse.[85] That explains why 58% of women initiate divorce.

Furthermore, addiction is linked to testosterone. That is, the higher your testosterone, the greater your risk of substance abuse disorders. High testosterone levels at twelve to fourteen years of age predict substance abuse disorders by age 22. Another study showed the relationship between high testosterone, breaking rules, seeking dominance, being aggressive, and later substance abuse.[86]

18% of women divorce their husbands
because of men's alcoholism or drug abuse.

High testosterone in men goes hand in hand with increased risk taking. In male teenagers, high testosterone goes with sensation-seeking and impulsivity. There is a parallel between the effects of testosterone (risk taking, sensation-seeking, and impulsivity) and substance abuse.[87] The abuse of substances can make men in relationships less available emotionally, more irritable and unpredictable.

The abuse of substances can make men in relationships
less available emotionally, more irritable and unpredictable.

Ann is frustrated with her marriage and says, "He gets over one addiction and is on to the next." They've been through several: his addiction to porn, to steroids, to TV, to computer blogging. "I keep waiting for life to *begin*," she continues, "for a time when we're not fighting his problems. He's absent, married to his addictions. It leaves no room for a true connection."

Jenny, 26, complains of yet another addiction. "He plays games on the computer, especially now that the internet allows him to play with opponents from all over the world, for several hours each night after work. It's his first love. He has little time for our marriage."

Addicts tend to believe that life should be smooth, nothing should be disturbing, and they shouldn't have to deal with much. If they do, it's overwhelming, so they do their addictive behavior to escape.

Higher levels of testosterone lead
to higher risk of substance abuse disorders.

"Evan used to dutifully help with the kids, methodically changing diapers or getting the bottle," said Cynthia, 42. "But he would never sit and look at the baby, in wonder of the new life, the creation. He wouldn't seek a true relationship with the kids. If buying something would shut them up and give him peace, then that's what he would do: anything for peace."

But then Evan broke down and confessed to his wife that he was a sexual addict. He made disclosures—painful, bloody, earth-shaking disclosures of prostitutes, affairs, secrets. His wife was appalled, disgusted by him. He pursued her in the old style: charming her, giving her gifts, and trying to win her as if it were a race to be a won or a land to be conquered. She told him to stop. She needed space. He had to get quiet, begin therapy, and search his soul, she said. She couldn't live with him. He pressured her to make "everything okay again" until she asked him to get a separate apartment. She needed him to find his way out of dependency—on her, on sexual addiction.

Months later, Evan invites his son to sit outside with him as the cold front moves in, just observing nature and feeling the change of weather. He asks his son to bring his guitar outside and show him what he's been learning. Cynthia knows he is moving in the right direction, but wonders if he can be genuine and relational over time. One thing is helping a lot: now when she is angry with him, realizing afresh the lies she's swallowed all these years and the STDs he's exposed her to, Evan knows to sit with her in her anger. He knows, from therapy, to let her cry, to examine the ugly stuff together. He's now able to be with her in their vulnerability, without trying to change her responses. It's the one thing that is making her consider a continuing relationship with him.

Men hear less well

Janel Caine's master thesis included playing soft music to twenty-six premature babies. Another twenty-six received no music. The premature girl babies who received the music were discharged nine and a half days earlier than the girls who did not receive the music. They grew faster and had fewer complications. But the boy babies, *with or without music*, didn't leave the hospital any earlier.[88] Why? Because females and males hear differently. Girls' hearing is seven times more acute than boys'. Girl babies have an 80% greater response to the range of sound used in communication than do boys.[89]

Women hear much better than men.

The difference increases as we age so women hear 24 times better.[90] Sometimes a boy can't hear his soft-spoken grade school teacher, while a teenaged girl believes her male chemistry teacher is yelling. And now you know why you're always repeating yourself to your guy.

In *The Female Mind*, Dr. Louann Brizendine points out that testosterone constricts the size of the brain area devoted to hearing, so when a woman feels her male companion is "deaf," she is, to some degree correct. Intimacy does not lend itself to shouting or to the continual repeating of oneself.[91] Furthermore, in the rare times when men's prolactin increases (causing testosterone to drop) his hearing improves. An example of this is three weeks before his female partner is going to give birth. Unfortunately, it only lasts somewhere between the child's sixth week of life to her first birthday.[92]

Not only do men not hear as well as their female counterparts, they don't *process* conversation as well either. Women often ask if their man is listening. This is because he's driving (or doing something else) and she knows he doesn't multitask well. Besides, he has a blank look on his face. He's irritated by the implication he's not listening and proceeds to quote what she's just said. But he says it with mere repetition, with no sense of really having understood. She feels like she's having a relationship with a robot. He hasn't digested what she said and he didn't catch her nonverbals, the part that portrays the feelings behind the words. Though he can repeat her words, he hasn't grasped her thoughts. Current research is showing that men's left hemisphere alone is activated when they listen, while, in most women, both the left and right hemispheres come alive.

A related problem with men's hearing—just as big—is that to listen well you must be empathic, dropping your own perspective and getting into someone else's world. A very nice middle-aged male client disclosed during marital therapy that when his wife brings up a complaint, it takes him significant time to process what she's saying. First, it takes time to realize he's hurt someone and to then feel guilty enough to do something about it. It may take days, he admitted. Empathy isn't at hand for him. He's not equipped to respond immediately, or even within the day. This conversation lag is one reason women need respites from their partners.

Men's left hemisphere alone is activated when they listen, while, in most women, both the left and right hemispheres come alive.

Now we turn our attention to the subject of empathy in men.

CHAPTER 3:

MEN LACK EMPATHY

The Research

Women have special brain equipment for empathy that men don't have. Mirror neurons in the brain allow us to *read* another person's actions and *imagine* the feeling behind them, to *anticipate* what someone else will feel and to become in sync with that person. Women's mirror-neuron system is both more active and larger than men's. In a series of studies, Yawei Cheng used MEG, spinal reflex excitability, and electroencephalography to study mirror neurons and gender responses. She found that females display a stronger empathic resonance than do males.[93]

Helen Fisher's *The First Sex* references tests of empathy from 1974 to 1993, hundreds of which show women have greater emotional responsiveness, nurturance, and empathy than males do, whether girl infants or older women are measured.[94] Across cultures and time women are perceived as the more nurturing gender, more likely to reach out to the sick or the young.[95]

Daniel Coleman also refers to the hundreds of studies finding that, on average, women are more empathic, as evidenced by their skill in reading another's unstated feelings, relying merely on nonverbal cues like facial expressions.[96] That is, women not only "pick up on" what others feel but they feel motivated to extend help, thanks to their brain structures.

Hundreds of tests show that women have
greater responsiveness, nurturance, empathy and
motivation to help when compared with men.

In asking the question, "Is it really true that females are more empathic than males?" primatologist Frans de Waal states the obvious: if any female mammal failed to respond quickly to the distress in her little ones, she would lose them. That, in and of itself, sensitized her to their emotional state and grew her sensitivities.[97]

Women have special brain equipment that men don't have.

Researchers speculate that a woman's left prefrontal cortex of the brain, where the ability to shut off negative feeling is located, is somehow different in men. Women allow themselves to feel the negative emotion and are then moved to do something about it. Also, because men's connection between the right and left hemispheres is lesser than women's and because they show activation in the left hemisphere *only* when asked to think sad thoughts, this compartmentalization allows them to separate from their feelings.[98]

The level of empathy is even found in what books the genders choose. Two researchers at Queen Mary College in London asked 900 adults which novels had shaped them. The men liked stories where someone was fighting to overcome obstacles or were isolated, as in *The Stranger*. Mostly, though, men read nonfiction. Women, however, loved novels that were relationally and emotionally rich (*Pride and Prejudice, Wuthering Heights*), and look to novels to transport them into a new world where they see life through another's eyes. A study in *Psychology Today* reported frequent novel readers score higher in social acumen, social reasoning, and—you guessed it—empathy. Reading novels is a way to practice intuition as the reader surmises the thoughts and feelings of the characters, as Lisa Zunshine of *Why We Read Fiction* points out.[99]

Men can more easily separate from their feelings.

Women are empathic partly because they have more connections to the right brain. This is where negative emotions are, and, as difficult as it is to have such direct access to tough emotion, it does allow one to empathize with others who are hurting, whether sad, lonely, slighted or discouraged.

On the sociological front, an amazing change has occurred, having directly to do with parents' recognition of the greater empathy in females. Though the birth of male children has been formerly preferred, the Chinese, according to a *New York Times* account, now wish for girls, believing a daughter will render more compassionate care as they age.[100] Aside from the hundreds of tests proving women's empathy, this change is living proof of the empathy of females.

In the end, it is childbirth that distinguishes women from men and grants them a disproportionate supply of hormones crackling with empathy. Once a woman gives birth, she is deluged by hormones that take her empathic abilities up several notches. (Though a father's hormones also adjust, it is nothing like the transformation a woman's brain goes through.) As she bonds with her baby, she is less and less self-focused and she readily leaves her own shoes to get into another's. It is the nature of motherhood and without a mother's empathy none of us would be here.

As a woman bonds with her baby,
she is less and less self-focused.

New moms report experiencing more understanding, warmth, and kindness, found a Turkish psychiatrist.[101] Indeed, mothers go through a profound brain change, making them different from men. Prolactin causes an explosion of new stem cells,[102] estrogens climb hundreds of times their normal amount, and cortisol levels double, making her more alert.[103] Estrogen fuels oxytocin, which makes a woman generous and giving. *She needs a transformed brain, after all, to keep her firmly connected despite the crying and relentless neediness of a newborn.* Facing mounting demands, her brain renovates itself into a more complex organ.[104]

A woman may feel frustrated with her guy's lack of empathy prior to giving birth, but afterwards, she faces a *greater difference* between her empathy level and his.

After childbirth, a woman's brain renovates itself
into a more complex organ.

How the Lack of Empathy Plays Out in Relationships

The effect on men's behaviors

Women want what they give—empathy—because it is the diamond of
all affiliate skills. Kindness, politeness and even manners—which stem
from asking, "What is the kindest thing I can do in this situation?"—all
spring from empathy. She wants and needs genuine concern, emotional
sensitivity, and for her male counterpart to anticipate her needs like she
does his.

Empathy is the diamond of all the relationships skills.

Men's lack of empathy affects romantic relationships in many ways.
Men don't have the force of nature that turns women's hearts to others.
They are free to consider just themselves. When Suzanne plans a vacation, she makes sure her husband has a place to fish, that the kind of
food he likes will be available, that his kids from his first marriage will
have video game access, entertainment, etc. When *he* plans a vacation,
he only considers himself. He puts her on the floor in a sleeping bag, in
a stinky cabin. He figures there must be a mall somewhere, so she can
shop, albeit alone. She feels like his companion for sex and meals, but
otherwise a non-priority. He will do what is necessary to keep her off
his back, but he doesn't otherwise extend himself.

Most men are able to give only a modicum of
what women want most in a relationship—emotional
closeness through empathy.

Naomi, a paralegal, age 36, married for 12 years, opened her heart and wrote Paul a long letter, expressing her appreciate of him. It was her attempt to encourage loving verbalizations in their relationship. However, he didn't respond. He didn't even acknowledge the letter. It felt to her like he'd never read it. He didn't anticipate that she would need feedback.

"I explain how it hurts; he sees me crying, but he doesn't change." Naomi continues and pauses to shake her head and grab a Kleenex. "I've decided it hurts too much to care. I numb myself out."

Is the key to better relationships educating men about having more empathic behaviors? As a psychologist, I continually teach men to say, "Honey, you're more important to me than anyone, and I want to know what you're feeling." It will not flow from a wellspring of emotion, but the words tend to help. The *true, underlying empathy* that she desires and expects isn't there. Women must understand that there are true limits on men's abilities to empathize. Though his words mimic empathy, his ability to spontaneously give it and tune into her when it's needed are limited.

Lisa and Steven were invited by Luke, Steven's old college buddy, to have dinner with him and his second wife whom they'd only met once. In the course of conversation, Steven recounted the fun double dates he and Luke used to go on with Luke's *first* wife. Lisa watched as Luke's current wife became uncomfortable. Lisa saw her eyes drop, her face flush, and the stricken look on her face. Lisa began nudging Steven's leg under the table. Finally, Steven turned to her with irritation and said, "Why are you kicking me?" Lisa flushed and dropped it. Steven wasn't able to communicate subtly or pick up on cues. He was unaware he was causing hurt because he hadn't noticed Luke's wife's face.

Robert had an affair. He knew his wife was terribly wounded. But whenever she started to express her hurt, instead of being present for her, he would say, "Why am I getting my ass chewed out? I know it was wrong." He was unaware of her need to receive his empathy. Couples need a year to eighteen months of rebuilding after an affair. If the wounded female partner is forced to repress her need to talk about it, the affair is probably the beginning of the end. Without openness, relationships, especially for women, can't flourish.

Men can learn to say empathic things, but their
ability to spontaneously give empathy is limited.

Arthur, 46, the head of a charitable organization, can't really imagine what his wife feels after he's had an affair. He can't get into her shoes enough to know what to say to her, so he says things that end up being deeply wounding. In the name of honesty, he recounts a conversation with a friend regarding his affair partner. "My friend says I light up whenever I talk about her. And I admitted that I have deep feelings for her." He expects kudos for being honest, and feels defeated that his wife just cries. He doesn't have enough empathy to gage what *not* to say to her, even though he's highly motivated to win her back.

John was too busy to be there for his wife when she had to pull the plug on her aged, ill mother. That moment will never come again. He wasn't there and the message inscribed on her soul is that she can't count on him. He neither anticipated her need nor understood the depths of it when it was stated to him. She was alone as she faced her mother's death and the hard decision leading up to it. "For me, the marriage will never be the same," Teresa, John's wife said. "I understood my aloneness in this marriage — but it was made concrete. As long as I'm with John, I will always be essentially alone." At her age — 56 — the only real need she has of a marriage is for emotional support. She earns her own money, acts independently in most every way, and has her own set of friends. What she needs from John is a sense of closeness and understanding.

Misty, 42, is a nurse to a surgeon and explains aftercare to patients. She tells me, "I am always concerned when a female patient says her husband will be doing the aftercare. A husband could get lost in TV, the newspaper, or work and not check on her. He could overlook her need for water or medications. He expects her to concretely state her needs, but what if she's not clear-headed enough for a few days to do that? He won't anticipate the loneliness she may feel while in bed recuperating, away from her regular social contacts. He won't offer extra dialogue for the sake of making up for her loss."

Candace, 49, a professor of social work, confirms the nurse's remarks. "When I first came down with cancer and realized I had to go through chemo, I came home and needed him to talk with me, lie down beside me, comfort me," she laments. "I asked clearly for my needs to be met, but he got up and did home repairs. He felt more comfortable doing that, I think. He just left me alone for hours on end. He couldn't read how upset I was. He's task oriented, but emotionally and in terms of nurturing, he just plain can't do it. It hurts. And though I was in the middle of a crisis, I thought about leaving him. I realized that, when I needed him most, he would be the most absent."

The effect on men's talk

Women's talk is filled with "I feel for you" responses, not reasons why someone "shouldn't feel that way" or ways the person's problem can be "fixed." Women's talk is warm, reaching out, loving, and filled with exquisite listening skills that pick up on more than words. Women possess the relational lubricant men don't have much of: emotional empathy.

While men rarely convey how much they mean to each other, women often do. They affirm others and use language to develop a back-and-forth dialogue that creates intimacy. They spend more time than men parleying understandings and making another feel heard.[105]

As adults, women often find that men either talk far too minimally, giving monosyllabic replies, or lecture without the listener giving so much as an "um." They just don't comprehend the idea of checking in with the other person. It takes empathy to understand turn-taking in dialogue.

Dave, 36 and married 13 years to Kendra, says, "I don't get all the fuss about talking. I mean, if Kendra has something she needs to tell me, that's fine. But I'd rather read the newspaper or watch sports when I come home. Talking is exhausting—I've had to do that all day." Dave uses talk to find out what Kendra needs or if she knows something he needs to know. He doesn't view it as a way to access her feelings or thoughts.

It takes empathy to understand turn-taking in dialogue.

The *mental component* of empathy includes dropping one's ego, de-centering, and coming over to the perspective of the other, considering what the other is going through and inferring from there what the other is experiencing. The *emotional piece* of empathy includes a desire to help, feeling sad when they're sad, feeling mad when they're mad, and feeling happy when they're happy. The woman goes into the head of the other, translating cues from their facial expressions, posture, and tone into an imagining of their experience. Truly, *empathy's attunement makes genuine communication possible*. Men's language is often filled with venting, lecturing, story telling, or just filling silence, but lacks disclosures and emotional truth-telling. Instead of finding the rhythm of back-and-forth verbal intercourse, men will hijack the dialogue for their own liking or for a whim. His lesser empathy causes him to be less aware of *her* needs. He doesn't think to provide her with a pause in his speech so she can be a part of the "conversation."

Empathic listening includes *tuning in* so that you can ask relevant questions. Being patient and attentive. Watching for the *rise of feelings* as the other talks. Staying with the speaker verbally and nonverbally, listening for *changes*.

He doesn't think to provide her with a pause in his speech
so she can be a part of the "conversation."

Facial feedback from him would help her feel integrated with his thoughts and feelings. However, men's nervous systems are not wired to the muscles in their faces in the same way women's are, so their faces often look blank. A woman's stronger link between her brain circuits and her face allow people to *see* what she feels. She uses eye contact, facial expression, tone of voice, posture, gestures, timing, and intensity of response to help others understand her and to convey that she "gets" the other person.[106]

Catherine, 36, with big blue eyes and auburn hair, speaks of her relationships with other women. "With my sisters or friends, there's this emotional flow to our dialogues. They pick up on what I'm *really* saying. Our words and feelings are mixed together and flow back and forth and everybody gets it. With my husband, there's this deadness. He listens for the factual side of what I'm saying. That's it."

She continues. "I mean, my girlfriends think I'm intellectually shrewd and ironic, that I'm funny, but he doesn't know that part of me."

This session is hard for Catherine. She wants to get it all out. "I try to get into that flow with him, but he interrupts with his not-so-right-on interpretation, or he offers a way to fix me—like my feelings are a disease or he wants to sexualize what I say. It shuts me down. I just stop. I figure, 'the meaning is lost on him!'" She throws up her hands and shrugs. Then she slumps, saddened. "But what I don't get is how can I ever feel close to him?"

Women use eye contact, facial expression,
tone of voice, posture, gestures,
timing, and intensity of response to convey that
she "gets" the other person.

One Opposite of Empathy is Presumption

Men want to show strength, not weakness or vulnerability; therefore, they want to be *right*.

Women are frustrated when men, as a show of superior knowledge, presume they know, better than they really do, what women need or want or feel. "I know how you feel or what you need better than you do," is the message. Juxtaposed to this attitude is that of women. Rather than projecting her thoughts or feelings onto another, she leaves herself and gets into the mindset of the other, striving to be sensitive and reading non-verbals. Research shows she's very good at intuiting what another feels. It is particularly upsetting when this is not only not reciprocated, but the opposite—presumption is offered.

Carman, a nice looking single 32-year-old administrative assistant, went out with a successful banker, though he'd made some slightly inappropriate comments when she'd met him with friends. She wanted to extend a second chance, but at the restaurant, he brushed her hair back and kissed her neck. She turned bright red. He said, "You're blushing and that means you're attracted to me." Actually, she felt so humiliated she vowed never to return to the popular restaurant where they were eating.

Women demonstrate intuition; men demonstrate presumption.

Low empathy allows one to assume they are right while everyone else is wrong. *Empathy* would recognize that another has a valid point, a partially valid point, or, at a minimum, feelings that cannot be ignored. Empathy knows that there are many ways to see the world.

One of men's most common presumptions is that because a woman is friendly with them, she wants a sexual relationship. She can be utterly surprised when the relationship flips, at least in his mind, and he's making advances. She would like to develop a working relationship or a friendship, but he presumes she finds him sexually attractive.

A man may presume his wife has changed her mind about not wanting him to fondle her breasts while she's doing dishes. He thinks, this is a new day and she may like it now. Sexual attunement requires two people to hear one another. He may perform sexual behaviors that are arousing to him but a turn off to her. If he isn't sensitive, she will turn off in a more permanent way because sex is no longer about feeling stimulated—it's about feeling irritated. More on this topic later.

A wife was cajoled by her husband into going to a strip club with business associates and some of their wives. He arranged for her to get a lap dance and she felt violated. She left after that, returning home in her own car. She cried and cried. She showered in the hottest water she could stand. Meanwhile, he thought she was the coolest wife among the wives there and was proud of her. He felt socially elevated among his peers. When he got home, drunk, he was all over her. He was insulted and defensive to the point of feeling violent when she meekly said, "I don't want to be touched." He couldn't read her before, during, or after the club experience.

Remember that, historically, men have been rewarded for rising to leadership, and the traits that went with leadership had to do with feeling superior, being intolerant and forceful, and expecting to be obeyed. These attitudes, in the military and elsewhere, allowed men to rise to the top.

The AARP report on divorce found that females could better sense problems in their marriage than could men. About *twice as many men* were surprised by their wives' announcement of divorce as were women. The men presumed everything was okay.

Due to the lack of empathy, men presume that everything is ok in the marriage even if it is not.

A similar study found that men presumed their marriages were going well, believing that everything from sex to finances, from communication to how much their faults affected their partner, was fine. They were confident they were doing well in all areas. However, interviews with their wives showed that the husbands were *underestimating* the problems.[107] Their wives weren't fine.

Many women come to the place of leaving their husbands when explanations, tears, and pleadings don't work: he wasn't empathic enough to be moved by them. She finally says she's leaving, she's been through so much pain, that she's truly made up her mind. At this point, he finally believes she's serious and realizes he actually must make a change, at least a superficial one to appease her. He doesn't get in touch with her suffering; he just knows that to keep her, he's going to have to give in some. But she was in deep pain during all the lesser confrontations and has had it. As one divorce attorney said, once a woman has made up her mind, it tends to be permanent. The husband's suffering may just have begun at the *end* of the marriage when he decides he has no choice but to "conform" to her relational needs.

Jessica needed to leave her marriage after 25 years. She couldn't grovel, asking for her needs to be met, one more time. Dan was and always had been very attracted to Jessica, but he thought her bouts of crying would blow over, and sure enough, they seemed to each time. Now, he was dumbfounded as to why she would leave him. He was willing to change, he read the books I'd asked him to, he had written her letters explaining how he realized he'd goofed. Still, he just didn't think they had the kind of marriage that a woman would leave—there was no abuse, after all, and his attraction for her had never waned, and, for goodness sake, he loved her. She felt though, that she no longer had it in her to put herself out there for more hurt. It was too big a risk, given their history. Jessica had experienced his presumption that everything was ok and that he didn't have to change one too many times.

A man's presumption is a woman's frustration.

Sociologists Regnerus and Uecker studied 18–to 23-year-olds and found that most (74%) young men expect that a married woman will contribute steadily to the family income.[108] The key word is "steadily"—that is, the men don't anticipate that pregnancy, childbirth, infant or toddler care will interrupt her contributing. The same sociologists found that college women hold more negative assessments of their male counterparts and of their relationships with those men than men do of the women.[109] Unaware of women's dissatisfaction with men and with their romantic relationships, these men nevertheless come with their demands. Despite their expectations of a woman's uninterrupted wage earning, the men probably assume they will need to contribute very little to housework.

A religious male client, now 45, told me he had "kept himself" for 25 years—that is, he bypassed sexual relationships he could have entered into, thinking his denial of self would guarantee him, by God, a good marriage. His sacrifice, he believes, should be rewarded with a relationship that is fully gratifying to him: the relationship shouldn't require any work; it is, after all, compensation, a prize for his sacrifice. It never dawned on him, as he was waiting for a relationship to come along, that he might study how to be a good husband or sexual partner. When he finally married, he became resentful that his wife was unhappy with his level of skill. His presumptuousness is even greater considering his disclosure that he was raised with three brothers and had "zero relationship with girls." He didn't date because "I was taught that God had just one special person for me." He did not have the empathy to anticipate that it takes effort to learn to understand the opposite sex.

Presumptuously, a guy may minimize a woman's feelings. He does this because his own feelings aren't that strong, as we'll see in Chapter 4. He therefore doesn't experience the woman's emotions as all that important. He may say the equivalent of "just don't let it bother you," because that's what he can do.

Another Opposite of Empathy is Selfishness

"The relationship always required I give up *my* dream for *his*," Connie, married 12 years, says. Women enter marriage believing both are committed to the other's success and growth, only to find that he's either intimidated by her paycheck or sulking because she's not sacrificing enough for *his* success. Further, he won't divide domestic chores and child care equally, leaving her so burdened, she questions the marriage. Inasmuch as her title or success reflect well on him, he likes the prestige, but that doesn't carry over into actual interest in her career or freeing her up by giving more at home. Ambitious women who earn top salaries are four times as likely to get divorced.

A husband in therapy confesses. "I just blurt out whatever comes to my mind," he says in reference to how his romantic dinner with his wife got spoiled on her birthday. "I didn't mean anything by it when I looked at this girl—we were both looking at her actually because of her curvaceous figure—and I said, 'I wonder what it would be like to have sex with *that*.'" He explains how it's foreign to him to stop and consider how his words will make his wife feel.

His wife says, "I've learned to put on a thick skin since being married. My husband's insensitivity wore me out till I hardened myself. What he doesn't realize is that I shut down the best parts of me—my openness to him, my sensitivity and softness. That may not bother him but my sexual desire left as a consequence. They're connected."

Sexual disharmony is, no doubt, one reason women find
the work of a marriage not worth the trouble.

Sexually, women experience men's selfishness, too. They skip over her need for romance, nonsexual touching, or clitoral stimulation. In fact, while three-fourths of males report almost always orgasming, less than 30 percent of females can say the same.[110]   Many men don't acknowledge what Alfred Kinsey proved long ago: that women need clitoral stimulation to orgasm. The must-see movie *The Kinsey Report* documented his findings and the movie *The Good Mother* illustrated it. It's shocking that so many women have never orgasmed until post-divorce dating. Another common problem is men's premature ejaculation. Women who can climax through intercourse, don't receive enough stimulation. Some clinicians say premature ejaculation should be considered "normal" since so many men do it. Yet, a man can learn, by holding back and surrendering his own immediate gratification, to pleasure his partner. Sexual disharmony is, no doubt, one reason women find the work of a marriage not worth the trouble.

A major challenge for a man is being unselfish enough to keep a woman engaged sexually. Sex helps maintain the quality and stability of marriages, and replenishes the couples' bond and emotional reserves, according to Judith Wallerstein and Sandra Blakeslee who followed couples in California's Bay Area for thirty years. They found divorcing couples commonly endure seven years of sexual deprivation.[111]

Darwin, writing in 1871, saw the female gender as being tender and less selfish than her male counterpart. Empathy inhibits selfishness and causes other-centeredness. Laws and moral codes are relatively unnecessary for the highly empathic female because she can't stand the thought of hurting someone.

Many women find that, however well a relationship begins, men, after time, manifest a growing selfishness. They are efficiency-based, as we'll see in Chapter 4, and only put forth the amount of effort necessary to keep her okay but not happy.

Laws and moral codes are relatively unnecessary
for the highly empathic female who can't stand the
thought of hurting someone.

An area requiring empathy is thoughtful gift giving. Many women are hurt by the gifts men give them, the last minute purchases, done without forethought. This is in contrast to her giving consideration and care to the gifts for him. Tanya's husband gave her wild flowers picked on their way home from church on Mother's Day. "It's like he had forgotten completely, but when the minister's sermon reminded him, he grabbed what was easy. The flowers wilted in a couple days." Tonya, on the other hand, had had flowers sent to his office from the best florist in town last Father's Day.

Paul Zak's lab found that testosterone rises when men *win*. Winning is another way of "getting your way," and relates to selfishness. A man in an argument with his girlfriend pushes to get his way, not really hearing her, but since he perceives he's "won," his testosterone rises. The elevated testosterone causes his relational skills to sink.

Men put in minimal effort hoping for maximized reward.

Researchers set up a money game to test whether testosterone made men selfish. *They found that the more testosterone, the greater the stinginess.* Here's the game: 25 male students were asked to split $10 with a second student. (You would think the guy would say, "Here's $5.00; I'll keep the other $5.00. But that isn't what happened.) Mind you, if the other student thought the first student's offer was unfair, *no one got any money.* Putting a testosterone gel on the students making the offers made them 27% stingier, with offers going down to $1.57. That is, a gamer offered only $1.57 out of the $10 to the second student, *even though, if the second student rejected the offer, the first guy wouldn't get any money either.*

If a more powerful testosterone was used, offers sank to 55 cents. Those guys with the *least* amount of testosterone offered $3.65 (out of $10.00;) that is, their offers weren't even 50/50 (and you expected him to pitch in 50/50 with housework and childcare?) Also, testosterone blocks oxytocin, the generosity hormone found in plentiful supply in females. At the other end of the spectrum, researchers in 2007 administered oxytocin to male gamers. These made them *more like females,* and, guess what? Generosity was boosted by *80 percent![112]*

Men's testosterone causes stinginess;
women's oxytocin causes giving.

"I gave and gave and gave and then I realized I was a dry well," says a 35-year-old wife.

A male client told me, "I just need to grow up." Before marriage, he did "whatever the hell I wanted to do. After marriage, I'd get pissed off at my new wife for bitching at me, so I would rebel against her, and go out more, drink more, watch football more. I paid no attention to how my behaviors affected her." He admitted to a deeply established pattern of wanting to get his own way. Currently, he wants to spend money on a boat when they need furniture. He measures the relationship by how much sex he's getting, without an understanding of the deeper parts of the relationship. He's clueless about her real feelings.

Why wouldn't a woman act this way? Because women's brains are eight times more activated than men's while thinking about something sad.[113] If women feel that acutely, and are equipped to sense what others feel, they loathe the thought of inflicting hurtful feelings. This intense brain activation, along with her lesser impulsiveness, keeps women from selfishness.

John's manner of arguing with his wife is all about him and his needs. He pouts, "I should never express what I feel. I should stop being honest. Every time I am, she gets mad." The thing he's "honest" about is how he can only be happy if he's living in Boston. This is impossible because her work and their kids' schooling is in a different city. He wants to be applauded for what he feels, as though his wish to live in Boston counts as a disclosure that would bring them closer. I suspect that behind those feelings is the wish to indulge in pleasure with no responsibilities. John, 54, envies, after all, his 40-year-old friend who's single in Boston, plans to remain single, and can play golf anytime he wants.

Women's brains are eight times more activated than men's
when thinking about something sad
so they're more careful not to inflict hurt.

Granted, women can also be shallow, but their hormones predispose them to be relationally oriented and, once they bear children, their hormones dictate their devotion to their children's well-being. This can propel even a shallow woman into the demands of baby care, cooking, cleaning, decision-making, and earning a living.

Glenda and her boyfriend of two years got pregnant while sophomores in college. When he found out, he ignored her for days. Finally, he drove up to the parking lot where she and her classmates came after class. He signaled for her to come to his car and then coldly handed her the money for the abortion. Months later, she asked him why he'd abandoned her at such a hard time. "I got scared," he said.

"Hello?! Do you think *I* was without fear?" she countered. The left brain, devoted to rational thought, is uncomfortable with feelings. But the clincher came a few days after the abortion. He booty called her. The profound insensitivity left her flabbergasted. He cared only about his own interests, his own need for sex, unable to imagine how she felt.

A husband had affairs each of the three times his wife was pregnant. He wasn't getting enough attention. Rather than seeing her pregnancies as something he'd helped to create, rather than becoming a partner who would see her through the difficulties of pregnancy, he was consumed with himself. He wasn't getting enough sex and her focus was more on the new child than on him. He lacked empathy and therefore, persepctive.

Though David, 42 and in his second marriage, traveled for his work *ten* months out of the year, he wanted to be married. The separation and re-entry into the life of his bride was hard enough on her, but she also didn't like his continual use of porn, his hanging out in bars with single guys, and his using steroids to build his muscles. He would lie that he was no longer using porn, and then she'd find it on his computer.

She confronted him, and suffered emotionally, confused and filled with doubts. After seven years, she's had it. The years of confronting had made her realize her guy had no intention to change. She was done.

His response? He said he deserved someone who wouldn't give up on him and that if she loved him she wouldn't leave him. He told her he'd made mistakes, but "nothing a rational person couldn't forgive." He wanted her to go with him to a Christian counselor and start attending church, things he'd never mentioned before. "When you make vows, you accept that person for who they are," he said. *He believed marriage was a guarantee that he could do whatever he wanted without losing her.* He didn't have to change jobs so he'd be home and could keep doing things that offended her (the porn and partying with single guys) or scared her (use of steroids.) She felt bullied by him.

Some bachelors get bored with playing poker, sleeping alone, and doing whatever they want. They want to add a woman, and what she can provide, onto their bachelor lives. He feels warm about the way she creates a home, nurturance, emotional support, children, and, of course, free access to sex. Quite frankly, he likes the idea of adding a second income to his. Marriage does not mean change or giving up his bachelorhood or, most importantly, taking on a new set of skills. He is messy and doesn't expect much of himself. She can do it. He is selfish. He doesn't intuit the cost of children on her time and energy and focus. He doesn't expect her to need much from him. He doesn't want her to need anything from him. He is very surprised by how deeply unhappy she is in the relationship and he's threatened if she asks him for change.

For most women, preparation for romance should include
how to maintain and further their selfhood and autonomy.

Now that almost 40% of women earn more than their spouses, it behooves a woman to be careful about men's less empathic, more selfish nature in another arena: finances. It's happening more and more: men taking advantage of women's money. Rachel, 50 and single, talked for two months with a guy over the internet. He seemed impeccable—wonderful to talk with, great resume, involved in humanitarian causes. He could work anywhere as a business consultant, so it made sense for him to move near her. Sometimes she'd go to sleep early and he'd go back to his apartment, locking her door behind him. Seven months after he'd moved to her city, she discovered he'd been taking her credit cards and using them to pay his bills over the phone or online. Unsuspecting, she didn't notice for months because her office staff paid her bills. Once she did, she felt a profound, numbing betrayal, and since he used *her* phone or computer to pay his bills, the credit card company would not see it as fraud and she had to fork over the large amount of money.

Jonathan is a romance addict. He knows how to get the attention and sex he craves. He's one guy who shows interest in what interests a woman. He sends flowers when she's had a bad day. He admits he needs to grow up. He's married, but is having trouble leaving the single life behind. Meanwhile, his wife is bleeding inside, always sensing that something is terribly wrong with their marriage. But she shushes her intuitions. She saw one email he accidentally left up where he says to a girl, "You've got a nice ass." She confronted him and he said it was no big deal; he was just joking. She's confused, terribly lonely. I ask him why he doesn't end the marriage and remain single. "I don't want to; I like having a wife."

Preparation for marriage or relationship for most women should include how to maintain and further her selfhood and autonomy. For men, preparation should include how to unify, adapt and become more relational, giving up some of their selfishness and autonomy.

Is it narcissism?

Beyond selfishness is narcissistic personality disorder, where a person is incapable of forming true relationships, but only uses others. According to the *Diagnostic and Statistical Manual of Mental Disorders*, the disorder includes taking advantage of people, feeling shame or rage if criticized, feeling super important about exaggerating achievements, believing one's problems are comprehended only by "special" persons, being hung up on attaining amazing success, ideal love, handsomeness, intellectual prowess, or power, feeling entitled to special favors, needing a lot of admiration, lacking empathy, and being obsessed with jealousy.

Despite a narcissist's presenting as grandiose, his self-esteem is fragile, and in romantic relationships, a narcissist sees his partner as an object to buoy up his own esteem.

Susie, an articulate, middle-aged owner of an upscale restaurant, says of her husband, "He's developed this overinflated ego because he got kudos with little effort, just for being male. Yet, I know that, as a kid, he would drop out of favor quickly if his dad caught him being 'like a girl.' So there's this dynamic where, though he's pot bellied and bald, he assumes these gorgeous successful women 'want' him. He has the nerve to rank order my friends' attractiveness. At the same time, he's overly sensitive to any criticism. I'm sure he believes that he's won me forever...just because he's Who He Is, so there's no need to pick up a book or try to understand me."

Many women feel their husbands have narcissistic traits, whether or not they qualify for the full diagnosis. (Only 2–16% of the population has the full fledged disorder and of these, 50–75% are men.)

When Tami, 27, talks about her boyfriend, it's easy to pick up on his narcissistic tendencies. "He's all about himself—what he wants, needs, aspires to be, how great he can be. He will lie if it gets him what he wants. Plus, he's one person in private and another in public, like he needs everyone to believe he's such a great guy. At home, he's critical of the kids and expects to be waited on, even though I work as many hours as he does. In public, though, he'd give the shirt off his back cuz it would bring in praise. His temper never shows in public."

"How do you handle this?" I ask.

"I never disagree with him. It's not worth it. The kids and I work around him. I've stopped making legitimate requests for help with the kids or the house. I'd rather be overworked than be the subject of his anger."

Narcissists are incapable of
forming true relationships.

On a date, many men present a monologue of their achievements and thoughts, as though a woman wants to hear this. She may be bored and recognizes the narcissism of his presentation but, out of politeness, continues to show interest, smile, and ask questions. But think about it. Why does he *assume* she's so interested in him? Why doesn't he think *she* would also like to be known, understood and maybe even admired? She walks away from the encounter with many question marks: Can he meet my emotional needs? Will he eventually want to know about me? (If she's looking for a success object, however, she might have soaked in the litany of his achievements as evidence that he's right for her.) This phenomenon, however, is partly why women take longer to decide if a relationship will work for them.

Teresa, 59, has dated Randy, 62, for the last three years. "When I tell him how I feel about something he has said—usually about our relationship—he listens to what I say and gives me the impression he will change. He doesn't, and I find out later that it is Randy's way. It's his life and that is the way it should be, but he insists I go along with his plan. And if I go along with his plan, I'm someone he just might consider marrying. He gives off little innuendos, like, 'Teresa, when you do such-and-such you get points,' like he is teasing, but I think it's true—he's got a point system. I found out last night that the loan on his house has been approved, and he kept referring to 'his' house the whole evening. We had talked about moving in together, after dating for three years. I was going to sell my house for my share of the down payment, but there is, in fact, no 'ours.'" Randy's narcissistic belief in "ideal love" could only abide a completely selfless woman. Therefore, he felt justified stringing Teresa along for three years to weigh how selfless she was.

John, 28, lives with his girlfriend whose parents are both sick and dying. As the therapist to him and his girlfriend, Chloe, I was surprised at his perspective.

He explained. "Several of my guy friends tell me they don't know how I've stayed with her. They sympathize with my having to put up with her emotion, her worry, and finally, going through the death of her parents with her. It's required a lot of listening and hearing her cry."

Think about if these roles were reserved. It's doubtful that a woman's friends would say the same thing about a boyfriend who was helping his sick parents and then grieving for their deaths. They would assume it's her responsibility to *undergird* him. If *she* were in the supportive role, she would feel comfortable with his feelings and draw closer to him as he expressed them. Women are not afraid of negative emotion in the way men are.

Another opposite of empathy is denial

Men live mostly in the logic-driven left brain, unlike women who have better access to both hemispheres. In *The New Feminine Brain*, Mona Lisa Schulz, M.D., Ph.D., speaks of the denial that occurs when a person lives in the limited emotions of the left brain, like cheerfulness. The attitude is blindly positive and allows one to experience a general denial of life's problems. She explains how women cross over to the right brain, where the bulk of the emotions reside, once a month for a couple weeks as dictated by the menstrual cycle. Also, women have greater access in general to their emotions because the bridge between the two hemispheres has more connections. Women are, then, *unable to ignore* the bad, while men, living easily in the uncomplicated left brain, can turn a blind eye, feeling artificially blissful. This cluelessness is frustrating for women.[114]

Living in the cheerful left brain
allows a man to deny problems.

This is why men don't see marital problems coming. It's probably why they don't work to prevent their own health problems. It may also be why they just don't see the needs of their children that are pressing in on their wives. He may tell her not to worry about things, to let it go. He tries to smooth over something she sees as a warning signal.

Linda, for instance, feels she and her husband need to get an attorney because they're being audited by the IRS, while he believes he'll *charm* the female agent assigned to them. Ramona suspects their neighbor's daughter is being molested by a babysitter. Carla thinks one of her husband's employees is stealing from him. Stephanie senses their daughter is feeling overpowered by her gymnastic coach. In each case, the husband just doesn't see it. It's not on his radar.

Because the husband doesn't receive the right brain information she gets, he may count her fears as needless. He may get lost in the details while she sees the big picture that propels her to seek change. Bottom line, the wife feels alone with the difficulties.

A striking example of men's propensity toward denial in comparison with women comes from the onset of the AIDS pandemic. Even though middle class females were hardly at risk at that time, *they eagerly sought testing*. They wanted to know about their own health and felt responsible not to spread AIDS to their sexual partner if they had it. In contrast, men, because of their riskier past sexual behaviors, were far more likely to have AIDS. *Denial prevailed* in the men: they simply did not want to know if they were carriers.[115] This also means that they didn't care to know if they were transmitting a deadly disease to their sexual partners. Empathy would drive a person to find out.

In summary, men do not have the brain structure, the hormonal makeup, or the unique experience of giving birth that gives a woman her emotional sensitivity and empathy. This and the effects of testosterone encompass the fundamental differences between the genders. Understanding these is "Men 101." But wait, there's yet a third difference that's just as profound: men's systemizing, the subject of our next chapter.

Chapter 4:

Men Are Motivated to Build Systems

"I do not socialize because social encounters would distract me from my work and I really only live for that."

—Albert Einstein

Most men, according to Simon Baron-Cohen in his book *The Essential Differences*, are "systemizers." They value what is fixed, limited, and orderly, be it a pencil sharpener or computer data systems. They spot a system's rules and predict its outcome, assuming it will not change. Consequently, they like strategy games, want to know how machines work, "get" instruction manuals, like knowing the names of things like cars or bands and the dates of historical incidents, visualize how freeways converge, want to know the capacity of their car engine and hard drive, and like science, sports scores, grammatical rules, rules governing numbers, and technical features. A systemizer is more likely to see a person for what she can do. *Most male brains are hard-wired for valuing and assembling systems.*[116] (Baron-Cohen found that only about 17% of men have empathizing or "feminine" brains.) [117]

Researcher Richard Lippa studied gender as it relates to occupational preferences, finding that men prefer *things* (mechanics, building) while women prefer *people* (social work and teaching). Elaborating, we could say women like to delve into the untidy, complicated world of people—how they think, unconsciously function, and feel. Men prefer the precision of the seeable physical world, where clear and tidy laws can be implemented. [118]

Men are interested in structures and things
while women gravitate to relational skill.

In contrast, most women are "empathizers." They like being caretakers and being in relationships, are easy to talk to and can read why someone is upset and feel for them, feel upset when someone is suffering, abhor hurting someone and take responsibility if they do inadvertently cause hurt, predict the feelings of others and tune in to provide care, discern if someone has something weighing on their mind, make you feel understood, foresee what action another will take, spot emotional pain in others, provide acceptance so that others feel comfortable disclosing to them, provide emotional sensitivity, perceive deception and whether a person is masking true feelings, are careful not to intrude or tease or cause harm, reach out to newcomers and read them quickly, make a gesture of caring with no expectation of reciprocation, perceive facial expressions and tone of voice, discern even small shifts in mood. *Female brains tend to be hard-wired for empathy.*[119]   (Baron-Cohen found that 14% of women have "masculine" or systemizing brains.)[120]

Part of the baffling and even infuriating struggle in dealing with the opposite sex is that while systemizers must *detach* to observe a system and figure it out, empathizers must *attach* to discern another's feelings and how they affect her.[121] Obviously romance is about attachment. Women do this naturally while men detach on and off as an automatic way of being.

While systemizers must *detach* to observe a system and figure
it out, empathizers must *attach* to discern another's feelings.

When a woman goes in search of a romance, she will find, according to Simon Baron-Cohen, a researcher at Cambridge University, that some men have balanced brains. That is, they can both systemize and empathize. My guess is that a lot of women would find happier romances with these men and that women today are not as okay with the systemizers (54% of men, subtracting 17% as empathizers and 29% as balanced to equal 100% of men)[122] as they once were, when silence and lower relational skill was better tolerated by women. If a woman wants to be with a man with a balanced brain, she must face that this description fits only 29% of the male population. Remember, though, that even these men have the characteristics of testosterone we reviewed earlier.

On that note, I'd like to introduce and caution you about Matt, 34, married 15 years. His wife finally caught him, which landed him in therapy. He'd been sexting, going to dating websites, collecting videos and pictures of himself in sex acts, even having long-term relation-ships with women in different cities, something he could do because his work involves travel. But let's back up to Matt as a teen. He never liked sports, fixing things, or math. He liked girls. Now, as I meet Matt as a 34-year-old, I immediately note how engaging he is, how he sustains eye contact, how he understands emotional concepts readily, how easy he is with dialogue, and how he has close male friends. He's great at his job that requires high relational skill. Sound like a woman? But Matt has testosterone.

A balanced-brain guy is more able to get into your shoes,
to use empathy in dialogue, and to share more of your interests.

Matt sees women as his "sport." He likes flirting and having sex with a lot of women because it allows him to perfect his "craft." He also has the categorical thinking typical of men: when he's with his girlfriend, it has *nothing to do* with his wife and kids, and vice versa. He keeps a record through pictures of his "conquests," and there are so many his wife would die if she only knew.

So, although Matt is warm emotionally and has a brain balanced be-tween systemizing and empathy, he has testosterone. Does he ever!

Nevertheless, a balanced-brain guy is more able to get into your shoes, to use empathy in dialogue, and to share more of your interests. Just find one who reigns in his sexuality.

Now back to romancing with a regular guy, a systemizer. Being the more empathic one in the relationship translates into being more aware, kind, thoughtful, and able to anticipate the needs of the other. *The less empathic person will be the recipient of this good fortune.* The more empathic person will be short changed but may expect similar empathy from the other, especially a lover, because she gives it herself. But who will benefit most—the systemizer or the empathizer—from being in relationship with the other?

The male systemizer has the good fortune of being
the recipient of the empathic female's relationship skills.

Once, when women needed financial support from a man, his systemizing abilities made him a great asset to the relationship. But women are
finding their own way, excel in academia, and are nabbing good jobs.
This, I believe, is why women instigate most divorces. They are disappointed with the quality of the relationship.

"But it seems like men are empathic sometimes," you say. While men
can empathize (or they would be sociopaths or criminals), and women
can systemize, men prefer systemizing and it comes more readily than
being empathic. But when we talk about male empathizing, we may
be—except for some men—talking about a cognitive, not an emotional
empathy.

Systemizers give cognitive, not emotional, empathy.

Let's look at the male brain to understand the difference between the
empathy he gives compared to what women give. Men, like women,
have a special place in the brain for caring. It's the mirror-neuron system or MNS. A man's mirror-neuron system turns on when he sees or
hears emotional pain in his female partner, *but only briefly*. She sees a
flicker of emotional resonance in his eyes, but then something changes
and he's different. Immediately, he switches to the temporal-parietal
junction system (TPJ). Whereas the MNS is experienced as *emotional*
empathy, the TPJ registers as *let's-get-it-fixed* empathy. By late grade
school, boys prefer TPJ and puberty seems to buttress that inclination.
Untainted by emotional considerations, the TPJ keeps the man firmly
planted in himself, whereas a woman, remaining in the MNS, feels *with*
a person, leaving herself to get in another's shoes. During a dialogue, if
she changes emotion, his TPJ continues to doggedly work off the *initial*
emotion he observed and toward an objective analysis of the problem.[123]
He doesn't *flow* with where she's at.

Once the male brain spots an emotion, it jumps into problem solving, and usually, the man's face turns blank because he has left his MNS. She thought she'd caught a glimpse of caring when she began talking and she did—momentarily—but his brain went into solution-land, hunting for the answer that will flood pleasurable dopamine into his brain. That is, if he finds a solution, he's "won." This is the kind of empathy men give: *cognitive empathy*. It is a mental activation driving a man to come up with a solution to the problem presented. *Cognitive empathy doesn't move him to validate, show sensitivity, or even understand what you feel.* He doesn't walk around inside your experience or feel with you. "Let's get this fixed immediately!" is the motto of cognitive empathy.

What a dialogue means to her is that he'll climb
on her ship for a while and ride the waves of
emotional exploration. He, however, is back at the
dock, analyzing which anchor will stabilize her.

The difference between male and female empathy is often illustrated in couple-talk. Valerie, 36, says to Josh, "I'm so tired; I just want to take a week off work."

Josh, feeling responsible to fix her problem, says something that doesn't seem to fit. "You should really consider that job in Pennsylvania."

Since Valerie and Josh live in Idaho, his statement results in a knot in her throat. What Josh means is that the job she's been offered in Pennsylvania allows for 4 weeks off each year. It's a fix.

But now Valerie, who was just trying to vent and gain sympathy, feels annoyed. She doesn't want to think about a job change and moving across the country right now while she's so tired. They get into a quarrel about his comment and he defends himself, knowing he had come up with a solution. Since men receive a mood boost when they land an answer, they feel good, and don't understand why their remedies turn their female partners sour. Such is the difference between the validation of feelings and caring expression Valerie wants and the remedy Josh gives.

Men fail to appreciate the true emotional texture of a woman's sensibilities. To find out why, let's revisit male history that included inflicting pain, watching a slow death, knowing another's life is being stolen. Men couldn't get into the "shoes" of the animal or warrior bleeding before them; they turned off the distress that emotional empathy would bring and switched to a mere mental recognition.

The women's curse is believing her love can change a man. Instead, she needs to know what to expect. A man, tuned into the cognitive empathy part of his brain, wants to know what, factually and concretely (and often briefly) he can *do* to be successful (remember that testosterone searches for victories) as your mate. Hearing your feelings or your complex processing only frustrates him, so you have to do it alone or with a girlfriend. But he will often provide the actual behaviors you want.

Women just want to vent to their men and receive
empathy; instead, men try to fix the problem.

When Sylvia found out her twin sister had cancer, she was overcome with sadness. Her husband responded with a series of questions about the name of the hospital her sister was in, how long she'd been there, what the names of the doctors were, when she was scheduled for chemo. Frustrated, Sylvia shut the door to the bedroom to be alone, away from the fact-finding. Her husband then assumed she needed time alone. But feeling the loneliness on top of her sadness made Sylvia cry all the more.

A man's expression of compassion is of a more objective kind and not as deep. It doesn't move a human to hands-on caring the way women's empathy does. It is not as personal or directly caring, though the objectivity can help a man figure out how to save a life. Our focus here, though, is on its affect in the most personal relationship of all: romance.

But there's another phenomenon about men that baffles women, also relating to men's lack of feeling empathy. One of the most loving men I've ever known disclosed that if his children get hurt, he feels furious and yells at them. He says things like, "Why'd you do that, you knucklehead," even though he doesn't normally call his child "knucklehead."

He admits that he is angry because the one he cares about has injured himself. "Why did my son hurt himself when I don't want him hurt?" he thinks. Furthermore, it takes a while for him to recover himself from his anger. Somewhere in there, he tells his child where to find the Band-Aids and first aid cream.

Many women are mystified by this kind of response because it's so different from the emotional empathy natural to them. Women viscerally feel the pain of someone who's sick or injured, actually allowing them to experience it personally. They cringe or wince. Their instinct is to comfort, to take the physical and emotional pain away as soon as possible, and to immediately move toward the hurting child with reassurance.

The initial angry response to a child's pain given in the example may be explained by Harvard researchers who found that infant males get emotionally charged faster than infant girls. Adult males seem to retain this agitation. Just as my male friend referenced above confessed to having a tough time recovering, so the researchers found that parents had to spend more time trying to settle sons down compared with daughters.[124]

The male extreme — or not so extreme?

The extreme systemizing brain, according to Baron-Cohen, is *autism*, where a person, usually male, talks only of work or to gain facts. Autistics ask few questions because they are uninterested in what others think. They are indifferent to what somebody else knows because they prefer to solve problems alone. They are oblivious to what's going on around them. They don't like conversations much anyway, but ones involving imagination are of little interest. They don't make eye contact while talking, may suddenly walk off, may interrogate you, or touch you inappropriately. When an autistic gets off work, the last thing he wants is to talk or socialize or hear family problems. You may feel invisible to an autistic because the relationship must be on his terms.

In 1944, Hans Asperger wrote in German that *autism is the extreme of male intelligence*. Oddly, the translation of his work didn't reach the West until 1991. He found what many women feel about their partners: that they are kind of autistic — that is, they like to solve problems more than they like to develop emotional closeness.

Systemizers are Less Relational

Babies and attention to faces

Because systemizing tendencies start in babyhood, they are inborn and not about how we condition boys and girls. Researchers Connellan and Bakti videotaped more than100 day-old infants. They didn't know the babies' gender because the mothers were instructed to keep that secret. The babies were given two things to look at. The first was a lady's face and the second was a mobile. The mobile was an odd configuration of the lady's facial features (nose, ear, eyes,) but rearranged. The researchers lovingly called the mobile "The Alien."

The significance of the study is that girls looked longer at the face, while boys showed more interest in the mobile.[125] It is believed that girls' interest in actual faces leads to reading faces, empathy, and thus a greater propensity to develop relationships. While boys are not uninterested in relationships, their *greater* interest is in putting things together (faces, computers, cars, political systems—or, in this case, the ears, nose, mouth).

Males and females see the world differently,
literally, even as infants.

Infant girls look long and hard at faces, compared to infant boys who, though they also look at faces, show greater interest in moving things, shapes, and objects.[126] Boys come by this tendency from the most basic of origins: the Y chromosome. Gender interests related to looking at faces or movement have something to do with differences in eyesight. While boys have more M cells, having to do with detecting motion, girls have more P cells, having to do with texture and color.[127] That is, the genders literally see the world differently, which affects our interests.

As further evidence of greater relationship-interest in girls, researchers found that little girls cry more than boy babies when exposed to the cries of another baby.[128] Later in life, women will reach out to comfort others, even strangers, more than men.[129]

Baby boys pose a surprise to their mothers. Although 5-to-7-month-old boys can discern if their mothers' faces show anger or fear, by twelve months, this ability is *gone*. A change occurs in the boys' makeup that makes them less able to read mom's face. For girls, the tendency to discern facial emotion grows and grows.[130]   The thought here is that as boys grow into being systemizers, they must leave behind their empathic tendencies.

One-year-olds aren't androgynous

One-year-olds played on the floor while their moms sat in chairs near them, and researcher Svetlana Lutchmaya filmed them. She watched to see how many times each tot glanced at mom. The girls searched for their moms' faces significantly more than did the boys. Further, when researchers showed these babies films of cars and faces, boys looked at cars longer while girls looked at the faces longer.[131]

Girls seek eye contact with their moms
more than boys do.

So, kids aren't androgynous at birth, with parents and schools later determining their interests according to their sex. Concordia University studied 77 one-and-half-year-old toddlers and found they were *clueless* as to their gender. They barely scored above chance at assigning themselves or others to a gender, yet when boys were offered a doll or truck, they wanted the truck. Their preference obviously wasn't grounded in some rule that "boys don't play with dolls;" they weren't even aware of gender.[132]

In fact, every mammal studied showed gender differences in play behavior, with boys preferring rough-and-tumble play.[133]   If the amygdala is damaged in young rats of both genders, the males decrease their roughnecking, but the females don't change, showing that males are wired for that kind of behavior.[134]   Even female monkeys prefer dolls, while male monkeys prefer cars.[135]

Preschoolers have story and toy preference

In another study, the majority of stories told by two-year-old girls were about people, while only a small minority of the boys' stories were accounts of people. Later, at age four, *all* story telling by the girls was people focused, while only 50% of the boys' sagas were about people. Even boys as young as two chose violent fairy tales over warm, nurturing tales.[136]

At all ages, females show greater
interest in relationships.

Preschool boys used objects as weapons or equipment (i.e., using beans as bullets and spoons as flashlights) six times more frequently than girls did, found researcher Eleanor Maccoby.[137]

Monkeys aren't socialized like humans, so they give us further understanding of innate gender qualities. When given a wheeled vehicle and a doll, almost all males chose the vehicle. Girl monkeys in this study played equally with the toys.[138]

Grade school girls and boys treat newcomers differently

Back to fairy tale preferences, most girls like nurturing stories, but when a 5-7-year-old girl shows preference for violent fairy tales like boys do, it is a predictor of a psychiatric disorder![139] So, while violence is a normal trait for males, it is unnatural (a mental sickness) in females.

Researcher Eleanor Maccoby tested the degree of relationship skill in children by introducing a new boy or girl to a group of established playmates. Researchers found that when a new girl enters, she will most likely wait and observe the group, pausing to figure out the rules and mores, and eventually offer a suggestion to assist others to be successful. The group responds to her sensitivity by welcoming her in.

If the stranger introduced is a boy, however, his behavior is the opposite. He interrupts, and tries changing the rules, grabbing the attention, or otherwise commandeering the game. The boy is concerned with displaying his toughness, not his relational skill. This research illustrates that, by the age of six, girls show greater desire to extend kindness.

Maccoby found that girls, whether in the role of newcomer or host, show more emotional sensitivity and higher empathy than boys who don't care about the newcomer's or the stranger's feelings. Maccoby speculated that this explains why the genders separate into same-sex groups—their styles are so different![140]

Our relationship expectations
come from our gender-specific childhood experiences.

Girls like small groups of same-sex friends where the focus is on each other, conversation is rich, establishing a hierarchy is shunned as detrimental to friendship, and making self-disclosures is seen as the key to closeness. Boys, on the other hand, like groups of up to 12, where the friendships are really about a shared activity, conversation is minimized, hierarchies structure their solidarity, and personal revelations are circumvented.[141]

So there you have it: the beginnings of what's wrong, from a female point of view, with romances in adulthood: males are oriented in ways that hinder the one-on-one development of emotional closeness. Now you can see where our expectations come from—our childhoods! Females come into romance believing they'll share the close ties they had with girlfriends. Males come into romance believing they'll establish a hierarchy and engage in little conversation.

Girls prefer small groups that focus on conversation
with one another, friendship, and self-disclosures. Boys
prefer larger groups that are structured by hierarchy.

Here's another kicker. Psychologists asked kids around age ten what they'd do if someone grabbed their soccer ball away during a game. The boys usually said they'd hit the kid and would feel no guilt. The older the boy, the more likely he believed the hit would result in his getting the ball back. Girls weren't sure hitting would work and knew they'd feel guilty and upset after hitting someone. Unlike the boys, they couldn't expect other girls to approve of hitting.[142]

Furthermore, girls can more accurately judge if there's a *discrepancy* between what a character in a story is feeling on the inside when showing something different on the outside. Later, this will translate into adult females drawing men out to get to their real feelings. And here's another way girls' kindness is shown: they can better discern when it's best to *suppress their feelings* so the other person's feelings can be spared, as when given a dumb birthday present. Girls are also *seven times* more likely to recognize a comment that would register as a *faux pas*. All the above—the ability to read people, the appropriate suppression of feelings and using careful language—are indicators of empathy, the pearl of relationship skill.[143]   No wonder girls, and later women, are frustrated with males for their lack of relational awareness, *especially when they expect the same*.

Adults and closeness

Women smile more and sustain eye contact longer than men do, using the small relationship skills that bring a sense of closeness. Women respond sympathetically, letting the discloser know they're understood, while men offer less verbal support. So while women encourage the sharing of the heart, men do not. For a woman, it is secret-sharing and dream exploration that brings on the closeness she calls "romance."

Being systemizing is so fulfilling to men, why would they seek change? They enjoy full concentration, and the solitude that kind of focus requires, without the need for interacting with someone. In fact, people can get in the way of the systemizer's task. Think about the development of systemizing—from tracking animals to pre-industrial tool repair, to writing grants in our day. Men focus to the exclusion of relationships. When they do relate, it often has a purpose—to find facts, to find or keep one's dominance. This is unlike females who relate for the sake of gaining or sustaining a connection.

Men rarely shine in emotionally close relationships. This does not mean they can't be friendly salesmen or cooperative on a project. We are speaking of relationships that are deeper and more personal. Except in short-term relationships when they rise to the challenge of winning a female, most men's forte is systemizing.

It is women who shine in relationships.

Many skills that are prominent in women make them especially able to promote and sustain relationships. Most women (67%) are superior at discerning non-verbals compared to the average guy, according to psychologist Judith Hall (1984) who analyzed many studies. Compared to the average male, 70% of women show more emotion in the face, 84% are better at conveying emotion to others through their faces, 74% smile more, 75% gaze more at other people, and 72% express themselves more in gestures. All in all, women make a lot of effort to communicate, showing strong relationship orientation compared to men. Conversely, compared to the average female, 83% of men keep more physical space from others, 85% show less careful movements and gestures, and 88% say things like "ah," "er", and "um" to fill pauses. Put together, these show that men are less concerned or aware of others, more anchored in themselves, and less flowing in conversation compared to the average female.[144]

Different brain structures

The difference is actually in brain structure. Females' affiliative style is related to neocortex capacity, say Lindenfors and Dunbar, while male conflict and cutthroat style relates to subcortical units.[145] That is, the brains of women and men develop different orientations, which affect what's important to each gender. Women seek closeness while men gravitate to *power* and *competition*.

A couple sits down to talk. They are reflecting on an important conversation they had three days ago. He remembers the plain data—facts and figures. The woman remembers the facts too, but also remembers the emotional aspects, including every feeling she felt during the dialogue and every feeling she believed he felt. She can entertain the memory of these feelings, but if she tries bringing them into their discussion, he won't relate because he was never aware of them in the first place.[146] Women have more brain area allowing feelings to *enhance their memories*.[147]

Women have more brain area allowing
feelings to enhance their memories.

Women deepen relationships

What makes relationships happen is making admissions about oneself of a personal nature. Interestingly, both men and women find themselves telling their secrets and confessing their weaknesses to *women*, not men.[148]   Later we'll see how men are more likely to feel pride and feel it intensely compared with women. Unfortunately, talking about how proud you are of yourself does not facilitate closeness; it facilitates *competitiveness*.

Women disclose their sadness more than men do,[149] which tends to draw others in empathy toward them, while men articulate what makes them mad,[150] which tends to be off-putting. Here again, we see how women facilitate relationship compared to men. This leaves women in a bind when, in romances, they rely on men for relationship.

Women are by far the biggest buyers of self-help relationship books. They strive to make relationships work. It is important enough to study and they are willing to learn. Why don't men buy them? Quite possibly, they don't feel the need in that their interests lay elsewhere.

Because Men are Systemizing They Seek to be Efficient

How systemizing affects dialogue

Women use dialogue to create emotional intimacy while men define closeness by how few words they can get away with. For example, Jon says to his middle-aged golf buddy, "Car. 6:30. Tuesday." They both give a slight nod and that totals their communication. But, for them, the brevity marks a common understanding. Since men seek efficiency, the fewer words the better. A woman might say, "Will you be able to meet Tuesday around 6:30 or do you have to take your daughter to tutoring that morning? I can help with transportation if you need me to. I was thinking 6:30 because we would beat the crowd, but I'm flexible."

While dialoguing is not men's forte, it is what women crave.

Rebecca, 36, comes into therapy upset about how Alex, her 38-year-old husband, acts when she's attempting to solve a problem in their marriage. After she presents a concern, he either stares at her or talks in a stunted, robot-like manner which she sometimes calls his "attorney style."

I ask Alex to explain his perspective. He says he is afraid to speak. After all she'll remember every word he says, including what intonation it was said in. And he could make a mistake, he says, using the wrong word or expression. He is well aware that he is entering dangerous territory. Further, he believes that whenever she voices a complaint, he is required to come up with some kind of magic to fix it for her, as illustrated above in our discussion of cognitive empathy. It is his personal job to make her happy, he says. And she seems so upset. She expresses her feelings so deeply and clearly, in a way he could never do. He figures she must be terribly, terribly unhappy. He feels shamed: he is not being a good husband. He has failed in his role. The powerlessness he feels is not ok and makes him less like of man.

Plus, he goes on, as she begins talking about her feelings, he's trying to find her bottom line. That is, what does she actually want from him? He can't listen to her feelings because he's so busy trying to figure out how, specifically, he can redeem himself.

So we decided she would, on her own, figure out what behaviors she needs from him. Maybe she'd talk it over with a girlfriend first. To him, she would say, "I have a bottom-line question for you." He'll then be able to respond positively to a relationship talk. She'll then present what behaviors she needs from him. He, like many men, will most likely respond with a yes to what she wants once it's clear—that is, not emotion-laden. After that's settled, she'll say, "I need to talk about my feelings now. I need to know you understand how I feel." At that point, he's free to listen because he already knows how to solve the problem. In this case, she's asking for him to take her out on Saturday nights and to copy her on any email he sends to his ex. He feels confident that he can do both. No more staring, no more protective/defensive attorney talk.

On a practical level, this arrangement will work for Rebecca and Alex. However, it lacks what Rebecca really seeks. It seems stilted. Alex will sometimes have trouble carrying through because, why listen to her feelings when he already knows what to do? But he'll try, he says. She agreed to modify her expectations.

The promise of romance is really short-term conquest behaviors

Men act one way during courtship and another after marriage. Women do that too—usually in response to men's behavior, but men inherently do it because they love conquest. They will do whatever they have to do to win her: bring flowers, talk about feelings, and be more emotionally present than they will ever be afterward. Ideally, what one acts like in courtship is an advertisement for what is to come, but with men, this is not the case.

Men act one way during courtship and another
after marriage, which is false advertising.

Men turn on selfless behaviors in order to succeed with an attractive potential romantic partner, reports the *British Journal of Psychology* in 2012. Women don't do this—their behavior isn't affected much by being around a cute guy. The researchers see the good behavior as tantamount to peacocks fanning their tales. [151]

For men, then, courtship behaviors are not a sampling of things to come, but are recruiting behaviors. Systemizing efficiency says, do the minimum you have to do to reach your goal: in this case, commitment.

Despite our Cinderella-inculcation, we must face that, because of men's efficiency-seeking, romances are short lived. The male behaviors that accompany the beginning of a relationship—pursuit with verbal and physical affection, gifts, and attentiveness—usually die off. At the fourth year of marriage, there is often a crash.

The woman who understands men no longer lives in a fairy tale, but realizes that a relationship will be partially fulfilling and paved with some difficulties. Rather than allowing myths of romantic love to distort what is truly reality, she faces head on what is the truth. In this way, she can plan to broaden her life with many fulfilling pursuits, rather than hope romantic love will fill her cup. She's savvy about romance and the chemical cocktail it brings. She realizes her date, filled with the dopamine of a new relationship, will escort her to dance lessons and act charming with her grandmother now, but may not do that in three years. She understands that she herself is feeling empowered and expansive due to the chemicals in her body, but not because *he* is an everlasting fountain of love.

Remember the childhood gender pattern: activities are the centerpiece of male relationships, while, for girls, the relationship itself is of prime importance. The problem is that most women feel like they could do side-by-side activities with a stranger. Doing activities together is far less personal than what she'd expected.

In an interview with a middle-aged male client of mine, he admitted that courtship is like an advertisement for what can be expected as the relationship goes on. It only makes sense, then, he said, that husbands continue to do whatever they did in courtship because this is what the woman has a right to expect.

If you think about it, you realize that courtship behaviors are the only ones we have to use to make a decision about whether we want to continue the relationship. If they're not representative, they are indeed false advertising. Of course, men complain that women are often less likely to keep up the level of sexual activity expressed in courtship, but how can she give the symbol of love (sex) when she is painfully aware that the foundations of the relationship (emotional closeness) are not in place?

Men think sequentially, that is, they think in a straight line. You get one thing done and then move on to the next. You court a woman, win her love, and then move on to other priorities, like work.

Though this seems incomprehensible to women, a man feels that when he's expected to do the things he did while courting, he's being demoted to the first rung of the ladder, explains John Gray. Further, affection-ate touching is what you did before the sexual relationship fully began and feels, to men, like reversing progress.[152] A guy doesn't naturally understand that, at the beginning of an evening—even after decades of marriage—nonsexual touching turns her on more than sexual touching, building her desire.

Men don't naturally understand that non sexual touching turns a woman on more than sexual touching.

Men often fail to consider the ongoing nuances of a relationship, the subtle emotions that emerge. Once he perceives he's secured a woman's commitment, the deal's done, and everything should be settled: she's committed to him and no further discussion is needed. The bottom line of marriage for men is that it provides, not a deepening emotional connection, but a structure (and a hierarchy) from which to operate. "Our marriage provided a box out of which we lived," says Sarah after ten years of marriage. "Everything was in place, but, for me, it was empty."

Women can pay a high price to be in a relationship with a man. Of course, these bad behaviors most likely don't show up in courtship. It is little wonder that men have been so protective and cautious about their daughters dating. They know what men are like. They know the selfishness she will be subjected to. They know her date can give her what she needs long enough to win her and then drop those behaviors because he no longer sees them as necessary.

This is one reason marriage, or a secured relationship, may not continue to be the best format for getting the best from men. The exception is when two people connect for the purpose of raising children, and the contribution of each is needed. Men relax into their selfishness in the security of a legal contract. It may not be the best format for women either, who need to keep their options open and not become locked in to someone who's unable to fulfill their deepest needs. Currently, women have that format in place: divorce. When author Gail Sheehy interviewed middle aged, single women, one said she liked dating a man for a couple years; after that, men begin exhibiting less favorable behaviors.[153]

Men believe that relationships shouldn't require much effort

James, 43, married 16 years with three children, wants to be seen as a great guy and see his wife as the idealized woman. This adds to his reluctance to work on a relationship. The Great Guy and Ideal Woman do not have problems, he thinks. They don't need to have relationship talks, they don't need counseling, and they don't need to read books. He just needs to come home from work and find her waiting. They have a peaceful evening and then sex. This is his unrealistic mindset. Add to this the facts that men's vital signs tend to go up during a relationship confrontation and that their verbal skills are lesser than women's and you have a gender that struggles to do the necessary and minimal work of keeping relationships healthy.

"I can't believe we're talking about toilet paper," he said.

"But if you don't put it on the list, I end up having to go to the grocery store twice," she says. He sighs. In his mind, he shouldn't be criticized for this. Somehow, toilet paper should appear. It shouldn't be an issue.

Kendra, 39 and married 15 years, turns to her husband Randy during therapy, and says, "I get it. If you don't invest much into our relationship, you have little to lose." She turns to me, frustrated, and says, "Work is so important to him and he knows darn well I'll be the one to make our relationship last."

Any marital therapist will tell you that couples must keep up the fun and romantic part of their relationship, through weekly dating and regular out-of-town trips. Sandra feels discouraged because she has to remind her husband of their dates. It's so easy for him to forget. She ends up planning the date alone and in the end it doesn't feel romantic. Taking care of the relationship just isn't that important to him. He believes the relationship is a given; it will always be there.

You may feel disappointed that he doesn't intend
to spend time working out problems.

A wife in her thirties, married six years, talks about her marriage in an individual session. "He can discuss work and sports, but not our relationship. He would rather leave the house than work through a problem

113

together. He picks everything else over our marriage. Every last girl-friend I know has the same marriage: you get 4-5 good years, and then you're expected to fit into the guys' world because they won't fit into yours or meet your needs. Their marriages aren't a priority; they focus on work and their own hobbies and having fun." She goes on. "Sex is disgusting. The relationship is important to him but relating is not. The relationship started out the way I had expected, but then I have been so disappointed. He leaves me feeling insecure. Yes, I'm gonna pursue cooking classes and jewelry making. He's happy as a clam if I pursue my activities and he does his. I was hoping for a different kind of mar-riage. I'm squeezed in, but I'm not his main interest."

"What about marital therapy?" I ask.

"He won't follow through with it. His attention span isn't that long and it's not a priority. I mean, he'll come into your office out of obligation, but honestly, he wants to work, hunt, and watch sports." She wanted to show her kids a marriage that could work. So she's invested in her own therapy, tolerance, and hope. She is following the course of women from another generation, believing the female is the one who must make the relationship work.

Men who make minimal efforts in a relationship, skimming by, have no motive for promoting relationship growth, and stop certain behaviors just short of their female partner's getting upset. Their wives live with a chronic sense of dissatisfaction. This is not, however, because men are trying to hurt women, it is because they are systemizers, putting priority on other things.

Systemizers don't typically work to
promote ongoing relationship health.

Tracey, a very articulate 47-year-old, tried explaining to her husband that a relationship is like a car. It can take you places you've never been—to mountains, valleys, oceans. It can exhilarate you. If you take care of it, it can give you pride and you'll love to show it off. But if you don't, it may barely function, your worry about it will supersede your enjoyment, it may break down and you'll be left on the side of the road. *It's the same with me,* she said. I have a list of needs and if you meet them, our relationship will take you places you've never been, it will exhilarate you and be a source of pride. I need romantic behaviors; I need attentiveness to me as a female. I need a sense of order and cleanliness around the house and I need you to help make that happen. Otherwise, I'm grouchy or hurt. I stop wanting to meet your needs. The relationship breaks down. But it's all about choices. If you choose to meet my needs, the relationship will run smoothly. If you don't, we'll break down."

Her husband understood, but did not have the motivation over time to carry through.

The woman finally detaches

A disappointed woman, not knowing what else to do, often detaches. Disengaging in this way is obviously the opposite of being intimate, so her needs for closeness are more crushingly unmet. She's taken aback, though, that he's more comfortable because there's now no conflict. He isn't oriented toward emotional intimacy and doesn't feel the need for it. He prefers peace. If she could be happy on her own, that would be great, he thinks, and maybe this is what's finally happening. She's making no demands now, so he feels no failure, and they have no conflicts. He doesn't realize, though, that she's actually left him. She's stopped investing in their relationship. She's done because she feels the relationship is dead.

Jasmine, 41, had waited all day for her husband to come home from work. Their two-year-old and eight-year-old were demanding. She envisioned him walking in the door and saying, "Hello, Sweetheart, I've missed you so much today." They would embrace, she imagined. But that's not how it happened. After gobbling down, in silence, the meal she'd prepared, he picked up the two-year-old, saying he was going to wipe off her hands. He couldn't find a clean dish clothe though, so, getting agitated, went to the drawer where clothes are kept and jerked it open. Not finding the right kind, he slammed the drawer shut. His aggression, though unsaid and indirect, was clearly felt by Jasmine and probably by the two-year-old. Jasmine felt teary now, and very alone. He did take their toddler outside to play for a few minutes, fulfilling, in his mind, his family duties. But his attitude left Jasmine disquieted and hurt. Because he's home in the evening, and she is continually trying to develop a relationship with him, she has little time to develop friend-ships with women.

After weeks of disappointing evenings with her husband, she arranges for a babysitter to come after dinner so the two of them can go out for a glass of wine. But as they sit across from each other, she finds him out of words. She works hard at drawing him out, but he gives succinct an-swers. She changes the topic to what she believes are his interests—his work, his mother, current events—but these, too, go nowhere. As they drive home, she feels empty. She considers making love that night, but feels inauthentic to have a physical relationship with someone she has so little emotional connection with. She decides to go ahead, neverthe-less, in order to make him happy, but feels she's giving away a piece of herself. Contented, he falls asleep quickly, having gotten what he needs from the relationship. She lays awake, trying to find her self.

At first, a woman is tempted to teach a man
how to be in a relationship.

An attorney who's practiced family law for 30 years says that some men's egos make it so they only *begin* hearing their wife once she files divorce papers. Before that, the talk, including couples therapy, doesn't register. What the talk wouldn't do, a behavior (like moving out or fil-ing) will. Unfortunately, by that time, she's had it. She's out.

Systemizers are Hierarchical in Their Thinking

While girls want best friends to share secrets and dreams, boys want to build a social structure with everyone rank ordered. When put into a group, boys seek a system and push to the top. We have looked at the male drive to social dominance earlier, but now we will look at how it takes their focus off relationships—that is, their minds are busy doing something else besides relating.

The dermal premammillary nucleus (DPN), buried in the hypothalamus, is larger in men than in women, making them hierarchical and seek to be "one up," aggressive, and territorial.

Frans de Waal, Ph.D., primatologist, points out that anytime men congregate—be it in the Masons or church or the armed forces, they arrange themselves in hierarchical order. He submits that men are miserable without this display of who has what power. It feels right to males to order the home also—with themselves at the top and everyone else—wife and children—underneath. This is true even though the wife knows he's out of touch with the needs of the home.[154]

Landmark research was conducted by anthropologist Ritch Savin-Williams who studied a teenage summer camp. Girls and boys were assigned to gender-specific cabins with strangers their same age. Within hours of arriving, boys began their vie to be at the top. How? They'd ridicule and bully boys in front of the others. The girls waited over a week, building friendships first, and then through talk and eye contact, used a more sophisticated and indirect means of establishing dominance. The subtleties made it difficult for researchers to discern how one girl was viewed as better than another, but, somehow, the girls at the top did it without harming the emotional connection with the girls she chose. That is, she didn't push or bully. That would have been unacceptable.[155]

The important point here is that the aggressive boys didn't care if their victim felt hurt or offended, if it cost them intimacy in other relationships. The overriding aim was control, power, and the access to resources that this brings. Relational connection was of lesser value.

Further, while the hierarchies the boys established endured through the summer, the girls' soon split up into groups of two or three, sharing themselves emotionally. Rather than challenging girls at the top, they overtly acknowledged their leadership, asking them for support or advice and showing admiration—in other words, they attempted to turn what hierarchy there was into friendship.

Those who think in hierarchies have a hard time apologizing and doing housework

Being much less hierarchical, women inherently know that apologies are part of the lubricant between two people. It makes relationships work by soothing a difficult moment. Apologies say I will do my part in making this work; I will take responsibility in the relationship.

You will wish he could apologize in a heartfelt manner.

He may not think to apologize or the apology may catch in his throat. He may glibly or defensively, say, "Sorry," but then justify what he's done. He may name things he's done right or things she's done wrong as though evening the ledger. Or he may say "sorry," but before a second passes, he turns to watch TV. Why? He doesn't want to admit blame in the first place, but if he does, he wants to get away from it as soon as possible

Justin, 32, asks me, "When I goof up, why doesn't she see all the good things I do?" She's upset that he isn't emotionally sensitive to her and wasn't there when she was working through her childhood sexual abuse. She had overlooked many difficulties in the relationship, but she did expect that if something big happened, he would know that she needed comfort and he would be emotionally present for her. He was not.

He sees this as a "goof." She sees it as a relationship breaker, an indication that he's truly not there for her. He doesn't realize all the insensitivities she has overlooked. To him, saying "Sorry" means defeat, and it evokes power issues. "If I apologize, being humble, she'll be in a one-up position with me. I believe in never admitting defeat," he says. It is this armor, though, that threatens their relationship.

All relationships run through a three-part cycle, going from attunement (which we love,) to deregulation (which makes us uncomfortable), to (hopefully) repair. When men see apology or giving assurance as a power play, they do poorly at the essential skill of repair. That is, due to his hierarchical thinking, he may see her apologizing as meaning he's now on top, and that feels good and right to him. It doesn't, however, bring about true repair. Often, she's left to either withdraw her full emotional self from the relationship or do all the "repairing" herself. He may be unwilling to apologize or offer assurance (i.e., "Baby, I just want to be close to you, whatever that takes") because doing so would put him in a one-down position;in his mind, he's "lost the battle." *What battle?* she wonders. She just wants to return to the feeling of attunement.

Men don't willingly do housework or child care because they view themselves as too important to stoop to that. She can do it. Let the woman take care of you. Females are destined for "lower" work, on the hierarchy of life. Until he asks how it must feel to live with someone who views you that way, he won't get it. So men leave a trail of opened mayonnaise jars, dirty socks, and newspapers. Women keep picking up, thus inadvertently saying, "Not only will I do this for you, but I acknowledge I am on a lower rung." He then unconsciously feels justified, and the loop feeds itself on and on.

Systemizers Have Categorizing Minds

Mark Gungor's Utube presentation "The Nothing Box" humorously explains how men's brains are composed of little boxes (sex, money, his relationship to you, and his relationship to the children) and how none of them touch. In women's brains, everything is connected—for instance, how he treats you at breakfast relates to whether you're open to sex that night. Further, men's *biggest* compartment is "The Nothing Box" where they don't care, they think about absolutely nothing, they're blank. Women don't get it because women care about everything!

A man says in therapy to his wife who's trying to process his affair, "If something is irritating or hard or troublesome, it's gone. I don't remember it. I have an editing memory." He can't respond to his wife's past hurts because he's edited them out. So there's no one to resolve her past hurts with.

Another male client told me, "I can make my affair go away. I forget about it and go on. I was a son of a bitch, but I don't like looking at that." His wife, however, says she needs to talk about it. His mind compartmentalizes his affair, putting it in the "I want to forget this" file. She wants to understand his affair, perhaps so she can prevent another one. He says, "It makes me so depressed to look at it." His wife put the secret dates of the affair on a time line to see what else was going on in their lives at the same time. She was facing tests for cancer at the time. He then asks, "How could I have done this, left her alone, been so inconsiderate?" It's easier for him not to face the pain. If his wife weren't unsure about whether she wants to stay in the marriage, I doubt he would be facing this.

Men really do have selective memory;
it's called compartmentalizing.

If compartmentalizing goes too far, a man won't see how an affair has anything to do with his wife or marriage. He may even be surprised the wife is bothered by it.

Men's ability to categorize keeps them emotionally immature. They don't really process things because they don't face them. They can, much like an alcoholic uses alcohol, use a distraction like sports or the newspaper to forget about the problem. Women, having blood flow to the whole brain all the time, are more likely to think holistically, thinking about all aspects of their lives at once. She doesn't forget it: she wants to process it. We all categorize, but the tendency is much stronger in men. An example is the man who's reading the paper and his wife is shouting because one of their kids has cut himself. He doesn't hear.

Questioning the Ability of Men to Change

"But can't I change him?" you ask. And isn't this all just the result of conditioning? To answer, we look first at whether parents do, indeed, condition boys, say, not to feel.

Remember that Harvard researchers discovered that infant males get emotionally charged quicker than infant females, and once worked up, they are more difficult to calm down. Parents, therefore, spend more time trying to settle their son's feelings than their daughters'. This is interesting because it means boys receive more emotional attention and soothing than infant girls. When you consider the effects of environment, then, or parenting, the boys are favored, in this sense.[156]

Boys receive more emotional attention
and soothing than infant girls.

Further evidence that conditioning *slants in favor of males* is the finding that boys receive twice the verbal warnings from their dads at age one than do girls.[157]   That is, if conditioning were going to make males thoughtful and empathic, why don't the warnings help them?

Despite the egalitarian styles of second-wave feminist moms, boys still use dolls as weapons and girls still cuddle cars if that's all they're given to play with. Boys spend 65% of their leisure time competing, while girls spend half that.[158]   The icing on the cake is that girls take turns *twenty times* more often than their male counterparts![159]

For most men, systemizing is their hard drive. To understand if this is true, we first ask, how early does this orientation to things rather than intimate relationship building occur? Previously, we saw how even one-year-old boys prefer to watch a film of cars (non-personal), while baby girls prefer watching a face speaking. By age two, boys choose cars (involving mechanics) and bricks (involving building), while the majority of girls choose dolls to play with (involving empathy.)   But aren't the toy choices just social conditioning, you ask. It's doubtful. Researchers asked two-year-olds which toys were meant for girls and which for boys, but the kids didn't know if a doll was for a girl and a car was for a boy. Even so, these same kids were already making gender-typical choices.[160]   That is, their preferences *predated* conditioning.

You can't change a systemizer's natural
proclivities and motivations.

First we ask if the patterns occur *early* in life. The answer is yes. Then we ask if this object-vs-relationship orientation is universal. Sure enough, men around the world choose jobs like building weapons, boats, tools, computers—that is, the crafting of a system. Weapon-making, for instance, is done by only males in 121 of 121 societies studied.[161]

We also ask if the trend is *enduring* over time. Adult males lean toward engineering and jobs using math and physics, the male-to-female ratio being 9:1 in 1970 and *about the same today*.[162]   Furthermore, men naturally value math as a system, liking its rules, so they gravitate toward learning it, and score fifty points higher than women on the Scholastic

Aptitude Math Test.[163] Women can, of course, excel in math, but most women aren't interested unless there's an empathic draw, like becoming a doctor or wanting to teach math.

Well done research shows the two genders are parented with the same amount of conversation, sensitivity, rules, support, and kindliness. Surprisingly, evidence shows parents *try harder* to get their sons to be empathic, including moms *demonstrating* empathy by replicating their sons' facial expressions *more often* than they mimic their daughters' non-verbals. The moms attempt to train empathy into the boys.[164]

Parents try harder to get their sons to be empathic.

The Gender Differences of Our Brains

Finally, you cannot change a guy's actual brain. (Over time, evolution modifies our brains, but only out of felt-necessity.) Three brain parts are smaller in men: the corpus callosum, the anterior commissure, and the mass intermedia that connects the two sides of the thalamus. In women, all three of these are larger. In a woman, the first two allow for rapid communication between the two hemispheres of the brain, which is exactly what being empathic and communicating requires, because the woman's left brain (the facts) is connected to her right brain (her feelings.)[165]

So, are females essentially gifted with empathy, having inherited something boys don't possess? Yes, say researchers. Sex chromosomes, X and Y, shape the brain according to gender, stamping inclinations toward certain behaviors. Some genes are linked to one gender and mold the brain accordingly. Contrasting identical twins (sharing all genes) and fraternal twins (having different genes) further clarifies that empathy is indeed inherited, as researchers have shown.[166]

Additionally, sophisticated MRI imaging shows how emotion is handled in the brains of children 7 to 17 years old. Girls go through an interesting change. At first, they process negative feelings in a part of the brain that hasn't changed much over the course of evolution. The seven-year-old boy or girl handles negative emotion in the amygdala, a place that looks about the same as a mouse's amygdala and that's why these young children can't explain to you what they're feeling. However, a seventeen-year-old girl's brain transforms so that the processing of emotion *moves up to the cerebral cortex where higher mental functioning*—like reflection, language, and reasoning—takes place. She can now *easily explain why she feels as she does*. However, negative emotion remains in the primitive brain for males, so that asking a 7-year-old or 17-year-old-boy why he's mad or sad renders the same "I don't know."[167]

Many women get caught in hoping
the problem is just conditioning
and therefore changeable.

Men are less developed than women in terms of relationship skills because of other brain differences. The dorsal premammillary nucleus (DPN) is bigger in men's brains and is sensitive to territorial threats from other men. It immobilizes men to defend their turf. Furthermore, the amygdala is larger in men and triggers an alarm if any challenge occurs, making him alert and ready to defend what is his. In the bigger picture, this has to do with why it's men, not women, making and fighting wars. But in the more personal realm, it explains why boys and then men don't develop the kind of friendships with other guys that women tend to have with girls and then women. This special brain structure disallows the development of friendship skills and intimacy skills females bring into marriage.

PART II: WOMEN IN A BIND

"Sometimes I wonder if men and women really suit each other. Perhaps they should live next door and just visit now and then."
                                                              —Katherine Hepburn

"Men and women, women and men. It will never work."
                                                              – Erica Jong

Women are in a bind because they are caught between their heterosexual drive to form a relationship with a man and the fact that men seem unable to meet their deepest needs. If either end were changeable — women's drive or men's inability — it would not be so painful.

Women's expectations of romance pose a difficulty for women in several areas: Women expect sex to be a symbolic part reflecting emotional closeness, women expect heart-dialogue that promotes closeness, women expect to deal with conflicts by dialoguing until they are resolved, women expect to grow together with a man through exploring feelings together, sharing empathically, and developing a strong private life based on dialogue. This chapter reviews what a woman *can* expect from a man.

It isn't that men intend to be difficult,
they are just different.

When relating to a man, a women has to be careful not to develop a false self, where, to make the relationship work, she only speaks factually, presents only a cheerful self, and gives in to him. That is, because women can read what a guy wants, she can cut herself short, becoming a bare image of her true self. Dropping her more interesting, intuitive, socially fluent self because he doesn't "get it," she can become a pseudo self. He may be happy with this arrangement, but she will become soul-dead.

But what about counseling, you ask? I recommend it, but it has its limitations. Therapist Terrence Real, in "The Awful Truth: Most men are just not raised to be intimate," says men are raised to become rotten partners. The very way we define masculinity assures this. In therapy, Real begins by siding with the woman, who has been suffering with the man's insensitivity. Then he confronts the woman, who has often been passively hiding behind the man's wrongdoing. I take a similar approach, but add the rearrangement of her expectations, the subject of our next chapter. Terrence sees the male issue as one of conditioning. I agree that patriarchy has acculturated men to be non-relational, but behind that are the effects of testosterone, an inability to match a woman's empathy, and a systemized brain, and these are unlikely to change in many lifetimes.

Chapter 5
What To Expect From A Man

Expect Sex to be his Main Motivation and Source of Connection

What women expect but often don't get

Basically, women expect they will not have to speak up for their needs in the sexual realm, but that isn't so, and here's why.

Men get erections when around women they don't care about, but women have trouble having orgasms unless they love a guy.[168] It's easier to have sex for sex's sake if you're high in testosterone. It's also easier to separate sex from true relationship.

Evolution gave men the undeniable, unquenchable fire to keep the planet covered in humans. Testosterone creates a sexual tension that keeps sex on the brain constantly. Meanwhile, women seek a committed, emotionally close affiliation, with sex as a part of the whole. Men are more interested in sex for sex's sake, according to researchers. [169]

Women seek a committed, emotionally close affiliation
with sex as a part of the whole.

But don't assume women dislike sex. Not so. Among women age 40–60, for instance, who enter a new relationship after a divorce, 54% have sex at least once a week.[170]

The movie *Hysteria* humorously conveyed the desire for climax in middle-aged women, which resulted in the invention of the vibrator.

Sometimes a woman wrongly assumes she has something wrong with her sexually. Ron, 48, upon hearing his wife, Sandra, was leaving, suddenly wanted to change their relationship and became more caring and talkative. She'd often wondered if she needed an antidepressant or hormones because she'd lost her sex drive. She read lots of self-help books, searching for ways to fix herself. He would pout and make life miserable because she wasn't more sexual.

Ron, Sandra, and I put our heads together to figure out what had *really* gone on in the last 25 years. He admitted he'd been quite selfish, stemming partly from plain old chauvinism: he didn't believe women mattered much. His attitudes were easy for her to read and turned off her sex drive. Then, a few years ago, she caught him sexting with a woman on a dating site. She forgave him, but her willingness to be sexual ended altogether.

Later, Sandra met a man and discovered there was nothing at all wrong with her sex drive. She didn't need medication; she needed someone who took her seriously.

Women wrongly assume they don't have to speak up. Many men are so driven to sexual gratification that they don't consider a woman's needs. Or due to having a systemizing brain, they just want the bottom line of sex—orgasm—not the foreplay women need. Consider that 50–75% of women who orgasm need clitoral stimulation and are unable to orgasm through intercourse alone. Stimulating the clitoris may take about 20 to 45 minutes before a woman climaxes. Women who do orgasm through intercourse still need clitoral stimulation and find it through prolonged intercourse and specific positions.

~~~~~~~~~~~~~~~~~~
Say:
"Foreplay turns me on and once I really have enough, it makes me love intercourse."
~~~~~~~~~~~~~~~~~~

Interestingly, throughout history, men have said that women could have all the power over men they wanted just by limiting sex, using it as a reward or punishment. This seems more than obvious to men, but women are not, by nature, interested in using sex like this. Sex, for a woman, is symbolic of emotional connection. To objectify sex and use it to get something she wants feels hollow. What she wants must come from his heart.

What a man has to know is that she has a door inside her marked "caring." If he doesn't open that door by being romantic and loving, she can't open the inner court marked "sexual responsiveness." She simply won't be able to access it.

Many men are so driven to sexual gratification
that they don't give enough consideration to a woman's needs.

Women wrongly expect they won't have to clarify, be persistent about, and even demand what they need sexually. With low sexual desire being the most common complaint reported to health professionals by women, the question rises, "What's wrong?" Twice as many females as males report they just can't get aroused. But, from the start, women envision sex being a part of the whole relationship and symbolic of the shared emotional closeness. It is not as physical, orgasm-driven, and, quite frankly, non-relational as men see it. The fundamental difference between the genders requires *ongoing, clear communication from her*.

This may seem like a funny place to talk about chores, but in the mind of a woman, chores and sex go together in a full partnership. Nothing shuts the female door to sex like feeling taken for granted and being overworked. One Gallup poll found that the majority of husbands (73%) say they help with cooking. It sounds like the burden on wives has been lifted! However, only 40% of the wives themselves report that this is true. While almost all (89%) of husbands report there's a fair division of domestic labor, only 55% of the wives agree.[171] Family therapist Virginia Goldner reminds us that historically women's domestic work has been mandatory; men's has been discretionary.[172] This no doubt leads men to believe they're doing a lot of giving.

Back to the actual act. The rise in testosterone in men that comes with sexual excitement can cut off their supply of oxytocin, which, you remember, is the cuddling and generosity hormone. Women want sex to include physical and verbal affection, not just the raw deal. When men are aroused, though, they experience a rise in the male hormone that makes oxytocin unavailable to meet those needs in a woman. Because of this, many women find that men are better lovers at middle age and beyond, once their testosterone supply declines. Rather than shutting down sexually, a woman has to lay it out there and say what she needs.

Rather than shutting down sexually,
a woman has to lay it out there and say what she needs.

Kim, 48, faces a difficult situation after 25 years of marriage because she feels no emotional tie. All the sacrifices in the relationship must be made on her part. There is no verbal affection before sex. He doesn't have the social capability to fit into her social group or family. He can monologue if prodded but cannot dialogue, so there's no sense of shared communication. He doesn't get what's going on with the home and kids unless specifically told. His doing things for the kids feels to him like "giving and giving with no payoff." He doesn't find intrinsic joy or value in being with the kids. Anything he contributes is "for her," meaning she is then indebted to him. They are not partners. Being sexual with him feels empty, like it's with a stranger, because they don't share life. He seems to have one need: sex. It feels unnatural for her to have sex without an emotional connection, but he says he can't give any more (i.e., share childcare or domestics or try to communicate differently) because he hasn't had sex in a year. This is the bind many women face. For awhile, Kim can go against her nature and give him sex. In the long term, that won't really work without Kim deadening herself. When I asked Kim what emotions she feels after sex, she reported, "repulsion and avoidance. Feeling dirty, stupid, weak, violated, and vengeful." Not the stuff great relationships are built from.

Emotional involvement is to women what sexual involvement is to men. So, for instance, men feel upset when imagining their partner having sex with somebody else. Contrarily, women feel upset and jealous when they imagine their partner being emotionally involved with another woman. While women's sexual fantasies include the personal and emotional traits of their imagined partner, men's fantasies focus on sex in the raw—just physical—without making the partner a real person.[173]

Emotional involvement is to women
what sexual involvement is to men.

Women's sexuality is more flexible than men's. Women who are unable to find a suitable male partner will still have sexual needs. Women are less prone to shaming sexuality. Women, after all, have never invented the male counterparts to the words like "bitch," "whore," "nymphomaniac," or "slut," all names invented by men to shame women sexually. As women become more of the decision-making fabric of society, they will support increasing ways of expressing sexuality while disentangling it from judgment.

It is women who will separate
sex from judgment and shame.

Women have specific sexual needs including, for most, nonsexual touching that leads to sexual touching and clitoral stimulation that either enhances or brings on orgasm. When a woman's attended to, sex becomes of much greater interest. It is shocking how many women, married for years or decades, have never had a partner-stimulated orgasm.

Resolved conflicts pave the way for her sexual openness

Often a man wants to make up after an argument by being sexual. He doesn't want to talk, but he wants to feel close again. This goes against the evolutionary grain of females who need emotional and verbal resolution before their affection and sexuality can kick in. He may feel slighted, however, if she can't immediately be physical. (Contrast this with true "make-up sex," where a long talk, including the disclosure of feelings, results in the desire on the part of both to unite physically.) Men are concerned about preserving their pride in a relationship. (Studies show that men feel pride more frequently and intensely than women.) They approach a relationship less as a union and more as an individual. Solving relationship problems or functioning as a couple is less on their minds than maintaining their self-respect. This is one of the reasons men do poorly with confrontation. Rather than focusing on solving the problem, men focus on maintaining their pride.

"It feels repulsive to me when he wants to kiss when I've had no resolution to my anger," a woman says. If she puts her own needs aside and has sex while upset, her sense of mistrust mounts and she's worse off than she was before sex. She may even, consciously or unconsciously, see him as a perpetrator.

I believe that when women's voices are more equally felt in a relationship (and in the world), women will be more inclined toward being sexual. Being heard and being sexual go hand in hand. Likewise, once an argument is verbally resolved, a woman may feel very much like having sex. One husband in marital therapy told me, "I believe all our marital problems would be resolved if she and I escaped for a sex-filled vacation." The wife turned away in frustration, hurt by his suggestion, seeing it as a blurring over of what must be faced.

For a woman, being heard and
feeling sexually responsive go hand in hand.

To a biochemist, the gender difference is no surprise. When men feel stressed out, they release testosterone and want to use sex to discharge the build up. When women are stressed out, they want to talk because talking releases oxytocin, the soothing, bonding hormone.

A possible reason why men don't seek resolution comes from psychologist Janet Lever. She watched elementary school-aged kids playing and noticed boys clash about *twenty times* as often as girls do. More surprising, though, she noted that the boys became *better friends* after their fight and went on to play together. Girls don't fight much, but if they do, the bitterness lasts. Lever found the same thing with chimpanzees. Males are twenty times more likely to fight but the fighting doesn't harm male relationships and may be a first step toward friendship. Female chimps rarely fight, but if they do the hostility can last for years or forever.[174] Men may see fighting, then, as *not needing a resolution* in order to bring closeness; the fighting itself brings closeness.

Women expect dialogue to open the door to sexual expression

Talking face-to-face, gazing into one another's eyes, and sitting close together make women feel intimate, says linguist Deborah Tannen. [175] Women feel evaded when a man avoids her eyes, and the avoidance doesn't give her a chance to build trust and thus ignite romantic longing. While women feel intimate when talking about personal issues, people, and emotion, men feel intimate when talking about sports, politics, world affairs, and business. These are the worlds of win or lose, of top dogs and underdogs, of status and hierarchy—worlds men understand.[176] A woman feels like making love when her lover demonstrates that he can listen, show support and patience, bridling his desire as they talk.[177]

~~~~~~~~~~~~~~~~

Say:
**"Sitting and talking, especially when
you make eye contact with me, makes me feel
romantic toward you."**

~~~~~~~~~~

Shelley, 58, talks about how Michael acts out (slamming doors, being critical) when he's upset about something at work, but won't talk. He's sarcastic and biting toward her, but she intuits it's not about her. She tries to get him to talk about what he really feels. If she tries to empathize he feels weak, and then he gets angry all over again. She knows what the problem is—he needs to talk about his work problems—but she can't get him to do it. She's been married to him for 32 years. We talk about what would help. "Sex," she says, tossing up her hands. "Sex would help. It's the only way he finds permission to be vulnerable emotionally." If they have sex, afterwards he'll talk. He'll be open. On the other side of sex, for many men, is openness.

The problem is that it's hard to give like this over and over again. It's hard to initiate sex with someone who's angry, critical, and sarcastic. She can do it, but it's difficult not to resent him. Furthermore, he never guesses how much she's giving. He doesn't admit how difficult he's being and how hard he makes it for her to be sexual.

~~~~~~~~~~~~~~~~~~~

Say:
**"Kindness and sex go hand in hand for me.
I just don't feel aroused when you're angry."**

~~~~~~~~~~~~~~~~~~~

In fact, she has to go against every evolved cell in her psyche. Being sexual, for women, requires the prerequisites of love and affection. From way back, a woman had to weigh a sexual encounter against the possibility of being stranded with a pregnancy and years of childcare alone. She seeks a guy who will stick around to help, one who doesn't just want sex, but wants a continuing affectionate friendship.

It's hard to initiate sex with someone
who's angry, critical, and sarcastic.

Affection, for men is, "white sex." It's on the same continuum as all sex, just a lesser form. It's less exciting, less important, and less mean-ingful than "real sex." This is quite different from the way women ex-perience affection. Women see it as a pleasure in its own right, standing alone, not necessarily related to being sexual. The reason? Women emit oxytocin (the bonding chemical) when non-sexually touched. No doubt this, too, comes from women's history with childcare. Women's respon-sibilities required that the affection they gave children be in a category all its own, separate from sex. If women had not had separate categories for touch and sex, it would have been a catastrophe, endangering the psyches of children if boundaries were crossed.

Molly, a 27-year-old attorney married to Zack for six years, has become discouraged with sharing feelings or confiding anything that happens to her that matters. She's tried reasoning with Zack, laying out what she needs in a calm, straightforward manner, but Zack shuts her down when she starts expressing feelings. He can't access empathic language or keep from offering quick fixes. Molly is trying to decide if she will stay in the relationship. She's gradually started sharing her true life with girl-friends and spending more time away from Zack. She only has so much leisure time outside work and home responsibilities. But she finds that without the emotional connection, she can't open herself up sexually.

She craves a viable sexual connection, but without an emotional one, sex feels inauthentic. Zack is becoming more disgruntled. She regrets that though Zack is a good man, he can't meet her primary needs.

Robby, 35, is surprised that after seven years of not going to strip clubs, his wife is still worried that he will. He believes his behaviors should prove everything she needs to know. But she, being female, needs words, explanations of how and why he changed. Women heal through words.

In the Australian movie *Alexandra's Project*, a wife's birthday surprise for her husband is a video tape in which she explains how she feels he has a relationship with her *body* but not with *her*. As long as he has access to her body, she says, he believes the marriage is in good shape, but she is miserable. He thinks she needs Prozac. He doesn't know her heart or her mind and doesn't seem to want to. She tells of their honeymoon, where he wanted more and more of her until she realized it was only her body he wanted. When she awakened to this, she was pregnant and had not yet established a way to earn a living. Then comes the part that blows his mind. She ends the video by disclosing that she's decided to earn money by being sexual with men—at least then it's her choice. After the birthday party of the once happy-go-lucky husband, he cries alone, watching the video. Perhaps he cries because he's lost his wife, but more likely it's because she's shared her (his) body with others.

A woman's sex drive rarely exists in isolation
from true closeness.

Marriage had prepared her for having sex with strangers. At the beginning of her honeymoon she surmised that her husband's desire to be sexual with her was an expression of emotional connection. Only after some time did she understand that he wanted a relationship with her body and not particularly with the rest of her. As she continued to meet his sexual needs, her own needs waned. A woman's sex drive rarely exists in isolation from true closeness.

What You Can *Expect*

Men love sex. They are good at initiating it, keeping it moving, surprising you with new sexual explorations. After years or decades together, he is still driven to find that connection with you. The same body you are critical of, he finds endlessly alluring. Not only is the extra fat on your hips okay with him, it's fascinating. And the freckles on your back are endearing. He gives you the incentive to keep your body in shape, your clothes in style, and your lifestyle active. My husband of 22 years told me he married me partly because he knew I'd look good bald. A man I dated told me he'd always be committed because of the way I walked.

Expect a man to believe that sex, not dialogue, *is* the emotional connection with you.

His passion is a blazing fire that can't be put out, despite rough spots in the relationship. It can feel like unconditional love. To be so desired is exhilarating; to be the one who satisfies him is deeply fulfilling.

Expect to keep sex a major focus in order to keep him engaged. Men love to talk about sex. Talking about your shared interest and experiences can feel fun and deeply intimate. His saying "I love your breasts" feels more emotionally intimate to him than if he were to say, "You look great in that outfit." The secrets you share, the sexual vocabulary you invent, the innuendoes you laugh over keep the relationship hot.

Expect to see your body through his eyes in order to keep your sexual connection titillating. He finds your skin erotically soft, your curves enticing. He buries his face in your hair. He delights in the tiny movements that only women do, from the lowering of your eyelids to the tilt of your hip. He validates your femininity. Experience your body through his eyes. If the sexual connection is strong, he will be fascinated, too, with your perspective. He will see how you help people and admire you as a fountain of love. You do things that are beyond his reach.

Experience your body through his eyes.

Expect him to help you transcend. He tends to you sexually in a way that allows escape from the mundane minutia of life, allowing you to travel to a pleasure palace and beyond, where, losing control, you orgasm. Your perspectives begin shifting, your boredom lifts and you see life with a brighter attitude.

Expect to broaden your appreciation of sex. His touch invigorates your immune system; his semen regulates your mood and menstruation; it protects you from cancers. Sex supports your cardiac fitness. The gift of his insatiable sex drive supports your mental and physical health.

Expect that when you enter a sexual relationship you have made an *unspoken promise* to enjoy regular sex on an ongoing basis. Men have semen build up every 3 days and are in a better mood if they have sexual release that often. Expect that if you are sexual out of "duty," he will feel rejected. He believes that what holds the relationship together is your essential attraction to him—not emotionally, mentally or spiritually, but sexually. If you initiate sex sometimes, it will lift his spirits. This becomes more needful as men grow older.

A man feels cheated and disappointed
when his female companion's sex drive wanes.

A man feels cheated and disappointed when his female companion's sex drive wanes over time or if she gains significant weight. Either is a statement about how much she *values him and the relationship*. Being good friends is no substitute for sex in his thinking.

Expect to keep yourself sexually alive if you want an ongoing romance. If you feel you need more emotional connection in order to be sexual, tell yourself men aren't naturally geared that way. However, asking for what you need *in light* of being sexual works well.

~~~~~~~~~~
Say,
"I feel so sexual when you do dishes with me."
Or
"I find it erotic when we cook together."
~~~~~~~~~~

Expect that his sex drive will be higher than yours, especially after childbirth, and, in general, you will be the "low drive" person in the relationship. Therefore, expect that he will feel controlled by you if you disallow him access to what he finds most meaningful — your body.

Expect to rely on your understanding that sex is good for you, even when you can't access the mood for it. Many conflicts in long-term romances are, bottom line, about a guy's irritability that he's not getting enough quality sex. To feel physically and emotionally comfortable, most men need sex every three days.

Expect him to promote your relaxation. That will, in turn, increase your sex drive. He thrives on making decisions, finding the directions, and planning your shared leisure activities. Because of his testosterone-endowed social dominance, he will like being the activities director of the relationship. Let him do this while you relax. Feminine sexual arousal is helped by relaxation. He will also, if you let him, pull you out of your subjectivity (your inner world of thoughts and feelings) into concrete ways to have fun. When this happens, your dopamine goes up and it makes you feel like having sex.

~~~~~~~~~~~~
Say:
**"It turns me on when you
kiss my neck"** or **"Slow down,
Baby, I like that."**
~~~~~~~~~~~~

Expect to tell him what you like sexually. He doesn't, after all, live in a female body. If he doesn't experience it as a criticism, it will turn him on. So word it positively. Explore the kinds of touch you like either with him or on your own.

Expect Communication to be Fact Driven

What Women Expect But Often Don't Get

Women expect men to be in touch with their feelings

137

In Al and Tipper Gore's audio book, *Joined at the Heart,* they quote from a survey where women were asked, if they had to pick between a husband who would be a good provider and one who could talk about feelings, 80% said they'd chose the latter. Women expected to provide for themselves.[178]

The IQ scores of men and women are about the same, but their relationship to emotion is markedly different. Compared to men, women feel both positive and negative feelings, from joy to guilt, more strongly and more often. Women have rich emotional lives. The only feeling that men experience more frequently and more intensely than women do is self-pride.[179]

Women experience emotions more frequently
and with greater intensity than men do.

Because he experiences emotion on a lesser level, he may (1) think you're using tears to manipulate him, (2) not comprehend why you can't "blow it off" when he's insensitive, (3) speak bluntly, without softness, (4) merely say "fine" day after day when you ask him how he is, (5) not notice interactions where subtle emotion is shown, and (6) have trouble facing strong emotion (i.e., he won't talk with you about your mother's death). A woman has to help a man understand her femininity, standing up for her nature, so that she's not misunderstood.

~~~~~~~~
Say:
"I'm a woman; I have a lot of feelings all the time. I like the richness of my emotional life. It makes me feel alive."
~~~~~~~~

When a woman experiences how *emotionally neutral* he is, she (1) believes he's "bottled up," (2) has emotional problems he can't express, (3) is being stubbornly inexpressive. When a man experiences a woman's *intensity or frequency* of emotion, he (1) believes she's fragile, (2) keeps information from her so she won't be disturbed, (3) feels superior because he doesn't "give in" to emotion.

Women know how important their emotions are to their overall well being, their sense of direction, and their relationships. The emotional nature of women is a beautiful thing.

Why Men Can't Give it

Not only did men's brain structure and hormones form around killing. Later it formed around making money their bottom line, working in businesses where the highest value was profit.

The fundamental difference between the genders shows up on The Myers-Briggs Type Indicator, a much-relied-on personality test that you can take online. It consistently finds a gender difference in one area: men are "thinking" and women are "feeling."

Though everyone has both thoughts and feelings, *men pay more attention to and rely on* their thoughts and principles, while women *pay more attention to and rely on* their feelings, desires, and values. Thinking types (mostly men) hide their feelings, striving to contain them and lean toward *impersonal* facts. They pride themselves on being logical, noticing inconsistencies as you talk, and finding solutions as quickly as possible. A "thinker" may argue a point just for the challenge of intellectual stimulation. He likes being factually "right."

On the other hand, a feeling type (mostly women) doesn't feel like herself if her natural expressiveness is curtailed, and seeks connecting, intimate dialogue. She will apologize for the sake of bringing harmony; whether she's right or wrong is unimportant. She seeks to understand the point of view of the speaker, and will sacrifice to make the other comfortable.

Deborah Tannen, linguist and Georgetown University professor, found herself overwhelmed by gender differences related to the use of language. Comparing girls and boys, she discovered that second-grade girls were more like twenty-five-year-old females in terms of their ability to talk than second-grade girls were like their second-grade male peers![180]

I was blown away the other day when my barely-turned-six-year-old granddaughter, after telling me the ins and outs of her current friendships, said, "So, Mocho, now tell me everything about *your* life." Taken off guard, I hesitantly started sifting through what was and wasn't appropriate to tell a six-year-old. But she listened with such direct eye contact and facial responsiveness, asking me such appropriate questions, that I gradually loosened up and talked more freely. The experience was indeed similar to talking with a 25-year-old female.

Present-day !Kung San tribesmen of the Kalahari maintain a strict silence as they hunt, knowing any talk could activate the flight response of their prey, anthropologists have observed.[181] They give us insight as to how our forefathers developed: in silence.

Women's verbal fluency is substantially better than men's, meaning they dialogue in a flowing, connecting manner and can generate fitting words more readily than men.[182] The basic male hormone, testosterone, changes a person's facility with language. In fact, females who transgender into males receive testosterone supplementation and with it begin experiencing decreased verbal fluency.[183] This includes feeling blocked from finding words.

The basic male hormone, testosterone,
changes a person's facility with language.

Here's what happens. Sophisticated MRI imaging shows the interesting change girls go through. At age 7, girls and boys process negative emotion in the amygdala, and they can't tell you what they're feeling. Alas! By the time the girl is seventeen, the processing of feelings has moved out of the amygdala up into the cerebral cortex. This area is known for higher functions like the ability to reflect and reason. Now, she can readily talk about what she feels and why she feels that way. For the males, though, *there is no brain change*: his negative emotion is still processed in the primitive brain, so whether he's upset or content, he answers that he's "fine" or he doesn't know.[184]

By the time the girl is seventeen, the processing of feelings has
moved out of the amygdala up into the cerebral cortex.

Even so, there's a big difference between the communication of girls and boys prior to the girls' brain change. While females use language to connect, boys are more likely to use language that is careless of the feelings of others. They threaten, dare, mock, interrupt, dominate the floor, and override others. They are more likely to issue edicts, refuse to give in, top another's story, or to "grandstand," giving an egocentric commentary on their own activities, says Eleanor Maccoby.[185] Other researchers studying gender differences in children have found that boys display *50 times the amount of competitiveness* when compared with girls, and that girls, on the other hand, take turns 20 times more than boys do.[186] Taking turns is the epitome of relinquishing competitiveness and stepping aside to give someone else a chance. It is a female tendency that promotes relationship.

Women have special brain links connecting feeling to language. It turns out this is a pretty big deal because researchers discovered 412 distinct and mutually exclusive emotions that have separate words to describe them.[187] There are so many emotions that define the human experience, so many to talk about and to read on other people's faces.

Because women use both their left and right brains when they speak, they are more likely to give and seek genuine communiqué, from the heart. Women like using language to get personal and intimate, quickly moving dialogue into the sharing of feelings to promote closeness. They use compliments to signal others to remove any obstructions to closeness. Men talk with one another about objects, like their newest possession. They talk about how bad the traffic is, and share information about sporting events or cars, researcher Baron-Cohen found.

A woman's ability to find the right word and do so fluently makes her easier to understand. Eleanor Maccoby and her colleagues used a communication task in which a parent and his or her six-year-old child were given four ambiguous pictures. The parent described the picture and the child was asked to pick out which of the four pictures was being described. Mother–child pairs were more successful than father–child pairs at identifying the intended picture: women communicate more clearly.[188]

When women expect men to be like them, they fall into terrible disappointment. Just as a woman would feel disconnected and flat if she mimicked the blunt, factual talk of men, so he feels uncomfortable in her world of feelings. Thankfully, some of men's behaviors—asking her out, buying her jewelry, planning a vacation, being committed to the relationship—often arouse emotion in her that feels good. Often, too, sex serves as an emotional conduit for both.

What You Can *Expect*

Expect to enjoy communication with your guy on a myriad of topics. There's a lot to talk about that doesn't involve much emotional exploration: work, future plans, finances, politics, weather, hobbies, house issues, technology, history, and the factual information that surrounds your life. Because men are systemizers, they are data banks of information—from rock bands to cars to sports statistics; he can make life interesting.

Just as you don't mind a limited foray into the world of cars or sports, so he doesn't mind a brief journey into your private world of feeling. Just as you'd do better with some parameters, though, if he were to launch into some of his favorite topics, so would he. Spell out the goal.

~~~~~~~~~~~
Say:
"You can relax because I don't need any help with this, but I want to talk about my feelings about work. What I need most is to know you understand what I'm going through."
~~~~~~~~~~~

Becoming a two-paycheck family has caused a shift in relationship expectations. When women were at home they coordinated and initiated social and family relationships. Now women, having little time after work, depend on their spouse for closeness. They are too spent to pursue much more. If male partners can't meet women's emotional/relational needs, *they go without*. As research shows, the most relational gender—women—are unhappy, at least in America.

Expect to supplement your romance with activities or people that *let you feel*. Time with female friends or relatives, especially those similar to you in emotional intensity, helps greatly. Book clubs, journaling, going to movies, reading, and other activities can facilitate your feeling whole.

Couples who share activities that are an *outlet for feeling* do better than couples who don't. Skiing or dancing together, nurturing a garden, or sharing spiritual readings act as conduits of feeling for women while men love the comraderie of shared activity. Planning the activities and reviewing them together later allows the woman to share feelings while he's still in his comfort zone: talking about doing an activity. Both genders find fulfillment. Also, having couple friends helps because the two women, in or out of the company of their mates, can open their hearts with full genuineness. Though these activities take time and planning, your happiness is contingent upon it.

Expect to ask clearly for what you need when you're really hurting. Don't project onto him the empathic response *you* are able to give others during hard times. The temporal parietal junction (TPJ) activates faster and to a greater degree in males, so that when a man sees distress in a woman, he moves out of emotion into analyses of the facts and solution-finding.

~~~~~~~~~~~~~~~~
Say:
**"I'm sad and need you to hold me. I need to talk and cry.
I know you want to help me, but I just need to feel."**
~~~~~~~~~~~~~~~~

Accept that, because of your hormones, brain structure, and the developmental history of females, you have by far the greater capacity for emotional relating. Take pride in that! But also understand that his limitations must be accepted and worked into your life plan. Don't get trapped in loneliness. Don't sentence him to feeling like a failure because he can't give what you want.

~~~~~~~~~~~~~~~~
Say:
**"When I'm making a disclosure it hurts when
you try to debate facts with me because I'm speaking out of
a deeper part of myself. I just want you to
listen and understand."**
~~~~~~~~~~~~~~~~

Expect that you can relax in silence with him and he won't care you're not "carrying the conversation." Communication in marriage is vital to a woman's satisfaction, *though that is not true for men*, as found in a study of 264 couples.[189] Another couple study by psychologist Ted Huston found that intimacy for wives *means talking about the relationship itself*. But men shy away from directly talking about the relationship. During courtship, men will make the effort to discuss the relationship, thus fulfilling the woman's need for intimacy, Huston found, but after marriage—especially among traditional couples—the husband *grows less and less willing* to spend time talking. Further, men are unaware of how unhappy their wives are.[190] Men prefer to find closeness by having side by side activities. Expect, therefore, to find other outlets for talk. Women don't do well emotionally when they're not expressive, so journal or find a female venting partner.

Expect a guy to be ok with silence. His mind is often in neutral, without much feeling going on. This isn't abnormal for men. He will feel drained if he has to "entertain you" with talk or strain to do it. Most women need more rest time from their thoughts and emotion anyway. Don't interpret his silence as a lack of relationship. It doesn't have meaning. He simply likes being in your presence without talk.

Don't interpret silence as a lack of relationship.

Expect Conflicts to be Set Aside

What Women Expect But Often Don't Get

Women, already having had a long childhood history of one-on-one female relationships, enter romances expecting conflicts to be talked through and resolved. They get the opposite from men: stonewalling.

When girls disagree, they do so carefully in the form of a question.[191] A girl might disagree using words like this: "I know what you mean, I've thought about that, too. Once, though, I experienced…and I'm wondering what you think about that." Girls get that each person has a *subjective* realm—that is, each may interpret things differently because of their life experiences and feelings, says Baron-Cohen, allowing another's viewpoint to stand, even though it's not her personal viewpoint.[192] That's empathy: she creates space for differing viewpoints.

Boys are more likely to believe their opinion is *objectively* true and defend it as such.[193] While she's hoping for a discussion that will lead to greater insight into one another, solid compromises, and figuring out what's really behind his strong stance, she finds him defending his side.

In adulthood, if a woman hurts someone, she's more likely to apologize, explain, and seek restitution. She expresses anger *indirectly, restraining herself* so she doesn't hurt another's feelings. Men, on the other hand, are more likely to withdraw, shunning both contact and repair attempts, finds Baron-Cohen. Males are also more likely to misjudge another's intentions and assume someone is antagonistic when they're not.[194] *Couple's arguments can get very complicated because of this.*

Men are likely to withdraw,
shunning both contact and repair attempts.

Several researchers have found that women spend more time trying to bring about understanding, affirming others, and listening when compared to men.[195] These gestures help ease the hurt of difficulties in a relationship. The same researchers found that, in contrast, men use language to impress others by displaying their status or know-how. Without considering their partner, they interrupt to show off their opinion and show diminished interest in where the other person is coming from. Though men are not biologically suited for arguing in a close relationship, women are. In an argument, a woman will lay aside her point and use self-control to restrain herself from blunt or cutting remarks, whereas the man will not. She will offer comfort, despite the other disagreeing with her on a point. As she opens up and shares, her generous supply of oxytocin is released and begins soothing her. Her mirror neurons and other brain structures allow her to view her partner's perspective. Her ACC (anterior cingulate cortex) gives her self-control.

A University of California psychologist (2000) found that women, thanks to oxytocin, respond to stress by tending-and-befriending, while men flee or fight.[196] So, in relationship arguments, the guy stonewalls (flees the discussion) or starts a fight while she's kindly trying (remember that oxytocin makes one generous) to help him consider another point of view.

Why Men Can't Give It

Men stonewall because their blood pressure rises at the beginning of an argument, even if *they* start it, found psychologist John Gottman, who rigged couples up to stress monitors as they talked. Men are not biologically suited for confrontations. Men are more likely to see relationship talks and going over difficulties as *personal* attacks.

The anterior cingulate cortex (ACC) is larger and more active in women. It forms a collar around the corpus callosum, the bridge between the right and left hemispheres of the brain. It avoids punishment (i.e., trouble in relationships), stays away from conflict (but not resolution-seeking discussions), and seeks options. In contrast, testosterone makes males less concerned about getting in trouble—including hurting a loved one—while women's more active ACC causes carefulness so she doesn't step on toes and doesn't cause power struggles. If a woman feels like she's doing all the work in an argument, she probably is.

If a woman feels like she's doing all the work
in an argument, she probably is.

Even when men feel *low levels* of emotion, their fight-or-flight reactions are primed. That is, they get emotionally *agitated;* blood pumping away from their brains into their feet enables them to run *but not to think or cope well.* Furthermore, once they get into the fight-or-flight stage, they recover from it more slowly than do women; the agitation and heart pumping lasts longer.[197] This is probably why men avoid conflict, shut down once they're in a conflict, or get defensive when a woman brings something up.

Reiterating my point, another study found that when men are stressed, blood flows to the left orbitofrontal cortex *where the fight-or-flight response sits.* So say researchers at the University of Pennsylvania using fMRIs. Stressed-out women show blood flowing to the limbic system, where *nurturing and cooperative responses* come from.[198] You get the drift: in terms of biology, women probably have to be the ones to make arguments civil and reasonable.

In terms of biology, women probably have to be
the ones to make arguments civil and reasonable.

As his testosterone and cortisol fire his amygdala during the frustration of a fight, the circuits that would render sound judgment, the frontal lobe, *go offline*. Rather than the calm, emotionally explorative conversation she'd come to expect with girlfriends, she finds him getting angry and rash. Women have come to call this defending of turf (or opinion in an argument) "the male ego." The higher the testosterone in a man, the more he will pounce at being challenged. His need for dominance, though, is often her landmine: that is, she's merely talking (trying to connect or find a resolution,) and doesn't realize she just stepped on a bomb. Goodbye logic, hello irrational thought.

The male hormonal cocktail causes men to be sensitized to criticism, *real or imagined*, and this, paired with cortisol, makes a sit-down-feelings-exploration tough. He's more likely to go into fight-or-shut-down mode. If her face shows disgust, his amygdala lights up and cortisol prepares him to fight. Eons of battling and competing make anger an energizing male tool, allowing him to gather his strength. Because it causes a surge of testosterone and then dopamine, it renders a feel-good rush. This whole thing is clearly not what the woman was hoping for. Typically females don't like or even fear men's anger and will tip toe to keep it under wraps. This carefulness, though, is another way that women lose themselves in relationships with men.

Paul J. Zak's lab may have discovered why. When men feel distrusted, their testosterone spikes, leading them to retaliate or at least to withhold. Testosterone blocks ocytocin, which makes people bighearted. Women's testosterone does not increase under similar circumstances.[199] Similarly, if a woman is hoping to improve a relationship with a man by discussing what she felt, he can feel distrusted, like she's accusing him of something. His testosterone then hoists and he stonewalls her. Again, not what she'd expected!

Furthermore, the receptors for testosterone are located in primitive regions of the brain tied in with emotion. The upshot is that males don't take much time to reflect before their anger flares at others. This is very different from females whose empathy and high oxytocin impedes angry expressions and causes them to exercise self-control. In contrast, men's brain structure provides little buffer.

What You Can *Expect*

Expect that, in a conflict, the relationship will improve if you give him a concrete way to show he is a good partner. Testosterone causes him to search for wins. Your natural tendency would be to explain your feelings as if doing so will elicit in him an ability to amend his behavior, like it might in an empathic female friend. Instead, say, "Please find a way to make Saturday night romantic. I would love that." This is much more effective than saying, "I hate how our relationship isn't romantic. It makes me feel dead inside. I wish we would do things like we did when we were first dating."

Testosterone causes a man to search for wins.

Whereas he feels *overwhelmed* by the expression of your feelings, he feels clear when he knows what you want him to *do*. There is a high likelihood that he will *do* something you want. He better understands how *doing* things for you can help you love him while he doesn't get how *talking and expressing feelings* can make you love him.

A caveat to this advice is that, after you say what you want from him, *dismiss yourself*. Upon hearing he has to do something and give up some of his energy, he may act agitated, frustrated, angry, or "difficult." Get out of his way. Let him feel his feelings alone. Don't "fix" them for him or psychoanalyze them with him. Let him have his moment of agitation as he adjusts to the idea.

In the long run, as he sees that his behavior (i.e., giving you flowers Saturday night) can make you smile, he will want to do more of that. If not, though, just keep asking directly.

Expect that you can avoid many conflicts by understanding that he needs to engage in whatever makes him feel "manly"—from work to sports. These allow him to enjoy what is essential to his identity. Without the activities that affirm his manliness, he feels he has *little to bring to you*. In this way, his work and hobbies are indirectly about the relationship. Though this may not strike you as true, it does him.

Expect him to steady the relationship. He can be the *rock* because he feels less emotion, compared to you. He also expects less from relationships, so he feels fewer disappointments (as long as we're not talking about sex). His evenness can provide a constancy that feels like unconditional love. You can feel secure knowing he'll be the same.

His evenness can provide a constancy
that feels like unconditional love.

Expect to be in charge of *empowering* him to be the kind of guy you need. If you take on a victim stance—saying to yourself—he's impossible, he isn't romantic, he doesn't love me like I want to be loved—you can swirl around in those feelings forever and get nowhere. Take charge. Tell him (without a big explanation of your feelings) what behaviors you want.

"Yeah, but, it has no meaning if he doesn't think of these behaviors himself," you say. Again, though, you're expecting something that another woman would think to do. His voluntary, thoughtful behaviors *may* come later. Right now, if the relationship needs help, he needs to see that it is *possible* to please you, that his behaviors can actually make you happy again. If not, he will simply invest in work where "wins" are more assured. Bottom line: he needs to see you as the source of acceptance, as the one who smiles when he puts forth effort.

He needs to see that you deem him capable of pleasing you.

Expect that men will bring up few arguments on their own. Not as much bothers them. This frees you from feeling criticized and confronted. You don't have to navigate a complicated emotional terrain inside his head.

Remember that men have categorizing minds. Men turn their focus away from something, leave it behind, and go on to something else. When they switch from category A to category B, Category A becomes temporarily forgotten. This is why so many men don't take their wives seriously if they're upset. They figure she'll get over it, projecting their own abilities to distract onto her.

Expect to handle your need to confront *without him*, at least initially. Journal or talk with a friend until you land on one thing: a positive statement of what you want from him. He can't handle the criticism. Protect *yourself* by not putting him in the position to stonewall.

~~~~~~~~~~~~~~~
Say:
"Honey, will you text me each day at 4:00
to let me know what time to expect you for dinner?"
That would mean a lot to me."
~~~~~~~~~~~~~~~

In stonewalling, the male not only leaves the conversation, he goes into a rock-hard silence that smacks of disapproval, superiority, and distancing. In 85% of psychologist John Gottman's cases, it was the male who stonewalled in response to a wife's criticism and contempt.[200]

Gottman, author of *Why Marriages Succeed or Fail*, hooked couples up to measure their vital signs and found that men's blood pressure and other stress markers rise dramatically during conflicts. To lower his blood pressure and stop the feeling of "flooding," he stonewalls, or becomes silent, while his adrenaline flows. Note that stonewalling then drops his blood pressure ten beats a minute, giving him not only a sense of relief, but a physiological reward for *not* talking things through.[201] Still, his stonewalling may be his best choice: his thinking can get out of whack when his blood pressure is up. He may manifest odd defensive behaviors as he tries skirting his uncomfortable overwhelmed feeling and being hyper vigilant to any perceived attack.

When men refuse to talk during arguments,
their bodies reward them,
much to the frustration of women.

During conflicts with his gentle wife Connie, Ray experienced flooding; in counseling, he explains to her how it feels. "The pressure makes me think the back of my head will blow out; blinding emotion rushes up and takes my breath away. I'm helpless to stop it and I don't see it coming. It's frightening," he admits. "At all costs, I feel like I must stop it. So I shut down." He turns to me. "Sometimes I yell at her because I see her as the cause...the enemy...the one doing this to me."

The discomfort for men *doesn't* improve over time. Robert Levenson questioned 151 couples in lengthy marriages and found that the problem doesn't fix itself even after 35 years of marriage. That is, the husbands in his study found the inevitable arguments of any long-term relationship to be upsetting and very hard, though their wives didn't experience the arguments *as that big a deal.*[202]

Expect to calm yourself through self-talk or diversion when he won't engage in an argument. The woman's blood pressure is just fine during conflict. However, *once she realizes he's not going to remain engaged, her heart rate shoots up in high distress.* She fears they are not going to move forward as a couple. When Connie sees Ray bristle, she knows the next thing that will happen is he'll put on his stage face. "Then I know my real husband is shut down and gone. I'm dealing with a stranger." Don't set yourself up for the "disappearing husband." Give him a positive behavior to do that, once accomplished, will register as a "win."

Many men don't relate to the idea of using language to process feelings in a conflict. It's all they can do just to hang in there. A husband told me, "I try to endure her complaints. I focus on keeping my cool. I feel like that's my job." Don't put him in this difficult spot. Cool down and later, ask for what you want.

Many men don't relate to the idea of using language
to process feelings in a conflict.

Expect him to seek neutral emotion after a disagreement. He wants to touch as a sign that peace has returned. Your capacity for emotion and emotional expression is beyond him and more or less disturbing.

It's *harder for you* to leave emotion behind and arrive at a place of neutrality. Remember, though, that you need emotional rest and you need touch, too. Actually, kissing and caressing release stress. They reduce cortisol and up the bonding chemical oxytocin. (You may need to write out your feelings before you can do this, though.)

Kissing and caressing help relieve stress.

Expect him to be allergic to criticism, even if it's helpful. Men come into relationships fearing subjugation and use a display of superiority to ward it off. Facing faults, men believe, is putting oneself in a one-down, defeated, and scary position.[203] Patriarchy was not founded on self-love, but around seeing oneself as an instrument *to be used*. A man had to continually *prove his worth*, like a good wrench that could be discarded if it stops working. His self-worth teeters on his ability to be "useful." He's already in a quandary trying to understand you.

Expect the possibility that if your guy feels criticized, he may retort, "Then why are you with me?" or "Do you want a divorce?" Not only is he feeling criticized here, but believes he is *unable to please you*. Back off, let things cool down, and come back later with a specific request he can fulfill. (Expect that your guy won't understand why you don't see the *balance* of his behaviors. That is, he wonders why you don't first say the things he does right before you say something negative. Men commonly think this way, so you might try it.)

There's another origin of his shame. It turns out parents work overtime reigning in their *sons'* behaviors, using threats and punishments to tame them.[204] In one study of fathers and their one-year-olds, sons were chastised *twice as often* as daughters. The girls read their dad's cues, detecting which behaviors were not allowed, and decoded gestures and facial expressions correctly, something the boys weren't good at.[205] Boys get into trouble for just being "themselves," making them *feel unacceptable*.

Expect, therefore, to experience your guy as tough on the outside but wounded on the inside. Still, reign in your empathy so that you keep in touch with your *own* needs. Your life is not about protecting his ego or anticipating his needs. I'll repeat that. Your life is not about protecting his ego or anticipating his needs!

Facing faults, men believe, is putting oneself
in a one-down, defeated, and scary position.

A guy hopes a relationship will not only be a warm place to land, but an ego booster. Surprise. He comes into the harsh reality that he is unacceptable to her. She had expected him to be more empathic, responsive, and emotionally expressive, like she is. In the male world of dominance and hierarchy, incompetence is shamed and therefore men conceal weaknesses. Again, then, journal privately when you feel critical of him. Find the *bottom line* of what you want from him and say it briefly.

Expect differences of opinion about parenting, especially when raising sons. Expect him to prepare your son for the work world, which requires doing-what-you-don't-want-to-do. He will be louder and more forceful than you would be. Don't allow shaming or physical abuse, but do reign in your nurturance and empathy as you watch him parent. You don't want your son to learn that women go the extra mile to "understand" him and don't require much. That would haunt your son the rest of his life. He could spend his life searching for another "mama" who "gets" him, without acquiring the self-discipline it takes to be respected by other men. Part of the male psyche is a boy's seeking his dad's approval.

You don't want your son to learn that women
go the extra mile to "understand" him and don't require much.

Around the world, older cultures put teenaged males in positions to prove themselves. The boy who fought his way out of the jungle felt self-pride and learned to eschew laziness. The same cultures did not view teenaged girls as needing motivation or toughening. Females who give birth experience brain (amygdala) growth, which motivates them in life through empathy.

Expect Your Way of Growing to Look Different Than His

What women expect but often don't get

Women want partners who will grow with them by means of exploring feelings together, sharing empathically with one another, and developing a strong shared private life based on dialogue. This is an emotional–spiritual–relational growth unique to women (and men with feminized brains.) I've saved this subject for last because it's the toughest one.

We are always creating and re-inventing ourselves. That's what it means to be alive, especially in our fast-paced, innovative world. As the body is a living organism requiring attention to its changes, so is the soul.

Although both genders are experiencing great growth because of constant technological changes and new opportunities, women are changing *more*. Because the female brain has more plasticity, women are more open to personal growth. Women expect to be with someone who is growing similarly to them.

Although both genders are experiencing great growth,
women are changing more.

Kim would love to talk with her husband about topics she considers important. She feels she's growing at a tremendous rate while exploring how to apply faith to her life, but she can't get heard on a heart level and her attempts at conversation end up in arguments. She wants to converse with her husband about concepts, to draw tentative conclusions, to explore. She feels they would grow together if they could dialogue in this way. But she says, "It takes so much energy; it's just not worth it. He becomes like a teacher and treats me like I'm ten."

Because the female brain has more plasticity,
it is more open to personal growth.

Men have been less willing to come into the naked examination of psychotherapy. Many times when a male enters therapy, I have to ask his wife to come in. He doesn't know what's going on with him or why he needs therapy. He can't talk about it. *She* knows. I often receive resistance on the wife's part, though, because she is already exhausted from being his in-house therapist. She's been working on pulling him out, helping him gain more insight and empathy, and trying to help him know what he feels for years. She's sick of it. But, without her, I can't get enough information to do therapy.

Four years ago, Cassandra stopped trying to receive spiritual inspirations because she felt, if she did, she would grow way beyond her husband and they would no longer be able to relate to one another. Before, she would heed her inspirations, but when she tried to share them with her husband, they seemed to be beyond him or he had no grid for them. She began fearing she would inadvertently leave him behind if she allowed her musings to take her heart and mind into new places. She knew she was headed into different ways of thinking, living, and being. She also stopped playing her violin because it was then that she would receive insights for her life. The sacrifices she made for the relationship caused a grieving to begin in her. She changed herself to fit him, but lost what she most valued about herself. She figured she'd continue halting her growth until her children were through college. She put her time into child rearing and pursuing a career that would lead to a large income. Her husband liked this. She doesn't feel good about herself and feels she is living out *his* value system, not hers.

Stephanie, 26, says something similar about her spouse. "My spiritual life is deeply important to me. I'd like to share it, but he's disinterested."

155

Why women excel at personal growth and what women can *expect*

"Twenty-five years of teaching and giving workshops have convinced me that we usually get about as far with most men as their wives do."
— Terrence Real, Therapist, *The Awful Truth*[206]

Access to the right brain promotes growth

Women journal to reflect and take stock. They confess their anxieties, worries, fears, dreams, and weaknesses. Their open disclosures to others foster closeness and genuineness in themselves. Women far outnumber men in reading self-help books. Women are in touch with their feelings, a strong source of personal growth. They are pulled to the right side of the brain for half the month (PMS and menstruation), and thereby are forced to evaluate their lives in light of the holistic, relational values of that hemisphere. The American Indians had separate tents set up for women to enter when they came into PMS/menstruation, for a time of rest and reflection. They ceased from the business of left brain activities and entered the wisdom of the right.

Marion Woodman, a Jungian analyst, thinks of women as bringing men, women, and children to wholeness, that the role of the feminine is to bring about personal and cultural transformation.[207] We are seeing this as the third wave of feminism assists women from third world countries.

The either/or thinking of the left hemisphere, is not as conducive to wholeness as the right hemisphere which embraces ambiguity and opposites. The defensive, survivalist thought prominent in male thinking is dissimilar to the elastic, more open thought of the feminine.

The role of the feminine is to bring about
personal and cultural transformation.

Women's non-hierarchical view promotes growth

Building a hierarchy in relationships leads to judgment. That's how you figure out how to form the hierarchy: by figuring out who's better. Then you rank them. Females don't have that tendency in their genetic makeup. Instead, females seek closeness with others. Intimacy requires a belief in the emotional and spiritual equality between people. Being more empathic, women tend to think of each human as having his or her own road to walk, a path that the rest of us won't completely understand. This belief helps women grow, whereas judging others keeps us stuck. Personal growth takes a loving focus, free from trying to find one's superiority. Growth is much more likely to sprout from humility.

Expect that he will be most open and disclosing after having sex. What's ironic is that men don't get what really arouses love in women. A woman may be drawn to the way a guy looks or how successful he is or how he treats her on a date. But ultimately, he must show his need for her or a romance won't bloom. Not just sexually, although during or after sex is often the only time he feels safe enough to uncover his psyche. Being sexual with a woman represents her bestowing a *profound acceptance of him* and if he has performed well, his masculinity is unquestioned, so he is free to reveal a softer side of himself. Ultimately, though, a woman must sense a man's emotional vulnerability or it is unlikely she'll fall in love or commit to him. The vulnerability arouses her maternal instinct and empathy, and is believed by her to constitute "love."

Expect a man's growth to look different than yours. Whereas women grow through feelings, empathy, and the development of a strong private self, men grow through facing physical challenges, making tough decisions, and developing a strong public self to use in the work place. The latter includes the suppression of personal feelings.

Expect that he will role model leading, speaking up, taking risks, knowing and stating his opinion clearly and freely, and being unafraid. He will assert himself in circumstances where you wouldn't. His masculine energy may *rub off on you* and, after watching him, you'll find yourself strengthened in a new way.

Expect that your advancement may threaten him. The white knight archetype many men, consciously or not, bring into relationships works against them. He is primed to find a woman who is needful, dependent, despairing, and hoping to be saved. This assures his top placement on the hierarchy and his job as a partner is well defined. In rescuing her, he feels like a man and, in fact, his testosterone goes up. But this works the other way, too. He isn't primed to support or promote her success. He may not like her growth. He may even try to sabotage it. Her growth may make him angry because it makes him feel displaced, unimportant. It helps when a woman, conscious of his need, communicates the ways in which she *does* need him.

It helps when a woman, conscious of his need,
communicates the ways in which she does need him.

Making the unconscious conscious promotes growth

Growth has to do with making what is unconscious inside us conscious, so that we live in greater awareness. Women are particularly equipped to delve into the unconscious because of their brain structure. Researchers found that when subjects saw slides of angry faces, their *left* amygdala (part of the brain) activated. But when angry faces were flashed quickly before them—so quickly that the pictures weren't *consciously* registered— the *right* amygdala activated instead. It is the right amygdala that handles the feelings of the *unconscious* mind while the left amygdala is more involved in what is *consciously* known.[208] Because women's left and right hemispheres are better connected, women better integrate communication from both the right and left amygdalas. This is why women have a better handle on unconscious feelings.

Personal growth has to do with making
what is unconscious inside us conscious.

Expect him to resist exploring his unconscious, including how he was parented. Making friends with our unconscious selves has, in part, to do with evaluating our parents' effect on us. Being able to acknowledge the weaknesses and downfalls of our parents and how they shaped our development leads to individuating or knowing who we are. This takes psychological awareness and the ability to connect memories, thoughts, and feelings. Few men can articulate how their parents' weaknesses impacted them, much to the frustration of women who typically love this kind of exploration. Women fear that without evaluation, we are doomed to repeat our parents' parenting. Instead of living automatically in our parents' choices, values, and attitudes, we actively chose our own.

Sharing thoughts and feelings promotes growth

Expect him to wait for you to share. He figures you'll tell him things if you want to. Don't expect him to facilitate your sharing, though you might do this for him. Todd and Becky have drifted apart, but he hasn't noticed. He's lived relationships on a superficial level, not expecting much, so he didn't see it when she stopped coming to him to talk, stopped sharing deeply as she had been. It didn't bother him; it seemed normal. But Becky was struggling. She's noticed how he didn't meet her disclosures with the empathy she's come to expect from her close girlfriends. And, so often, he seemed aloof, in his own world, and unreachable. She felt desperately lonely. All the love she had expected to give to him was now uncomfortably buried.

He was not experiencing her growth, keeping up with the many discoveries that enhanced her pallet of colors and deepened how she experienced the world. New tones and rich hues had been added. She saw people, politics, economics—everything—differently. Her growth was happening so rapidly, she could barely find words to describe it. "It would have taken my patience, my drawing her out," he confessed. "Her girlfriends were doing that, but I wasn't." He knew her body and that, to him, was the ultimate way of knowing someone. Every other kind of knowing was less important and less intimate.

Because men reside more in the physical side of life rather than the emotional, they have less experience with feelings than do women. Also, being left brained, they experience anger and cheerfulness, but don't have the vast experience women do with handling the 400 or more distinctive feelings that nest in the right brain.

Men have less experience with feelings than women do.

Women seek truth through their feelings. Spiritual leaders have spoken of emotion as the conduit of our inner knowing and that our highest understanding is found in our most genuine feelings.[209]

Women's empathy contributes to their growth

Women are particularly open to personal growth because their natural empathy leads them to get into the shoes of others who live lives very different from theirs, thus stretching them. Women regularly experience the feelings of others and can imagine what it is like to be them, whether it's a worried mother in Iraq or a construction worker thirsty after a day in the sun. This is one reason men turn to women and not male friends for succor. Women's empathy also causes them to show interest in others, watching for their concerns, beliefs, and perspectives.

Empathy stretches women, leading to personal growth.

Whereas men tend to have strong public or false selves (so that they can appear strong in the workplace), women tend to nurture their genuine, real, and human selves. Fearing vulnerability that will put their masculinity on the line, men fear judgment. Conversely, women's dialogue is filled with self-disclosure and their listening skills and empathy bring out disclosures from others, allowing them to transcend their own life experiences.

She is strongly oriented toward wanting her romantic relationship to grow. Particularly, she wants it to grow beyond the arguments and difficulties they face, rather than dealing with the same issues over and over again. She needs to talk through them in order to reach agreement or compromise about differences.

"I imagined a husband and wife would talk and go to hear stimulating speakers or travel together," says Teresa, a teacher, married 11 years. "I thought we'd grow *together*. Instead, I'm finding that I'm growing and he's not." She kept trying to be optimistic about the relationship, believing something would cause him to catch up. But then she realized that if he did grow, she would continue to grow, and would be exponentially ahead anyway. The imbalance would remain.

Relationships require mutual respect of one another's growth

A relationship may begin due to attraction or shared activities, but must deepen into a commitment to hold one another's growth-experience in respect.

In the movie *Freedom Writers*, Hillary Swank plays a freshman English teacher to the school's low-achieving, disadvantaged students. Having forgone a career as a defense attorney, she's decided the difference has to be made *earlier* in kids' lives. Using creative methods and lots of patience, she teaches them about a real gang, Hitler's, and provides them with moving experiences. Her husband, played by Patrick Dempsey, decides to divorce her because of how time consuming her work has become, though she is clearly supportive of *his* work. She asks him why he can't support her like a wife supports a husband. He says he can't be her wife, though he wishes his statement didn't sound so terrible. He simply can't find it within himself to come alongside this woman who is turning kids' lives around.

Before feminism made its mark, men were frustrated that their wives weren't growing. It was no wonder, though, given their restrictive role and lack of opportunities. Now, it is women who are frustrated, and it is *not* because men are restricted from growth opportunities. It has more to do with how men are made. It is therefore less likely to change.

Both genders must guard against the lazy tendency to settle into the growth that easiest for them. Traditionally, men have avoided the emotional and relational development that is within their reach, leaving that for women to do on their behalf. Women have avoided their fiscal and personal power development, leaving that for men to do on their behalf. It is time, though, for both genders to grow up, allowing full evolving within each.

Women have avoided their fiscal
and personal power development,
leaving that for men to do on their behalf.

Expect that your personal growth in some areas will surpass his. These areas include growing through feeling, being empathic, and strengthening your private self. Emotional–spiritual–relational growth hasbeen the specialty of women, not men. The hitch in today's romances is that women are boldly venturing into leadership roles, facing physical challenges, and developing strong work images. This leaves no special arena for men, leaving them with less motivation.

Consciously manage your expectations. Reign in your projections: don't pretend men can be like women. Stop trying to change men. Get on with your life. Accept your disappointment over men's lack of personal growth.

Reign in your projections:
don't pretend men can be like women.

The problem with getting together with someone who isn't growing is that you may, like Christopher Robin, outgrow your Winnie the Pooh. On the other hand, you may find he stretches you in ways you didn't expect.

Chapter 6

The Mismatch Mix-Up

Finding a Life Partner is Getting Harder

Women are less and less able to find suitable male partners. While a lot of guys hope adolescence will extend into middle age, women are dynamically moving forward.[210] Men are becoming increasingly unequal to women, and the bind is this: women have always married up. In 1977, researchers scanned 800 personal ads and found women seeking financial security two times as often as men did.[211] In 2005, when the McNeese State University surveyed personal ads, they found that females sought financial security much more than did men, with females still requesting it 40% of the time and men 15%. (One caveat, though: When women asserted financial independence or success in their ads, they received 50% more responses).[212]

Women with plenty of money still seek men with even more wealth.[213] Across cultures, females want partners with more *something*—be it money, status, education, or ambition. Our foremothers actually needed this; today's woman, unfortunately, still sees men as success objects. Though it's outdated, many women remain romantic pragmatists, seeking a guy who will share his money and stature. Some sensible women are, no doubt, thinking about the expenses of raising children, some carry latent fear of being unable to earn a living, and some may have learned that the main thing you gain from a relationship with a guy is money.

Women have always married "up."

Money issues aside, though, women direct their romantic love toward someone much like themselves. Unlike men who like to rank *above* their lovers, women have traditionally not sought "lesser" partners. Across cultures, women seek men with similar IQs, attitudes, values, communication skills, and educational backgrounds.[214] Increasingly, today's women are unable to find an equal.

Men are becoming more unequal educationally and professionally

Louann Brizendine, M.D., explains that teen boys aren't wired to consider the future. Seeking the pleasure of doing war games on the computer sings to him more than does his homework.[215] Blatant statistics from the National Center for Education Statistics attest to boys' penchant for something other than academics. They say boys are responsible for 90% of classroom mayhem, encompass 80% of the dropouts, and represent 70% of students receiving Ds and Fs.[216]

While women's academic success is growing,
men's is declining.

These days, for every 100 white women graduating from college, there are only 75 white men.[217] It's curious that the number of men receiving diplomas has dropped so significantly beginning around 1980, even though throughout this period, most boys attended high schools with college prep programs. To a large degree, males haven't taken up the opportunity available to them. Furthermore, both college and graduate school classes include three women to every two men. Women receive more PhDs and master's degrees; most law students are female and nearly half of medical students are women.[218]

Granted, a female college grad CPA or nurse can pair up with a male bookkeeper or male nurse's assistant. But women prefer equality in their relationships and are cognizant of the possible cultural divide. A woman likes going to a museum with a man who isn't rolling his eyes and checking the clock. She wants to discuss the implications of a movie or book with a man who's learned how to engage in intelligent discussions in a liberal arts environment. As a college grad, she's been exposed to possibility thinking, to great thinkers and ideas. She's developed a thirst for what's out there, what people are thinking about. She likes exploring her own thoughts, enhanced through education. One's academic depth tends to determine the types of friends chosen as well as the standard of living one strives for. Couples need to match in terms of how they want to live.

Advanced education contributes to how a person thinks,
chooses friends, and expects to live.

Dr. Leonard Sax worries that boys' school performance in US schools has been nose diving for the last 20 years. The US Department of Education says the average male junior in high school writes like the average eighth grade girl. England, Australia, New Zealand, and Canada are showing the same disparity.[219]

Women prefer equality in their relationships.

Perhaps parents have done a better job of warning daughters to stay in school and become fiscally self-reliant or perhaps females are more suited for academia. Black women have long known they could not rely on marriage for financial support; soon they will account for the majority of professionals (dentists, attorneys, doctors) from their race. It looks like white females will supersede white males in the same way.

That males lag behind comes to sit upon another problem: husbands are already quite satisfied with a marriage that their wives find deficient. The man's needs are simpler, many of them physical. This includes not just sex, but food on hand, meals prepared, clothes ready to wear, and a house furnished. He also expects emotional support, especially cheers for his triumphs and commiseration for his setbacks. Many men avoid conversation they regard as rambling or having no practical point. If a man's never had a course in literature, he would find verbal explorations tough. The divorce rate was high before this academic disparity between the genders presented itself; the rate of divorce or breakups is likely to rise because another contributing factor is being added.

As of October 2009, females comprised nearly half the workforce and 51.5% of the lucrative managerial and professional spots. The Bureau of Labor Statistics predicts 9 of the 10 occupations destined for growth in eight years following 2009 will be filled mainly by women. While

Booz & Co. recognized females around the world for their emerging economic power, Maddy Dychtwaldm, author of *Influence*, speaks of a huge power shift where women could snatch the financial reins.[220]

Women have long thought of men as success objects, as opposed to sex objects, looking to men to contribute financially. With 40% of women now making more money than their spouses and that statistic likely to go up, women are faced with re-thinking the male contribution. *The change makes his lesser relational skills even more obvious.*

Women are in the lead for the best jobs.

Today's men lack forward movement

More adult kids in their 20s are living with parents, not moving into careers and committed relationships as early as their parents did. In Italy 37% of men aged 30 to 34 still live with their parents, mostly because they are attached to their mothers, according to *Psychology Today* 2008. Interestingly, though, *half as many* of their female counterparts stay at home. Italy's economic minister is frustrated with the "big babies," and certainly their peer females must feel the same.[221] Meanwhile the US Census found a third of males ages 22 to 34 living with their parents in a sort of lingering adolescence, whatever their race, riches, or location. Note the trend and the difference between the genders: while this is almost a 100% increase for males over the last 20 years, there's been no change for females.[222]

There's been a 100% increase in the
number of males ages 22 to 34 living with their parents.

The nuts and bolts of the disparity? Relationship experts have long advised women to ask for a man's help, making him feel needed. While this can improve the relationship temporarily, women are becoming less willing to defer or show needfulness. While women are on a march toward self-sufficiency, males are playing around in the virtual world. Rather than deferring to him in a disingenuous way, she may prefer the less complicated route of hiring a handyman and yard care.

Women are becoming less willing
to defer or show needfulness.

Because more females graduate from college or grad school, the earning power of 22 to 30-year-old single women now surpasses that of their male peers, at least in large urban areas, says the *Wall Street Journal*, September 2010.[223] Women are gravitating toward big cities like Dallas, Chicago, Boston, and New York City. In 2005, 53% of female workers in NYC were college grads while only 38% of their male peers had degrees. Comparing this with women's wages between 2000-2005, which then stood at 89% of men's pay, you see the climbing disparity.[224]

Tracking the trends, a 2005 study found 25.5% of wives earned more than their husbands,[225] while a 2008 study found that 40% earned more.[226] Truly, women are on an upward climb: their academic achievements are winning them good jobs. Half of Ivy League presidents are now female.[227] Barack Obama was raised by a single mom and married an attorney who earned more.

Young women in big cities are
now earning more than young men.

The popular movie *Failure to Launch* featured Matthew McConaughey playing a carefree, bright, handsome 26-year-old, living with his parents and defensive if questioned about his lack of focus or drive. Hanging out and playing computer games made his days pass undisturbed. Though females would gladly have sex with him, they wouldn't consider building a life with him.

Different theories have been proposed to explain the reduced performance of young males. The one I want to propose is that males, for years now, have found the fulfillment of winning and competing via video games without the stickiness of real-life working. Their testosterone and dopamine rise as they compete and they can even feel socially dominant over whatever creatures they're defeating. Video game stores are filled with 30-somethings as well as teens. We are no longer in the Industrial Revolution where male brawn and the sequential thinking of the masculine mind created machines. Men have liked jobs involving systems (i.e., mechanical trades) where there is high predictability and they readily feel the sense of control. Unfortunately, computer games are perfect for giving that satisfaction, but with no financial remuneration.

What men once found at work,
many now find in video games.

Women and Men Mismatch in Their Approach to Parenting

Because women carry the baby, because giving birth is a major milestone, because she breast feeds, because biology ensures mother–child closeness, her bond is different than what the father experiences. Several researchers have shown that moms are more insightful, observant, and nonverbally in sync with their babies and young children than are fathers.[228] Mother and baby share heart rhythms during the child's time in mom's womb.[229] Dads are less prone to holding their baby face-to-face, resulting in less exchange of facial or emotional information.[230] As one guy said, "For the first couple of years, a kid is just like having a dog. They cry and poop. You feed them. That's it."

A mother's bond with her baby
and young child is unique.

Moms match their speech to the child's level of comprehension, while dads tend to use vocabulary that leaves the child without understanding. Moms use shorter sentence lengths to match a child's attention span. Moms take turns, using a give-and-take dialogue with the child and empathize more readily than do fathers. Moms allow the child to choose a play theme, while dads impose their own.[231]

Moms watch their children more closely, keeping an eagle eye on their activities when compared to men.[232] Twenty-six thousand kids die *daily*. That is why women evolved to be multi-taskers, able to watch several children while still attending to other activities. It is why women are empathic, able to leave themselves and be in the child's mind, anticipating her next move. A mother is more careful than her male counterpart, wary of children putting themselves in dangerous situations.

Many dads intermittently play with children and administer discipline as needed, while moms offer continuous nurturance, mediation, and overall management of the child's life.[233]

There are loving fathers who play with and teach their children. There are men who serve as upstanding role models for their children and are evenhanded with them. Who doesn't love Veronica Mars' dad? But many children are raised by fathers they learn to tip-toe around. He has a billowing anger, alternating with a lack of feeling. He may be moody from work, entitled at home, and oblivious to the relationship dynamics and needs of the home life. Impatient with children, judgmental. Perhaps addicted to or abusing a substance, which makes him more scary and unpredictable. The children may yearn for a relationship and try to please him, but feel void of connection and fear his anger and loud voice. Many adults entering therapy with depression or anxiety speak of living in fear of dad while their mothers seemed helpless.

Whereas a woman's attachment to a child is deep and enduring, a man's may be contingent on his relationship with his wife. For example, a friend dropped by tearful and devastated. She had just gotten bad news. Her son is ready to go to college, and her ex's military benefits should have covered their son's tuition, room and board, and about $800/month in living expenses. This was due to her ex's rank when he was discharged as disabled from the military. But her ex is angry about the divorce. He has therefore exempted his children from the college benefit he could have given them. When this mother called the appropriate military office, the woman on the other line said, "You're in a line of thousands." Military marriages are hard to sustain. After all, if the military wanted you to have a wife and children, they would have issued them. Ha ha. The many women who divorce may find their angry exes cutting off benefits to their own children. She can appeal, but there is no legal recourse. "According to them, he has a right to do this," my friend, feeling numbed and afraid, told me.

Testosterone's tendencies don't always mix well with child rearing. Furthermore, systemizers become frustrated or avoidant of whatever they can't control. About three weeks before a man's partner gives birth, his prolactin increases and his testosterone drops. Nature knows a man's testosterone needs an adjustment, so he can bond with his child. However, things are back to normal somewhere between the baby's sixth week and twelfth month.[234]   In the manic American work culture, men's testosterone stays high; men with lower levels are more likely to take care of their kids, as shown in several East African tribes.[235]

A man's feelings toward his children are often
contingent upon his relationship with his wife.

When it comes to divorced dads, the stats are dismal. One child in six receives a weekly visit from dad, half haven't seen dad in over a year, and a decade after the divorce, two-thirds of kids have pretty much lost contact altogether with dad, often because the dads move.[236]   Shocking, too, is a Columbia University sociologists report that four of ten divorced fathers don't describe themselves as "fathers."[237]   Not many dads handle their children's emotional upsets, their problems with friends, medical needs, or daily homework.

There are several differences in how mothers parent compared with fathers.

Mothers use a more democratic style

Dads demand respect and compliance from children and deliver more edicts than moms, according to research.[238]   Because of men's level of aggression, impatience with communicating, and social dominance, mothers often fear that a father will be too harsh with a child. She is naturally oriented toward a democratic style, including listening to the child, empathizing with her, and teaching rather than punishing. Many a husband has pointed out to his wife that the kids readily obey him and not her. In truth, the kids feel intimidated and won't speak up with their dads.

The gender difference starts early. Consider the use of language by boys and girls. Boys' speech is filled with more direct commands ("Give me that," "Do this") and prohibitions ("Stop it," "Don't do that"). In contrast, an empathizer worries about how someone might feel devalued or inferior and avoids such speech styles. Girls say, for instance, "I'm sorry, but would you mind not doing that? My friend has a headache." She references the person's feelings and explains why she needs what she's asking for.

Research also shows that boys tend to bluntly assert that someone is wrong or to assert authority without giving any reason for the command.[239] As these traits carry over into fatherhood, men give direct commands to their children without honoring their need for an explanation. The mother, on the other hand, wants the child to understand the reasoning behind rules so he can grow into a thinking adult. It can be argued that the male parenting style prepares children to live in a dictatorship, while the female style prepares children to live in a democracy where evaluating candidates, voting, and shared decision making are common.

Mothers teach rather than punish.

To the left brain, rules become an end in themselves. Systemizers (male) become rigid, with rules that cannot be broken. At universities, for instance, the bureaucracy can be crippling, delaying any real action that would meet the needs of students to occur. Government can be the same way. The courts can be so left brained that obvious criminals win cases on a technicality. Parenting for a male systemizer can become all about The Rules.

But obeying for obedience sake is not part of the democratic society our children live in. Mothers tend to give explanations for what they want a child to do. This tendency begins in the mother's childhood. Girls express less direct anger, propose compromises more often, attempt to clarify the feelings and intentions of the other person, make softer claims, use more polite forms of speech, avoid blunter forms of power-assertion like yelling or shouting.[240] Girls carry these early traits over into mothering, showing less need for direct power over their children.

Sara, 36, realized that her husband who over-disciplined their kids, leaving them in fear and anger, was a bully. His inappropriate use of power stemmed from his perpetual need to prove his manhood and constituted an emotional danger to the developing nervous systems of their children. Recognizing their need to blossom in a peaceful home, she separated from him. At first, he proved himself again by fighting in court for the children, but soon he became bored with the day-to-day work of childcare and lost interest.   Sara found a peaceful home and greater closeness to her children. She has an easier, more satisfying life and loves watching her children thrive.

Julie, 54, presented in therapy with anxiety and stomach problems, saying her siblings all have similar issues. She remembered her dad yelling a lot. "He never hit anyone," she said, as though apologizing, "but he threw things." She constantly felt judged by him. In response, Julie, as a child, began strictly inhibiting what she did and said. She could barely digest her food at meals. She tried to be invisible. Having developed under these circumstances, she has been seeking help for decades.

Mothers show more flexibility and understanding

Jayne sighed. "My husband said the twins had to be in bed by 10:30, no exceptions. But, as juniors in high school, they have tons of chemistry and English homework and it's just not possible, considering they've got sports till 6:00 or after. Pushing them to do it faster leads to upset and then they can't get to sleep. He doesn't consider any of this." Her husband doesn't realize the emotional implications of his black-and-white decision. But the twins feel nervous around him and, consequently, avoid him.

Systemizers love predicting and controlling the world. Kids are unpredictable and uncontrollable, leaving many dads either frustrated or uninterested. Making a demand and having the child obey it feels good to a systemizer, but kids aren't machines. When kids aren't manageable, many men get angry, and mothers worry about the effect of their anger on the child's emotional development. Anger and loud male voices are particularly hard on girls ,whose hearing is so sensitive that they feel blasted and learn to submit rather than to flourish.

Many systemizers would like children to be
more predictable and controllable.

A rape crisis counselor helps college girls who've been traumatized by sexual perpetration. She tells the mother of a rape victim, "In our experience, we don't expect dads to give empathy."

"Why?" the mother asks, surprised. She saw this moment as one where her husband could rise to being protective, even valiant.

"They look for details in order to understand whom to blame," the counselor explained. "They don't focus on the daughter being hurt, and that's really our first concern."

"Right," the mother agreed, glancing at her daughter who was waiting in an adjacent room.

"They sometimes get angry if the daughter doesn't stay in school," the counselor says. This has been her experience. The mother realized she would need to step up and get the daughter everything she really needed. "What she'll need most," the counselor said, "is your emotional sensitivity."

Many fathers are a barely modified version
of their own patriarchal fathers,
who issued edicts and were satisfied
with a relationship of obedience.

At his son's bachelor party, a father in his forties was matching drinks with the young bucks, the son's friends there to celebrate his last night as a single guy. He was going to "show you guys how the Navy does it," by being tough enough to drink a lot of shots. He did this at the expense of making his son feel overshadowed on his special night when his son should have been the center of attention. But personal feelings shouldn't matter, the son was always taught, so he didn't say anything.

Many dads have no awareness of the effect of their lack of understanding. Children have individual differences and developmental levels which, if attended to, allow them to thrive. Many fathers are a barely modified version of their own patriarchal fathers, who issued edicts and were satisfied with a relationship of obedience. They don't envision having true closeness with their kids or the warmth that makes it easy for a child to grow and learn.

Mothers are more involved

Involved fathering is a rather new concept. As one client asked, "Did you know anyone who was close to their father in the '60s?" How many children have grown up hearing "Don't bother your dad"?

It is questionable how much fathers in intact marriages actually contribute to the parenting. In 2001, social scientists from the University of Michigan actually clocked dads' involvement. They found that, where both parents worked, mom spent *twice* as much time reading to and doing homework with kids as did dads. The dads spent very little time alone with kids, without mom there too. Dads spent 63 minutes on weekdays *minus* the 33 spent watching TV or eating with the family. The average rose on weekends to 166 minutes, but 54 of those minutes were spent on TV and eating, and moms were usually present for the remaining minutes.[241]

Dads spend very little time with their kids
without mom present.

Psychiatrist Dan Stern has specialized in infant development for 30 years, and emphasizes the importance of a parent being attuned to the nonverbal or physical signals of the infant or young child because this promotes bonding.[242]   Mothers tend to be deeply and truly present on this relational level.

Moms talk to kids more holistically, helping children understand the feelings underneath events. Dan Siegel, professor of psychiatry at UCLA, speaks of the child's need to hear an *integrated story,* where a parent explains not only what's going on, but what the feelings are underneath it. Women, having a stronger connection between the left brain (the sequential facts) and the right brain (the meaning and feelings behind the facts), are equipped to provide an amalgamated account.[243] A 5-year-old child says, "Mrs. Johnson was grouchy today." The left brain says, "Yeah, sometimes teachers are grouchy." The right brain says, "Honey, have you noticed that Mrs. Johnson is going to have a baby? She might feel tired sometimes, and when we're tired, we can feel grumpy. Remember when your sister tried to take your pillow last night and you were so tired that you snapped at her? That's not how you usually act, but when you're tired, you don't have as much strength." The second explanation integrates facts with what's behind them and gives the child a greater education about life.

Jenny, 16, tried to tell her dad about how depressed she'd been feeling but he wouldn't give her eye contact as he rummaged around the kitchen. He did look into her face long enough to see the tears in her eyes, but he turned away and asked, "Where's the pizza?" She finds she gets tongue-tied trying to disclose to him.

Currently, in my caseload, I have a female attorney, female ob/gyn, and female chiropractor, all raised by mothers who went through the women's liberation movement, all of whom are now raising preschoolers, and all of whom want to *quit work*. Each of these ladies realizes she's stretched too far, is too anxious, and feels guilty. Each is married to a modern-minded husband whose mother also went through the women's liberation movement and who is aware of his need to pitch in. However, each woman complains that her husband doesn't "see" what she sees or "hear" what she hears. The husbands miss cues coming from the child and related to the care of the child. They aren't gifted with empathy to see a child's needs. What's more frustrating is that the husbands believe they're contributing fifty percent to parenting. In fact, she's doing most of it and carries the weight of guilt and responsibility.

Don has two sons and Sylvia is the stepmom. The boys are 7 and 9. One night one of the boys couldn't remember where to find pencils in the kitchen desk drawer. When he couldn't remember, he began to cry. He cried all through dinner and would not be consoled. Sylvia, his stepmom, was concerned and wanted to get to the bottom of the trouble. Don, his biological dad, ignored the crying and took his son outside to play ball and then get a snow cone, which meant the child never got his homework done and would be in trouble at school the next day.

Sylvia asked Don later if he was going to follow up. "What are you talking about?" he asks, not remembering anything out of the ordinary having happened that night. He looks at her like she's crazy and is seeing things. Everything's peaceful at their house as long as she doesn't try to bring stuff up. There's no talking, no exploring, no getting outside help.

He comes from a family where, if his mother was upset with his father, dad would take off for the deer lease, leaving mom at home for 3 days hoping things would pass. Sylvia feels like Don does something similar and that his father prepared him poorly for having a relationship with a woman. She's perplexed: as a stepmom, she just wants to have a normal discussion about the well-being of his sons, but he responds with, "You watch too much Dr Phil."

Mothers rarely sexually abuse

Almost all child sexual abuse is perpetrated by men, whether the victim is a boy or girl.[244] Sexual molestation often begins when the child is very young and lasts a long time. The memories are then repressed and recalled much later and with difficulty.[245] The perpetrator is rarely a stranger, but in the majority of cases, the child's own father or the male companion of her mother.[246]

The greatest thing women can do on behalf of the progression of humanity is to stop incest and child molestation.

Why aren't women typically perpetrators? Probably because of their high oxytocin, the touch and bonding hormone. For women, touch is not "white sex" as it is in many men, but is a separate category in the brain. Generations of being primary caretakers structured a woman's brain to safeguard children from their mothers' crossing sexual boundaries. This phenomenon also shows up in the adult female–male romance, where she savors touch for touch's sake, while he can't help but be turned on. She wants more nonsexual affection, but touching her that way always leads to something more.

Women are touch-sensitive, compared to men, a responsiveness that lasts her whole lifetime. Infant girls touch their moms more than do boys. South African mothers of the !Kung San tribe touch their babies 90% of the day and sleep with them at night. Infants receiving a lot of touch grow and develop better and gain twice the weight.[247] Nonsexual touching is a natural part of motherhood.

Infants receiving a lot of touch grow and develop better and gain twice the weight.

No doubt the greatest thing women can do on behalf of the progression of humanity is to stop incest and child abuse. If a mother is financially and emotionally strong enough to leave a perpetrator, she can protect her children. In fact, though, the cycle of abuse works like this: Eighty percent of children who get abused have mothers who were perpetrated themselves. The mother doesn't necessary collude with the perpetrator, but she dissociates. Out of her own childhood habit, she may turn a blind eye, or use alcohol, drugs, work, or romance novels to keep reality at bay. Because she herself was perpetrated, she may carry a deep belief that children just get hurt, or that men are just like that and can't be stopped. Sometimes a formerly abused woman will go into a younger part of herself, cringing and hiding as though being abused herself when her own children are being harmed.

Twenty-five percent of girls are now sexually abused. Imagine, though, a generation of girls raised without abuse. Think of mothers being strong enough to leave on behalf of their children's wellbeing, able to fight, and able to earn their own living, so that a generation emerges with emotional health. That generation in turn will raise less damaged children.

Imagine a generation of girls raised without sexual abuse.

Currently, so many people stagger into adulthood with such childhood wounds that it takes decades to get over them, thus impacting the children they are raising. They work and work to heal instead of beginning adulthood at a good place and going from there.

Raising kids without men

Jasmine has been observing her friend, Christina. Due to a lack of money and because the father of her infant abandoned her, she found a friend, another single mom, to live with her in a small house. They painted and decorated together, collaborating on everything. They vowed to be friends and second parents to each other's children forever. They both have part-time jobs and coordinate times so one can always be home. They've decided to live cheaply in exchange for quality time with their kids. After a year of living like this, Christina has such a close relationship with her friend's two children that it feels like they are hers. Her friend feels the same about her children. And they truly co-parent, talking through decisions together, helping each other. They are both heterosexual and have dating relationships on and off, but they know that the deepest and most lasting relationship of their lifetimes is to each other and to their children.

What effect does growing up with two mothers have on children's emotional development? The answer comes from studies where lesbians used artificial insemination to start families. Researchers found that whether the 154 mothers were partnered or single, the children, (followed from ages 10 to 17), scored developmentally and socially like kids raised by heterosexual parents. The authors were surprised, though, that the children of lesbians scored *higher* in self-esteem and confidence, and were *less likely* to break rules and be aggressive. The biggest surprise was that children of lesbians *surpassed* kids with heterosexual parents in academic performance. It seems odd because the kids of lesbians have to endure teasing and discrimination, yet their psychological adjustment was undifferentiated. Why?

One of the researchers, a professor in both psychiatry and law, has studied same-sex families for 24 years and thinks lesbian parents are more involved with their children, communicate better, are more present in their schools, and make parenting a greater priority. Furthermore, they talk with their kids about diversity, tolerance and sexuality, enhancing their children's thought processes at a young age which may help them mature.[248]

Between 2002 and 2007, the number of single moms rose sharply, so that nearly 4 in 10 births were to women going it alone. Many of these births have been to the poor and young, but a new phenomenon is on the rise. Almost one-third of these births were to women 25 to 29—the woman's age suggesting her pregnancy was no accident. Birthrates for single moms 20 to 24 have risen 13%. But get this: for single *30 to 34 year old women*, birth rates have risen 34% between 2002 and 2007.[249]

What's going on? Whatever it is, it's not unique to the U.S. Well over half (yes, half!) of recent births to women in Iceland, Sweden, and Norway are non-marital, with the French and Danish not far behind. The upward trend in non-marital child birthing is matched by most developed nations, with numbers doubling, tripling, or more between 1980 and the mid-2000s.[250]

The number of single moms with non-accidental
pregnancies is on the rise.

No doubt these older women are intentionally getting pregnant and many can afford nice housing, good schools, kids' computers, iPods, and college. More are looking to sperm banks. Sociologist Frank Furstenberg doesn't believe a second parent affects a child's development much if one good parent is already in place.[251]

When polled, most American women still say they want to raise children, but more are prepared to undertake the 20-year responsibility alone. In doing so, they make a statement: a man is either not necessary to make a family or they just can't find one reliable or interesting enough to live with. Perhaps even more profound are the women who have already taken on the massive amount of compulsory work of childcare and still *initiate* divorces. They just don't feel the guy's contribution is enough to warrant staying with him.

For those women who cannot find a nurturing male to parent with, there remains sperm banks and the sentiment of Pauline Roland, an early feminist in 1821 who had four children by four different fathers. She said, "I want to become a mother with the paternity unknown."[252]

In 2002, Congress proposed allocating $100 million annually to reduce out-of-wedlock births. What they were missing is that some women *want* to parent alone. While some just can't find a partner who interests them, some remember the impact of their own father's aggressive or punitive actions. They want a more pleasant and softer experience for their children. Women instinctively know that they are guarding their children's fragile and newly budding nervous systems and want to raise them in a kind environment.

Many mothers-to-be aren't bothering with marriage in the first place, feeling they can do it on their own. Celebs like Jodie Foster, Madonna (who sings "Papa Don't Preach!" about a girl raising her baby alone), Ally McBeal's Calista Flockhart, and The Practice's Camryn Manheim, the very poor, and the many females who adopt children alone—potential mothers are not valuing the marriage certificate as they once did.

Women instinctively know that they are guarding
their children's fragile and newly budding nervous systems
and want to raise them in a kind environment.

Better educated women are more able to support themselves and a child.[253]   On the other hand, 82.1% of mothers raise their children on less than $35,000 a year. Most moms (68.4%) receive less than $5,000 a year in child support checks and 41.5% receive nothing. And while dad's living standard increases by 10% after a divorce, mom's (and her children's) spirals downward by 27%. Furthermore, a divorced man remarrying in his 40s or 50s may father again, resulting in less time and money to spend on his other progeny. Having children attests to his virility.[254]   These facts point to the need for women to educate themselves and find good paying jobs, a message that is coming into sharp focus.

Education and good jobs make supporting
a child alone possible.

We've seen how the genders are different in parenting. Now we return to other mismatches.

Women Are Far Ahead in Seeking and Maintaining Relational Closeness

A woman is often surprised when she enters a relationship with a man. First, she discovers they are worlds apart in terms of what a relationship is really about. He wants sex, a leisure companion, and a soft place to land. The differences prime her to work on the relationship—to create mutual understanding through talking it out. She is taken back finding he doesn't really want to talk. She had assumed he'd draw on his empathy to get into her shoes, but this doesn't happen. When she asks Relationship Question 101, "Can we talk?" he balks. She can't quite believe that he assumed relationships require no working dialogue.

Many women feel like they have to guide and prod husbands for years due to this relational disparity, their efforts ending in resentment. They find themselves giving men explanations that, over time, amount to giving a whole education in relationships. Though women find relationships with men less satisfying than their male partners do, women, ironically, are expected to sacrifice more for a relationship, including their work aspirations. Will women keep doing this? Maybe not.

A woman finds herself explaining to her husband why his saying, "So what's wrong with *you*?" isn't a good way to approach her, their children, or others.

"It feels bad and makes me want to disconnect from you," she explains. She tries to get him to understand that he's provoking the kids and how he jumps in the middle of her sentences. Though he rarely, if ever, predicts what she's about to say, he assumes he knows. He really doesn't have a clue what's going on in her head.

It isn't that males aren't in relationships, Baumeister and Sommer argue, but, while men value hierarchical groups (i.e., on a baseball team or rank ordered at work), females value nurturing, one-on-one intimate relationships. The researchers concluded that whereas males are clannish, women prefer relating in twosomes.[255] In so doing, males forego developing the deeper relational skills learned by girls.

Maccoby (1998), in studying children at play, found older boys preferred group, physical play with a hierarchical structure and girls preferred same-sex one-on-one pairings, enacting caring roles like doctor–patient or mother–child, using negotiation and reciprocal language. Girls learn early to work things out.[256] Girls show more reciprocity (now it's your turn), and cooperative role-taking (I'll be the mommy, you be the child). They make space for another person, sensitively adjusting their behavior to accommodate the other person.[257]

Many women feel, when it comes to relational skill,
that they have to raise their husbands.

All this carries over to adulthood, where Tannen found women's talk to be joint and shared and accommodating, while men's talk is competitive, self-assured, and forceful.[258] Men are concerned about showing independence, exhibiting control, and saving their pride in relationships.[259] Women center their attention on disclosing personal information, forming a sharing partnership, settling differences, and developing mutually cooperative roles.[260]

Beginning at age 3, girls and boys prefer to play with their own gender, locking in the boys' inclination toward relating in groups structured by rules and girls' inclination toward intimate dyads known for openness and emotional nuance.[261] With little experience, suspiciousness and often disgust, the genders suddenly magnetize to one another as puberty dawns. But at this point, the ingrained differences are like uniting Libya's government with the US. Yet women and men come together, with vast differences in values and perspectives, to perform the most important functions of life, including parenting and home and career development. The struggle to make this work lands on the female.

Bruce was my first love. A sunny blond with knockout blue eyes and an ever-tanned physique, he was four years older and in the popular crowd at high school. Our families were friends. His crowd of guys would come to observe me as a ninth grader studying in the library. They'd laugh and cajole, sometimes pushing him toward me and making me blush. Although this was flattering, I didn't get it. Why couldn't we just talk? It wasn't really his looks that drew me anyway. I'd known his vulnerability. I'd accidentally seen his mother beat him with a belt the previous summer when I was babysitting his younger siblings. I knew his parents drank too much. I thought the relationship between our fathers was interesting as I contrasted it with the relationship between our mothers. I also wondered how he felt about the Catholic faith he'd been raised in, since I was grappling with everything religious. We had a lot of private things to talk about, so how did this involve the gaggle of guys who teased him about me? Finally, he walked to my house, rang the doorbell and asked to see me. We talked outside, and his self consciousness made him adorable, I thought. When he suddenly kissed me, though, I was mystified. I liked it, but a kiss wasn't appropriate until we'd established more of an emotional closeness, my fourteen-year-old mind reasoned. It was, after all, a symbolic act. My jerking back and the flash of consternation in my matching blue eyes was more than his fragile initiation could sustain and squashed the flower that had only peaked through the ground. We were looking for different things.

The more relationally skilled sex must partner
with a less relational type.
This is the gist of the "irreconcilable differences"
in most break-ups.

The female agenda is all about establishing a close, mutually enjoyable connection, freely confessing fears and weaknesses, saying sweet things to one another, and working hard to maintain the friendship through direct eye contact, affection, and communication. Activities are okay, but the focus is about sharing your thinking, affirming one another, and lying bare your secrets. The male agenda is opposite: hiding flaws, maintaining a one-up position within a group, and being the expert rather than being close through sharing. Males choose their friends not so much because of emotional rapport, but because a guy plays golf or poker, and from there comes the primary focus: who's going to win and who will lose?[262]

The mismatch between the genders includes educational, motivational, and parenting issues. *But none is more hurtful than that the more relationally skilled sex must partner with a less relational type.* This is the gist of the "irreconcilable differences" in divorce decrees.

Chapter 7
What To Watch For As Women Emerge

Once women have put their expectations of men and romance into perspective, five things will happen: Women will restore balance to our workaholic world, find fulfillment in female friendships, overcome caution and take more risks, make themselves more known, and restore joyous and health-giving sex.

Women Will Restore Balance to our Workaholic World

Women, not men, will return life to a balance. Currently, many women work too hard, laboring outside and inside the home. But women will use their highly adaptive brains to find solutions. Many will continue to seek higher education that affords them better paying jobs. They will then hire nannies, personal assistants, cooks, or housecleaners to assist them. I used to hire a college girl to sort my son's Legos and my daughter's puzzle pieces and doll clothes. It made my life better. Oftentimes, a woman and her employees will form a loving community because she will treat them as equals.

Women are highly motivated to balance life because they are currently unhappy. In our world of gadgets and consumerism, the systemizing gender reports that *he* is happy. But, since 1970, women's spirit has been declining. Across various studies, demographics, and industrialized countries, we find the same lowered mood in women.[263] What most profoundly affects women's mood? Sharon Lerner, author of *The War on Moms*, says it's family size and work hours.[264] That is, she's working too hard and there are no standardized systems in place to help her. She's exhausted. In truth, women need to pursue a broader spectrum of relationships in order to feel happy. Marriage can be deadening because she gives so much to it, receiving so little in return, that she is too worn out to find fulfillment outside the relationship. Unfortunately, this is the plight of all the women she knows. It has become, at least in America, a sociological syndrome. However, since women voters outnumber men by millions, they will, no doubt, change current policies.[265]

Women are not happy in the systemized world men have created.

Gretchen Rubin, in her book *The Happiness Project,* asks what actually makes people happy. She concludes that facing challenges and experiencing novelty are potent sources of happiness. Money, if spent wisely, can also bring happiness.[266] The problem for too many American women is that they face a grueling routine of constant tasks with no time for personally chosen challenges, novelties, or freedom to spend their money as they want.

So how will women balance life? Many are already trying. When offered a top echelon job, women in powerful positions refuse because they see the death of family and personal life. Women will seek to be ¾-time attorneys or they will job share a physician's role. Many women, having shone in a career, step back and take a holistic look at life. Surprising everyone, a woman may relinquish the money and prestige of a fast-moving career because she's decided she wants more time for her relationships. She doesn't want her job being her primary focus and doesn't want to leave behind her primary value: relationships. Capitalism has proven itself as a successful way to organize society, at least in terms of bringing prosperity. But men, socially dominant and testosterone-driven to success, enjoy it more than women who want a more balanced life.

Women are having fewer children. Somewhere around 2050 we will really begin feeling the decline in the world population, according to *Demographic Winter*, a documentary. Statistically speaking, women who bear 2.1 children replace themselves, their husbands, plus a little extra. Since 1970, birthrates have drastically fallen: China from 5.8 to 1.6, India from 5.8 to 2.9, Japan from 2.0 to 1.3, and South Africa from 5.9 to 2.7. In the US there's been little change, falling from 2.55 to 2.1. The US statistic is expected to drop more significantly soon, though, because second generation immigrants to the US have fewer kids.[267] As consciousness about women's rights rises around the world, so the birth rate declines. Alas, women are pursuing other interests. They are more aware of how having a baby radically transforms their lives, calling on them to make huge sacrifices. Each child represents an agreement to years of intensive labor.

For a woman, each child born represents
an agreement to years of intensive labor.

Women who want to bring children into the world will seek help with their children and their homes. Rather than clinging to their kids or looking to them for their identity, women will allow children to blossom and find their autonomy because they value their own. They understand that children, as Kahlil Gibran said, are "life's longing for itself" and don't really "belong" to them. Leslie has a busy career she loves and has decided to raise her children with the help of an au pair from Nepal. The au pair has a six-year-old son and husband back in Nepal, but she accepts that to make life better, she has to be away from them to find work. Over time, they've come into a lovely friendship and Leslie trusts her completely. Leslie has gone above what she is expected to pay for her au pair and has installed video conferencing for her to use to speak with her family in Nepal. Leslie and the au pair have a warm, collaborative relationship that is satisfying for both.

As highly educated women take on more *leadership* roles in the work world, we hope they will maintain the balance that their double-brain abilities make possible and won't give in to the workaholism, addiction, or health problems of men. That is, women will need to maintain right brain creativity, attunement to feelings, and close relationships that keep them healthy and balanced. Women saturated in the male work world (i.e., sequential, logical) without rebalancing through right brain activities (free flowing dialogue, creative endeavors, nurturance) may jeopardize their health.[268]

As a child and teenager, Monica journaled prolifically. Her feelings went on paper. She knew herself. But when she graduated from college and went into the business world, journaling suddenly felt silly, like a waste of time. Efficiency was important. "What's the bottom line?" was work's mantra. Wanting to return to her writing, her left brain bargained, *maybe I could turn my journaling into a book of poems and sell it*. But the very idea seemed to take away her soul. She ran into a snag in her personal life and when it began affecting her work, she knew she *had* to begin journaling again. Once she did, she realized she had lost herself, gotten out of touch with her true self, and replaced it with the mechanics of productivity. She had entered the left brain, bottom-line, logic-based world of men. Today's women realize they can have a well-developed left brain without sacrificing the right. They can be whole, using both sides as needed, without ignoring either. But this takes focus.

Women will need to maintain right brain
creativity, attunement to feelings, and close relationships
to keep them healthy and balanced.

By the way, if the nurturing tendencies of women weren't aimed at giving birth, what would happen to our world? Would women tend the earth, bringing environmental reform, nurturing humanity into a more caring, humane social structure, and giving care to our unhealthy medical system? Is it possible there's a natural suppression in women that says until we straighten up our world, making it more woman-friendly, we needn't bring more children into it?

Further, women will monitor their empathy. Codependency can be defined as the need to have someone depend on you so that you have an identity. *It is empathy gone awry.* Women developed extra empathy to ensure the survival of infants and children, but her attunement can be wrongly allocated to, for instance, an alcoholic or selfish husband. She over-gives, ironically, trying to avoid appearing egocentric. A soul-and-energy loss results from taking on the burdens of others. Giving too much to a man is like breast-feeding a grown adult and requires more calories than one can take in. Being too open to the needs or perceived needs of others is like holding up a sign that says, "I am all 'give;' take what you want." Men naturally stake out their territory (i.e., what is and isn't their responsibility) and think in terms of efficiency to limit what they're going to take on, as women find out when their new husbands don't automatically chip in with household chores. Men have to strive to give more, while women have to work toward limiting their natural giving, protecting themselves.

Giving too much to a man is like
breast-feeding a grown adult
and requires more calories than one can take in.

As she reigns in her empathy, she steps back and evaluates her circumstances. The wise woman will expend her empathy carefully and with wisdom. She will shore up her gifts to use with little ones or the sick or disabled, but not with grown men in romantic relationships. Many women are in danger of sacrificing too much and being too responsible for someone else's life. Never use your precious maternal instinct to succor a healthy, grown man. Expect a man to be grown up and stand on his own two feet. He will resent you if you think about his care too much because he will feel put down.

Empathy can create a dilemma for women as they find themselves sensing and protecting a romantic partner emotionally. For instance, often women confront men carefully and softly, shielding men's feelings, until it is too late for them to repair their own resentment at having to overgive. In earlier chapters, we discussed why women do this and the amount of energy it takes to make themselves heard, but women have to stop taking care of men and start getting what they want from a relationship as much as is possible or get out and give their gifts to something or someone else. Furthermore, women *sense* what men need emotionally, whether it's accompanying them so they don't feel insecure or bolstering an ego even though the man hasn't verbalized his problem. She watches and observes and intuits what he needs.

Codependency is empathy gone awry.

"But he needs me." A college student sat in my office sharing, with tears, about her boyfriend who relies on her for money and who, in sharp contrast to her, isn't going anywhere educationally or career-wise.

"Your empathy isn't meant to be lavished on a grown male adult, though," I reason. "It's there for the infants you may have in the future." Empathy assures that, even though a woman's exhausted and wants to do something else, she will attend to her roving toddler. Her eyes will never divert from the four-year-old while playing around the swimming pool. She will give and give and give to her children to assure their well-being.

But it's not only college students who don't understand the proper use of empathy, it's women of all ages. Too often women do their sacrificing to immature or irresponsible or abusive men. They tolerate, excuse, and justify bad behavior. Greater self-love is needed. They do not set the boundaries that are necessary to either push a man into good behavior or end the relationship. In so doing, *women inadvertently tell men that they don't expect much*. Remember that men, being systemizing thinkers, only give what is necessary to reach a goal. Women must reign in their natural tendencies to empathize. Freud called women *moral masochists* because they sacrificed too much of themselves for others. Sacrificing, no doubt, comes straight out of a woman's empathy.

Men, being systemizing thinkers,
only give what is necessary to reach a goal.

Today's woman acknowledges that, although Nature calls for coupling, she doesn't have to give herself up for it. Nature calls for her to have children, but she knows the world is overpopulated. Society calls for her to marry, but she knows there are other forms of relationship that may suit her better. Men call for marriage, sometimes because they want to let down and stop working at a relationship, and she knows that. *She is aware*. Her behaviors stem from her consciousness.

Women Will Find Fulfillment in Friendships

It isn't romance that staves off loneliness, according to research, but friendships. It isn't how many friendships you have, but the quality of the friendship. Even family relationships don't heighten our well-being like friendships do.[269]

Friendships fulfill our needs for emotional closeness.

Linguists explain that the particular language we use shapes our thinking. English speakers lack ways to speak about love and affection in friendship, whereas Arabians have fifty words to express types of love. But love abounds in friendships, especially between women. Free from sexual games and the difficulties of romance, friendships fulfill our needs for emotional closeness.

Women's history is unusual in that, historically, they took on the class, religion, and values of the males they depended on, which divided them from other women. Historian Gerda Lerner comments that despite women's experience of life being so similar (i.e., both the rich and poor cleaned house and raised children), they were so completely divided. In their subordination, they were denied the emotional support of other women who would have understood.[270] As women consciously set out to break this barrier, they can at last find relational fulfillment, being open to women of all classes, religions, and values, using the nonhierarchical tolerance natural to them. I once hired a Nigerian woman to clean my house. Raised in poverty, she had come to the US with her husband who was a student. One of the most open, intuitive, and loving people I have ever met, she and I shared an immediate rapport, and I grieved when, after two years, she returned to Nigeria.

Because many women will go in and out of relationships with male romantic partners, they will come to see their relationships with women as *foundational and steady throughout their lifetimes*. Whereas, in the past, females have been threatened by each other, competing for men, women will gain more openness with each other. As romantic relationships become less important to women, female friendships will become, not only more possible, but they will flourish. As Jessica, 43, said, "I joined a singles group after my divorce for the purpose of meeting *female* friends. And those women have become my lifelong companions."

Humans have moved from being hunter/gatherer, to the agricultural age, to the industrial age, and finally to our current information age. Unlike other times, today's individualism can leave us without consistent communities of support because these steady groups tend to be held together by common values and trust. That is, the more deeply held the values, the stronger the group ties. However, today's individualism means freedom to shed certain values as needed—freedom to leave a church, a set of friends you've outgrown, or a special interest group you now disagree with. It can also leave us lonely, bereft of more enduring, binding relationships. That's part of the current trap: women are turning to one male mate to fulfill much of their emotional needs.

However, women have always trusted one another more than men have trusted other men. Furthermore, women have always trusted one another more than they have trusted men. Building relationships with the more empathic, nurturing, relational gender is easier.

Building relationships with the
more empathic, nurturing, relational gender is easier.

Several avenues for friendship-building are emerging, among them the following five. First, women, having trouble finding fulfillment in the male work world, may bind together with other women to create successful enterprises, sprinkled with feminine savvy and care. More tolerant of flex time, willing to bring in childcare, open to sharing one another's lives, women can build foundational friendships in these work environments. Second, women can form social action groups to create woman-friendly family leave laws. This will pave the way for females to enter or re-enter the male work world without penalty. Third, with about 35% of babies now born in America to unmarried women, it is probable that some of these women will bind together, share household expenses, and assist in raising one another's children. Fourth, "sister houses" may become more common, where retired women collaborate to create a caring home together. Fifth, for women in relationships, the glue and baking soda of many a friendship is lending support to one another as they live with the opposite sex.

Women have always trusted one another
more than they have trusted men.

In a 2004 law review article, Rachel Morgan argued that while first-wave feminism focused on political independence (i.e., getting the vote) and second wave feminism focused on economic independence (i.e., getting viable work) the third wave needs to focus on emotional independence. She contends that as long as coupling and motherhood are seen as the only viable relationships for women, the opportunity to build other networks of support remains invisible.[271] That is, we need to work toward finding fulfillment in and giving time to relationships like friends and business associates.

Further, women have formerly looked to men, the dominant culture, for validation. Men have also looked largely to other men, rather than to their primary female partners, for validation. Now, though, as women climb into higher places of work, community, and government, they will look to one another.

Most women can't find a romantic partner who listens empathically, but they feel fully heard by another woman. Responding to one another with positive regard, a woman gifts the other with human presence and caring. A feedback loop begins where this nurturance elicits disclosures from the other, and each blossoms. The imposing presence of a man is not there; there is a greater softness. The push–pull or manipulating that is an integral part of most romances is gone. The essential ingredient of mutuality, missing in her romances, resonates in her friendships. As she shares, she feels the genuine and full presence of her friend, a true person-to-person communication. Whereas she can rarely access the inner being of her male partner, she knows her friend is sharing her true self.

Finding and then pursuing your natural interests will lead you to a group of like-minded people. Pursuing the same dreams, having common aspirations, you will discover your soulmates. These people will "get" you. Here is where you find profound understanding, connection, and sense of belonging. Take the advice of Edgar Cayce, who told the lonely to find their distinctive talents and use them to help others. Once your energies are aimed at helping others, Cayce believed, you will inevitably draw relationships to you.[272]

Set out to experience joy in every interpersonal contact you make. You never know what another person will mean to you. You never know how a relationship will unfold over the years. We are all capable of being very broad and developing kinships with varied people. Some need freedom from an intense romance in order to do that; others feel good in one very close relationship, romantic or not. Always pave the way for love, being open to giving and receiving love whether it comes from a child, an old person, a neighbor, a pet.

Set out to experience joy in every interpersonal contact you make.

The title of this book, *The Mother-Daughter Book Club: How ten busy mothers and daughters came together to talk, laugh and learn through their love of reading,* says it all and opens a door for fulfilling times.[273] Start with the relationships you already have to build new ones. Inviting female and like-minded male friends to discuss how to better your world, explore alternative medicine, or share spiritual sayings is another way to deepen relationships. An intimate group can even meet to share their private journaling.

Be grateful for short relationships and for people who move in and out of your life. Each relationship has its own mysterious trajectory. Each matures and shifts you. A person may suddenly appear in your life who has precisely the right attitude, skills, vocabulary, or rapport to team with you for a specific purpose, and then disappear forever. Some relationships only need twice-a-year visits to stay fully alive. My best friend from high school and I lost touch for 20 years. When we got together for a high school reunion, our rapport was immediate and we seemed to take up where we had left off.

A French study revealed that *female* friendship is a major contributor to happiness, ranking above jobs (61% said this), above sex (69%), and above "heart and feelings" (75%). Coming in at 85%, it ranks just below family (89%)! Unclouded by romance and underlying agendas (like hoping to up one's socioeconomic status through romance), friendships are purely about liking someone. They offer acceptance and understanding free of formal rules. Although these women rated their jobs as disappointing (24%), most (85%) said friendships helped them flourish. Though they found the work world to still be male dominated, their friendships provided shelter.

Friendships are purely about liking someone.

German researchers found that when a man was joined by his significant other as he prepared for a stressful circumstance, such as delivering a speech, his female partner's presence lowered his stress levels significantly. If a woman, preparing for the same event, were joined by her guy, *her stress levels surged upward*. The reason? Probably because men give support by giving advice, which can feel like being pressured into something, while women offer acceptance and validation. [274]

Two women relax their guard, giving themselves to the friendship with no holds barred, connecting as two souls. The permeable personal boundaries of women that allow them to so let another in probably stem from their abundant circulating oxytocin, which contributes to "pair bonding." Research suggests that treating autistics with oxytocin may help them become more relational. The verbal and physical affection, the unrestrained laughter, the openness shown between two women is different than the suspicion, competition, and concealment evident between two men.

In fact, women may live longer than men *because* they seek someone to succor and find connection with when stressed, while men wear out their bodies by going into aggression or withdrawal, both with physical cost. When a woman loses a romance, she turns to girlfriends for support, while a man in emotional trouble tends to isolate, according to Ohio State University psychologist Janice Kiecolt-Glaser.[275]

In the movie *Emma*, portraying early 19th century female friendship, a woman tries to help a man understand his betrothed, telling him that he may not understand the need a woman has of another woman's company. She also admits that marriage would bring about a change in the level of intimacy she once shared with her girlfriend (his betrothed), and that this was the one drawback in accepting a man's proposal.

Men give support by giving advice,
making women feel pressured.

Books like *Smart Women, Foolish Choices*, *Women Who Love Too
Much*, and *Codependent No Longer* continue in popularity because
although women like being permeable, it doesn't work with men. Those
relationships require a woman to be more clearly boundaried. But in a
friendship with another woman, she can relax.

Until a UCLA study on women's friendships was published, scientists
believed that all humans responded to stress through "fight or flight"
because 90% of research on stress had been done *on men*. In targeting
female subjects, though, they found that women fight stress very differently — by tending children and befriending women. Soothing oxytocin
is released as she socializes and she feels bonded. In fact the joke at the
UCLA lab was that, when stressed, women would clean the lab, get cof-
fee, and bond with friends, whereas the men would isolate.

Men's testosterone, which goes up under stress, dampens the effects of
oxytocin, says Cousin Klein, Ph.D., one of the study's authors and assistants. A professor of Bio-behavioral Health at Penn State University
says this may be why women outlive men. *It also explains the potency
of women's friendships*. Many studies have found that friendships lower
blood pressure, heart rate, and cholesterol. Harvard Medical School's
Health Study found that women developed fewer ailments as they aged
if they had friends, and that not having confidants was as *health-debili-
tating as smoking or being overweight*. The unpressured talk and nurturance between women brings joy and health.[276]   Don't let a romance
diminish your friendships with other women.

Because women's friendships are potentiated
by oxytocin, they are more open and less competitive
than men's friendships.

One male client told me women give "kind ear. Guys don't understand."
He needed people to talk to about the death of his wife. "That's why I

seek a woman as a friend." That's probably also why men who are wid-owed seek marriage quickly compared with women who lose a husband through death.

Stephanie is considering leaving her marriage, saying that when she's around her husband, "I feel less like me."

"When do you most genuinely feel like yourself?" I ask.

"When I'm with my girlfriends," she smiles, remembering their last getaway.

Friendship between women is special because they share the right brain's crisp grasp of reality that doesn't fit well into mere words, be-ing bigger, broader, and deeper. There are no words for much of what a woman experiences. Two women exchange knowing glances, com-municating subtleties a man doesn't catch. Intuition flashes and with instant clarity, they both "get" what's funny or interesting or important. She reads a face or experiences a color scheme without the need or any attempt to slow down and translate this into words. She doesn't need to bother because the other woman "reads" her environment in the same way. Women don't feel the need to finish sentences because they believe you've gotten the drift from what they've already expressed and the rest can be picked up from gestures or looking into their eyes. Meanwhile, the male listener is waiting. He needs the concrete words. When talking with another woman, she's free to communicate volumes quickly through nonverbals. The full value of this trait has not been fully experienced by our world because men, with their need for verbal concreteness, have been dominant for so long. The TV show *Lie to Me* helps men understand the concrete proofs of what women do: they read people.

When talking with another woman,
she's free to communicate volumes
quickly through nonverbals.

Friendship between women is rich and textured with subtle and com-plex emotion. Men, living in the left brain, access optimism and cheerfulness, which, for women, can translate into a denial and ignorance of what's really, underneath appearances, going on. Another woman shares her right brain's depth and willingness to see the darker side. Both are familiar with seeing life on this level and both are equipped to link words to their feelings.

Of all images, the human face is among the most challenging to decode: facial expressions fluctuate, people try to hide things, people's faces change over time, and there is such a variety of human faces. Nevertheless, women readily read each other, detecting mood and even thoughts. Their right brains listen for which words the speaker chooses, and for hidden messages conveyed through pupil size, gestures, tone of voice, inflections, and other hardly noticeable nuances. Their left brains hear the content of the speaker's words. Whereas women get into arguments with men because the men pick up on only half the message—the lesser important half at that—their female friends share the underlying and often truer meanings. This causes a deeper sharing between women, a sense of being understood, and a common way of experiencing other people together.

Women readily read the complex human face.

Men don't like it when women interrupt, partly because they lose what they were saying and partly because they think linearly—only one thing should happen at a time. Yet a lively conversation of females includes lots of interrupting because women can hear it all at the same time and no one takes offense. In fact, it enhances the intimacy because they can "read" what another is saying without the obviousness of finishing sentences. Conversation is like an orchestra, you hear it holistically. To speak a sentence, wait, and then hear a comment feels unnecessarily protracted to women.

Speaking of friendships in general, author Tom Rath drew on 5 million interviews. He found that those having a *best friend at work* were seven times more engaged, had fewer accidents, were more likely to invent and share ideas, and had a 50% boost in work satisfaction. (Imagine, therefore, how female friends would flourish starting a business together.) A solid friendship between members of a couple was found to be five times as important as their sex life. And get this: the quality of friendships in one's life was the *best predictor* of life satisfaction.[277]

Rather than thinking of yourself as partnering with one person only, see yourself as a soul mate with an evolving and universal consciousness. This will open you to forming friendships with persons who might otherwise be invisible to you. Taking on a greater openness to a wide variety of unions brings greater joy.

Jennifer, a gorgeous 48-year-old, reports six years after her divorce: "A guy has to really be worth it for me to give up my time. I need it for work, leisure, girlfriends, and the family I've created with my ex and our three girls. I also need time for my guy friends. I get enough male energy the way things are."

Women like ongoing dialogue
between equals.

A professor at the University of Pennsylvania asked students who they would choose if they were stranded on a desert island for several months and could have only one companion of approximately the same age. Would they choose a male or female? Without hesitation, almost every male said he'd choose a female. *Most women also said they would want a female companion.* The guys sought to secure a sexual partner and wanted a woman's support to stave off loneliness. He assumed he'd be the one in charge. The women weren't thinking of sex or who's in charge, but about ongoing conversations between equals. Some also reported that, if with a man, she'd be expected to assign herself to his wishes.[278]

Women have devoted large amounts of energy and time trying to squeeze connection out of their male companions. They have given themselves over to the care and feeding of husbands. More and more, though, women, being more truthful about what a romance can and cannot give them, will be freed up to enjoy female friends.

See yourself as a soul mate with an evolving
and universal consciousness.

In this chapter, we have considered that, as women rise, they will restore balance to the workaholic world and find fulfillment in friendships. Now we turn to an essential ingredient in her rise: taking risks.

Women Will Overcome Caution and Take More Risks

Let us dare to read, think, speak and write.
— John Adams, 1765

Women have traditionally shied away from risk taking

The long history of financial dependence caused women to be more submissive than assertive in relationships. A 2010 study of students graduating from professional schools shows that the males were *eight* times more assertive in getting better starting salaries than women. Another 2010 study found the females were twice as likely to feel nervous about negotiating their salaries. It's possible the women feel worried about offending a potential boss whereas their male peers "know" they're worth it—that is, they're confident because of their testosterone and the culture's history of favoring male accomplishments.

The Holocaust Against Women

Why might today's women shrink from taking risks in business, or in political or financial pursuits? In the days when nonconformity held a high price, a woman learned to refrain from rocking the boat. Some forget that a genocidal attempt was aimed almost solely at women. Although the horror-inducing Salem witch trials around 1692 resulted in only 150 arrests and thirty-one "trials,"[279] Europeans conducted 110,000 trials. The writer Dworkin, basing his numbers on writings from the time, believes about 9 million were accused and faced possible death, with about 85% being female.[280] The accused were tortured, sexually examined, and imprisoned for an indeterminable time. *This kind of history doesn't escape our consciousness readily.* During the hunts, rape and other crimes against women increased but the number of females reporting such crimes went down. All a deviant had to do was accuse her of witching. She dared not press charges.

Forever before and since, it has been males who fill our jails. But there was no way to hide from random accusations and women learned to be quiet and bland, and to obey male authority to save their lives. If merely accused but not sentenced, a woman was still stigmatized, abandoned by her family and at risk of dire poverty with no way to earn a living. The long arm of traumatization would have reached the ears and eyes of every female in the Western hemisphere. To witness a woman being burned would never have left one's consciousness. *Having a female friend was too risky.*

The long arm of traumatization would have reached
the ears and eyes of every female in the Western hemisphere.

Even highly educated men committed themselves to the irrational male hysteria, believing the women of their communities were so threatening to church authority that torture and murder were necessary and justified. In a profound loss of perspective, they hunted women like animals, turning against their mothers, wives, grandmothers, aunts, cousins, daughters, sisters, and the female herbologists who had healed their illnesses. Women were effectively shut down.

During the witch trials, having a female friend was too risky.

This history of gender-select torture, as well as the unconscious biases we will address next, are what each woman must tackle in her own mind. *Once she understands her fears aren't about her own shortcomings, but come from historically-imbedded thought, she can stop making them so personal and forge ahead.* Women binding together to take risks, with conscious knowledge of where their fears come from, can be particularly effective, with the support they give one another empowering.

Our Unconscious Biases

Let's look at another reason women don't assert themselves. Our attitudes about what's appropriate for each gender operate on two levels: the conscious—what we *choose* to believe, and the unconscious—our unthinking, automatic, conditioned responses that don't involve cognizant choice. Try this on: With which gender do you pair the word "leadership?" How about "housework?"

Here's how it plays out. Researchers followed thousands of women and men from birth to adulthood, and found that *one inch* of height is worth $789 per year in pay. That is, a six-foot-tall man whose work is identical to a five-foot-five woman will earn $5,525 more per year. Compounded over a normal 30-year career, the shorter gender is cheated out of hundreds of thousands of dollars. Why? Because imbedded in our thinking is that height bespeaks leadership.

Here's another type of unconscious bias. A Chicago law professor enlisted both black and white women and men to perform a test. He chose those of average attractiveness, had them dress conservatively, taught them the same narrative (i.e., they were college-educated professionals living in wealthy neighborhoods interested in buying a low-priced car), and sent them to 242 car dealerships in Chicago. They were to bargain until the salesperson either accepted or refused their offer. The results? White men topped the group, getting the *best deal* on the cars at $725 above invoice. White women came in at $935 above invoice, black women at $1,195, and last, black men at $1,687. Despite similar professional status, verbal capability, and economic status, bias toward sex and race trumped.[281]

In our deep unconscious, assertiveness does not go with "female." We have learned several myths at the breast of society and the tutelage of religion: women are to blame if a marriage doesn't work, it is inappropriate for women to show aggression or anger; a woman should curtail her success, it's wise to attend to a male's perspective over a female's.

In our deep unconscious,
"assertiveness" does not go with "female."

Taking Risks for Success

Parents and teachers need to help girls take reasonable risks and have confidence in their abilities. Perhaps the reason men are still at the top —CEOs, politicians, and initiators of new businesses—is because females are averse to risk. Women still earn less than men do in the same fields of endeavor. As Linda Babcock, economist and professor, found, women don't ask for raises or higher starting fees.[282]

Females hesitate to expend energy toward success because they are conditioned from early childhood that their worth *doesn't come from their efforts* as much as it comes from *who they are naturally*, without effort. That is, little girls in a classroom are gems—quiet, interested in learning, respectful of the teacher, able to sit still and attend. In contrast, the boys are rowdy, jostling with each other, listening minimally, showing less respect to teachers, having trouble sitting still, and overall, being less ready for school. Teachers and parents constantly admonish boys to "do better." Boys grow up with adults pointing out ways in which they can "try harder." The girls just need to be who they innately are; the boys need to work at it. Parents and teachers may be loath to encourage girls to try harder or take risks because they fear girls will overtake the boys.

While girls just need to be who they innately are,
boys need to try harder.

As stated earlier, whereas men have been *success objects* to women, women have been *sex objects* to men. Again, men are motivated to work hard to *earn* success, while women are attractive simply because of their bodies. To give some of their greatest gifts to humanity, women need simply be female: become pregnant, give birth, breast feed, and bond with children. A man had better try hard and succeed at work or... what is he? Because boys are pushed early on and then through life, they still hold the top ranking positions in most fields. Most have never considered this concept regarding women's hesitance to pursue success.

Women must venture forth, push harder, risk, climb, and strain—they will probably do this as a team, especially with another woman. It's ok to lose sleep because you're crunching numbers for your new business. Some women have remained in jobs with lesser demands so they still have energy to work the "second shift" at home, but a 1984 *Newsweek* research report on Women Who Work found that 70% of working females would prefer a high-pressure job with possibilities of advancement rather than a lesser job. The 1990 Virginia Slims poll asked females about "mommy tracking," and 70% thought it was just a justification for paying women less.[283] Mommy tracking is where a company offers mothers benefits like flexible hours but also provides them with fewer opportunities for advancement due to these "concessions."

So, get this: A Harvard professor studied the outcome of women who do negotiate for starting salaries and found, in 2007, that they were penalized. Male managers hired men but not women who asked for higher wages.[284]

We need more policies in the workplace that limit male social dominance so the feminine spirit can be felt. If women weren't afraid of male bullying, they would be more plain-spoken or more initiating. As one socially aware organization paves the way, others will follow and, as Margaret Mead said, "A small group of thoughtful people could change the world. Indeed, it's the only thing that ever has."

As women reach higher positions and collaborate together, they will make our work-life more humane with day care centers and flex time that will benefit both genders. They will also fight male social dominance that continues to hinder women in the workplace, including the sexual misconduct that scares women into fearful and compromised situations.

If women weren't afraid of male bullying, they
would be more plain-spoken and more initiating.

Women have had to forge their way in the hierarchical man's work world, with rules and values men agree on and understand, but that women find to be cold. Men seek to eliminate the competition, so if she speaks assertively (following men's rules), men label her a bitch in an attempt to take her out of the running. Some women may choose to start businesses outside men's purview, joining with other women and men with feminized brains. These will be marked by cooperation, affiliation, and empathy (as in the all-female computer support company, where a staff member says to customers, "You never have to be alone with your computer problems again. We'll be a phone call away.")

Women will return to older roots of autonomy, assertiveness, and resourcefulness

"Go confidently in the direction of your dreams."
—Thoreau

Our main adaptation to life comes from our hunter-gatherer days, when women supplied 60-80% of the everyday victuals, says Helen Fisher. Goal-directed and autonomous, they ventured as far as necessary to get the job done. Then things changed. About ten thousand years ago, women were excluded from owning property or pursuing education, and were restricted to keeping house.[285]

Despite this newer history, women's brains are fully equipped for success at work, but with special right brain sensibilities to keep her balanced. She can be wickedly smart and financially skilled, while enjoying relational closeness and the richness of her feelings. Her empathy for the Earth will provide loving strategies for extracting resources; her sensitivity to people will give her marketing acumen; her ability to tune in to others will allow her to truly hear clients or customers. Despite her repressed past and despite her having to forge her way through the male-created work world, the feminine spirit will rise. Though she faces past oppression and a current glass ceiling, her brain comes fully loaded, so that, as Emerson said, "What lies behind us and what lies before us are small matters compared to what lies within us." Today, we have cars that pollute, jobs that numb, and foods that make us sick. The feminine will bring on a world where the spirit has more pull than the ego that seeks status, power, and monetary gain.

D. H. Lawrence said, "The essential American soul is hard, isolate, stoic, and a killer." He was, no doubt, observing how under-represented the feminine was in the culture he observed.

Once women have mastered their
expectations of long-term romance,
they will emerge in every arena of life.

What will automatically increase women's autonomy and assertiveness is money. Money talks and few groups can really have a clear voice in our world without it. The values of older, white males have dominated our world. Why? They had the money. Let's review. The US workforce, as of October 2009, was half females and of those females, half had landed the higher paying professional slots, says the Bureau of Labor Statistics. With more women than men graduating from college and the economy turning to knowledge-based jobs, women are primed to snatch solid work. *Almost all (9 of 10) of the occupations producing the most jobs in the near future are currently occupied by women.* Though women on average still earn less than men, childless women in metropolitan areas earn more: 108-121% of what's earned by males. Researchers have named women "The Third Billion," referring to women's global emergence in economic power. It will soon be possible for women to take economic control.[286] The feminine is rising and our once-patriarchal culture is moving on. Be ready!

We need a new loving power. Once women have mastered their expectations of long-term romance, they will emerge to put our world back into balance.

It will soon be possible for women to take economic control.

Women Will Make Themselves More Known

"Whatever you can do or imagine, begin it; boldness has beauty, magic, and power in it."
—Goethe

"Those who say it cannot be done should not interrupt the person doing it."
—Chinese Proverb

One reason women are leaving marriages in droves is because the masculine/feminine polarity is out of balance—not that women haven't noticed this before, but they now have the financial independence to do something about it. The masculine spirit is so overly represented, it is exhausting and women have simply had enough. One more "testosterone episode" and she's out the door. She's inundated with the masculine at work, at church, on the news, and at home. The marriage is one thing she can break off. She's overloaded and fed up with masculine energies and values.

The masculine spirit has been overly represented.

When a woman says, "I've got to end this marriage," what she often means is, "I cannot find enough of the feminine in my world to rebalance myself." She is desperate for change. She doesn't have time to pursue female friendships because she's working (and often striving to make a romance work). She has to go *inside* herself to find what she needs. She must awaken to the beauty of her own feminine soul.

Everything we currently see around us spells "left brain" and masculine efficiency, from the marketing signs on the freeway to the gray cement the freeways are built of, from plain grass to cut down on drainage, to the cars that go faster and have more features. We have all profited from male systemizing. But as the female mind gains greater expression, our world will include marketing based on warm relationship, freeways turned into art canvasses, flowering gardens by the wayside, earth-friendly carriages, more trains and busses promoting equal opportunity among peoples. She will promote quality of life and togetherness that helps us stop feeling robotish and allows for a joyous expression of ourselves.

You can't argue with people who have been consistently voted by researchers to be the happiest people on Earth. The Danes top the rest of the world, while the US scores 23rd. Granted, they drink from the great breast of socialism, secure, unworried, and unhurried, which gives them time to nurture friendships. Danish women don't dream of weddings and they feel no pressure to marry. They have children and cohabit, but marriage isn't a major part of their consciousness. They're granted six to 12 months paid maternity leave.[287] With more social freedom, these women feel better.

The US, scoring 23nd in happiness, is built on the naked motivation to acquire, the fear of not having enough, a forward march toward materialism and greater technology. In its wake are the sicknesses of stress and a dirty environment calling for more medical interventions in an endless feedback circle. Yes, America contributes technology and medical advances to the whole world, and happiness isn't everything. But what about a balance?

It's been a long, cold winter for women. Why? Long ago, as the fetal human brain enlarged, our African foremothers died in childbirth, their birth channels unable to accommodate infants' large heads. To prevent death, Nature caused babies to be born earlier and smaller—even premature in comparison with other mammals. Women have had to bear the brunt of these early births, devoting a couple decades to raising children who can't make it without help.

I remember delivering a colt on my parents' ranch. I put both feet on the rear end of the mare, which seemed to understand what I was doing, grasped the colt, and pulled hard. The colt emerged, stood on its own, walked around, eyes open, alert and aware of its environment. I was surprised at the colt's lack of dependence. Now think about being careful to hold a human infant's head correctly, to swaddle her, to guess what she needs, to take her to the doctor, to locate babysitters. Someone must be with the infant at *all* times and when she grows into toddlerhood, she must be incessantly watched. By the time she is four, she is more comparable to the newborn colt, but still unable to function in our complex world. Between the never ending care of the home and the care of children, our foremothers have been busy. Spring has emerged for women and they are freer to make unique inroads into every area of life, from business to medicine.

The masculine/feminine polarity is out of balance.

A beautiful illustration of a time when women's influence was honored comes from a historical event in the United States and from Indian culture. The Cherokee Indians traveled to Charleston, South Carolina, to meet with US officials to reach a peace settlement. When the Indians saw that the US delegation was all male, they were alarmed. They assumed the government officials were making a mockery of them, not taking them seriously, and treating them with disrespect. "Where are your women?" they asked. The government officials, steeped in patriarchy, couldn't grasp their meaning.

In these Indian governments, young men ran the council, but it was the grandmothers to whom they looked for wisdom. The laws of the Iroquois Indians, one of the most powerful tribes, gave equal rights to each gender. Though the chief was always male, it was the select task of women to choose him.[288] The male/female balance was intact. They knew that without it, they could be strong and fierce, but lacking the acumen of the holistic feminine spirit. The Cherokees believed that nature was to be treated respectfully or there would be a price to pay, and this meant, in part, that a female/male balance was to be preserved.

In an interview with the BBC, anthropologist Helen Fisher talked about moving forward to the gender balance we had a million years ago, something we'll look at next. She also said excluding women from management teams was like "hopping on one foot."[289]

Our long history of being out of balance

"The rise and fall of images, women's rights, and the sacred feminine have moved contrapuntally with the rise and fall of alphabet literacy."[290]

Before we begin this discussion, it's important to note that the American culture, which uses uses reading and writing, isn't smarter than those who use verbal interaction and memorization as their major ways of communicating. The reader must suspend bias to understand the concepts below. As we will see, brilliant thinkers like Lao-tzu, Buddha, Socrates, and Jesus preferred speech to writing. Speech, because it includes intonation, gestures, and facial expression is more relational and whole.

Though women and men both use both hemispheres of the brain, women tend to prefer living in the right brain. But surgeon Leonard Schlain, foremost student of left and right brain function, has shown how the triumph of literacy has marched right over right brain (women's) values. Speaking includes gestures and body language that not only cultivate relationship but also set the right brain in motion *along with its value system*. Pictures of the *face,* whether art or statues, also promote relationship and activate the right brain. Perceiving pictures of anything relies on the right brain's use of simultaneity, synthesis, and wholeness. Societies that have, at least for a time, promoted *speaking and pictures* have been steeped in right brain, feminine values. They were more egalitarian and tolerant of differences in belief, and promoted unity with and respect for nature, art, compassion, justice, and intuition.

Intuition is, by the way, a catch-all term for a process we don't yet understand. Quite possibly females developed the perception, insight, and foresight that we call intuition because, as a matter of life or death, they were forced to figure out the link between having sex and getting pregnant. The many deaths of our African foremothers due to the ever-enlarging of the infant human brain compelled her to develop intuition, while men did not face such a personal struggle for survival. She had to resist sexual desire, though she felt it. She had to veto insincere lovers and gauge their character, reading them, to see who would stick around to help provide for the new life.

Women tend to prefer living in the right brain.

Back to the link between brain hemisphere and values. Reading and writing, both solitary activities, activate the left brain male values, *especially because most men already have a lesser bridge to the right brain.*[291] Figuring out the meaning of "d-o-g," for instance, using letters that have nothing to do with Rover, takes the left brain's ability to analyze, string letters together (sequence), and think in the abstract, (that is, "dog" is symbolic for Rover). *Further, most pen with the right hand, which, like the spear and sword before it, turn on the left hemisphere.* (Reading-and-writing-based masculine cultures emphasize not only rank but also the marginalizing of women, patriarchal families, law and order, war, and dogmatic beliefs that are held as superior and may lead to religious persecution).

The left brain influences are particularly deleterious for males who don't have the automatic right/left brain balance women's biology prescribes. Even highly educated women who have developed their left brains don't become violent or aggressive in the way men historically have. Yet when alphabetic, left brained influences balloon, the male left brain becomes destructive, marching over the civil rights of others and starting wars over minuscule points. It is doubtful that women—more empathic, egalitarian and tolerant—would willingly kill over minute doctrinal disparities or, for that matter, could bring themselves to kill at all.

Because religion largely shapes whether feminine (right brained) or masculine (left brained) values preside, let's review three religions—Taoism, Buddhism, and Christianity. We'll see how each started out with right brain values, but was changed with the masculinizing effects of writing. (The point is not to eliminate writing, obviously, but to understand the upcoming changes as our world becomes more and more visual).

In China, Lao-tzu (speculated to be a woman) represented Taoism, a right-brained philosophy with feminine values like egalitarianism. Lao-tzu was a contemporary of Confucius who promoted the opposite—a hierarchical worldview and patriarchal family, including mothers obeying sons. Radically different, Lao-tzu of Taoism stood for controlling *nothing*, finding wisdom through intuition and Mother Nature, celebrating sex, encouraging artists to paint images found in nature, and leading by *example* rather than by law. Interestingly, Lao-tzu was suspicious of writing, thus keeping feminine values intact.

Confucius had little impact during his lifetime until, in 200 B.C.E., reading began to flourish once Chinese writing was standardized. Women's rights and presence in society were then sharply curtailed, slavery became prevalent, females were precluded from learning, the painting of women's faces or figures was disallowed, and wars constantly arose. The practice of foot-binding, believed to be sexually stimulating to men, began at the same time the use of the printing press made literacy widespread and their first code of written laws was introduced.

Later, history switched for a second time and Taoists again superseded Confucians. Reading was devalued, and the feminine, tolerant, and open nature of China presided again.

Then Taoist leaders switched to writing and a masculine mode. In the back-and-forth weave of history, they created a male hierarchy, while Lao-tzu no doubt turned over in her/his grave. Women were marginalized, Lao-tzu was elevated to god-status, and priests went celibate, despite their belief in the yin/yang circle that represented the balance between female and male. In spite of Lao-tzu's admonition to beware of language altogether, male disciplines wrote volumes.

Reading and writing activate the left brain and male values.

Buddha, like Socrates, disapproved of the written word, asking his/her (ever thought about Buddha's breasts and swollen stomach?) devotees to memorize, *not write*, what s/he taught. Her/his teaching was available to anyone of any caste—rather than to a chosen people—and s/he was merely someone who had discovered truths that anyone could experience. Nonviolent, speaking in parables (the language of the right brain), her/his teachings found acceptance among people without an alphabetic language. S/he promulgated universal love, wisdom, and compassion— the principles that show up in image and speech-driven feminine societies. S/he believed that imposing laws upon people led to despotism. (Buddha was unusual for a right brained thinker in that s/he abhorred sex and birth, but that seems to relate to the death of his/her own mother in childbirth and because s/he wanted to stop the wheel of reincarnation).

In Buddhist India, the story of creation promulgated that humans come from the lovemaking of a husband and wife, who are equal. The story was without sin, blame, or punishment. However, the alphabet-driven militaristic culture that invaded India brought its own much different creation story: the primordial mother was hacked to pieces by the god of rain. Most reading/writing cultures have not and do not see God as including the female in any important way.

Both Taoism and Buddhism began with right brain values,
but switched to left brain values once
reading and writing were emphasized.

Then Buddhism also switched to the masculine. Around 1500 B.C.E. Aryan combatants conquered India, implementing the Semitic alphabet. A warring culture, they were suspicious of women, excluded them from education, and burned widows on their husband's funeral pyre. Buddhism was eradicated, but proceeded to blossom in non-literate Asia. But as Buddhists followers, like Taoist followers, discounted the warnings of their leaders and transposed the faith into rules and writing, women's *status fell*. Buddhist nuns were given more restrictions and were junior to monks, no matter what their seniority. They were allowed less education and financial support than male monks. Some claimed females had to be reborn as males before finding Nirvana.[292]   These ways were contrary to the egalitarian Buddha.

So, we've looked at how Taoism and Buddhism switched from their original female right brained values to the male values of the left brain. But the religion affecting the US most is Christianity.

In Christianity, there's Jesus, who, speaking in parables, escorted humankind back to the right hemisphere. He never mentioned Eve's supposed transgression, spoke a humanistic creed, advocated nonviolence in the face of antagonism, and believed in the triumph of love and the soul. A rebel against hierarchy, he emphasized the spirit, not the law, and cussed out the self-righteous exploiters of those trying to please God. He didn't believe people needed to beseech the elite male class for spiritual guidance. He taught all, using stories out of women's lives. He stood for free will, healing, equality, compassion, justice, mercy, integrity, power to the people, and free thinking: a feminine agenda.

Jesus escorted humanity back to the right brain
through speech, not writing.

Like Buddha, Pythagoras, and Socrates, *Jesus did not write*. Rather, he spoke and interacted with people. He spoke against the left brain's darlings: time, family authority, and money. He predicted that time would end; he said your own spirituality is more important than family obligations; and he toppled the moneychangers' operations. He himself possessed nothing. In the quintessential sweep known to right brain thinking, he reduced all the picayune laws to a couple sentences: just love

God and people. Strikingly different from many of the world's male religious leaders, Jesus never ordered anyone killed, burned, jailed, or exiled because they disagreed with him.

Understanding Jesus' death is enough to awaken the right brain. He died like he lived. In masculine thought, the law is the pinnacle of the left brain: it's thousands of pages of precise language that rank order the sins of humanity. In a stunning act of defiance, he willingly received punishment by death. Rather than each sinner getting his due per the law (a left brained concept), Jesus was punished on behalf of everyone (a relational, egalitarian, and right brained concept.)

Jesus turned tidy masculine rationality on its head.

He skipped over the law in a second way, again defying hierarchy. He came wrapped in a *male* body and was, he said, no less than the *Son of God*. In patriarchal culture, no one is *more valued* than the son of a powerful father. Yet he willingly died for those *lesser than him—with no regard for gender, race or status*—turning tidy masculine rationality on its head. Women liked the non-hierarchical, loving Jesus.

But wait. Christianity then switched to the masculine. It's Paul who carried his brand of Christianity into future generations, with the help of Constantine, a militant, who favored orthodoxy (i.e., the linear thinking of the left brain), and sent police to destroy all pictures (i.e., shrines, images) and burn the Gnostic gospels. The Gnostics, one branch of early Christianity, embraced their sexuality along with feminine thinking and leadership. Striving for an egalitarian spirituality, they drew lots to see who would lead each service, and ended them with a kiss.

When Christianity changed from the oral teachings of Jesus
to the written words of Paul, masculine values took over.

Oddly, Paul did not emphasize the teachings of Jesus. When Christianity changed from the oral teachings of Jesus to the written words of Paul, masculine values took over. A book man, Paul had been steeped in the most legalistic (left brained) interpretation of Judaism.

In contrast, Jesus, at ease with women, dialogued with the Samaritan woman, confronted self-righteous males about to stone a woman, had an extensive relationship with Mary Magdalene, and was beloved by women who stood grieving as he died a slow death by crucifixion. Contrarily, Paul steered away from a relationship with a woman and recommended other men do the same, saying it would limit them. Though history records that Jesus' influence strengthened women's voices, Paul, in his dissertations that clarified the rules and defended doctrines, wanted women to be silent and subjugated (I Tim 2:11-12), reiterated the patriarchal family order (I Cor 11:3, Eph. 5:23-4), and referred back to the law—rather than Jesus—for authority (I Cor. 14:34-5), Though Paul himself is an example of finding contentment in singleness, he didn't do much for women.

TV watching and using computers may promote
right brained values.

Today, we can expect a continuing rise of the feminine. Shlain says equilibrium is on its way because computers use pictures plus type, we type with both hands (versus writing that requires just one hand), and the holistic (rather than linear) "web" of the internet has arrived. All spark the right brain. The emerging of ecological movements, women's increased status, putting a critical microscope to dogmatism, and promoting tolerance show we are trending toward greater balance.

Consider the power of TV and its emphasis on pictures. The feminist movement lay mostly dormant for five *thousand* years of patriarchy until a generation grew up with television. Then, the baby boomers questioned and opposed the reigning hierarchies and explored spirituality outside their parents' religion. Anti-war movements rose, the Peace Corp emerged, and civil rights grew. The age was marked with at least two pictures: a rifle posed as a vase for a flower and a photo of the beautiful planet Earth, evoking, yes, peace and love, with which the unbridled pooling of left brain thought, as found in all-male leadership, does not naturally align.[293]

Women Will Restore Joyous and Health-giving Sex

Where females fair well, so does sex. Many cultures, including China, Egypt, Greece, India, Japan, Mesopotamia, and Rome provide generous anthropological evidence that female gods were revered by both sexes. In fact, in the city of Athens, males voted to have the female Athena as their goddess rather than the contending male god. *Few of us are used to the idea of worshipping a female, but suspend for a moment what you're used to and consider what this would do to women's status.* The goddess societies celebrated fertility, sex, and giving birth. Women, as representatives of the goddess, were special, and the majority of the non-literate farming societies of prehistory were egalitarian.[294] Anxiety and emotional distance cause female sexuality to shut down; feeling equal leads to its expression.

Feeling equal leads to the expression of female sexuality.

The major shapers of Christianity—Paul, Augustine, Iranaeus, Origen, Tertullian, and Jerome—all confessed to sexual struggles, leading them to disparage women and bar sex. *Instead of loving a woman and entering the joyous celebration of sex as the goddess cultures did, they formed a theology of condemnation around it, making guilt, sin, and suppression of sex major church themes.* They weren't influenced by the fact that Jesus never linked sex and sin or that God was seen as the originator of the human body with its sexual proclivities. Terrified of women's power, they blamed Eve, leading to a history of male leaders blaming women for plagues, storms, and their own personal downfalls.

Consider the difference. While the Goddess religions made sex sacred, the Christian fathers saw sex as the antithesis to spirituality; if you were really holy, you'd refrain altogether. Augustine is next up in influencing Western Christianity. Women's (that is, Eve's) sin permanently crippled human judgment, he said, so one's free will could not be trusted. Lots of rules, spies, and police were therefore necessary. God was punitive, unhappy. In a spark of weird logic, he said Eve's wrong justified subjugating all women, a belief that, oddly, still holds in Christian thinking, at least unconsciously. These dour attitudes continue to sour sexual expression. (I wish I had space here to go into the actual writings of these male Christian thinking-shapers. It's mind blowing.)

The success of romantic relationships is largely dependent on ongoing sexual interplay—from flirting to climax and back again. As the male meets the females' need for romantic connection, she responds sexually, meeting his deepest need, and so they go round and round in a feedback loop that replenishes itself. Throughout pre-history and history, it is the picture-based, right brained, feminine cultures that are open to sexuality. Early India is known for tantric yoga, sexually explicit art, the Kama Sutra, and joyous celebrations of the erotic. Time after time, patriarchal, alphabetic conquerors radically changed the freer sexual expression of feminine cultures, both tightening female expression to its narrowest confine and disrespecting women so they lost their affection for men. Where women have more rights, they are happier and more open to men in general and to trusting sexual connection with men.

Yet, while most romances begin with frequent and intense sexual expression, most peter out. Often, women lose interest and almost any man will tell you he wishes for more sex in his relationship. Sexual disorders are among our most often reported psychological problems in women.[295] The prevalence of females lacking erotic fantasies and sexual desire is reported as a whopping 46% in some studies.[296]   The inability to orgasm is reported in up to 41% of females in other studies.[297]

Sexual disorders are among our most often
reported psychological problems in women.

One of the great ironies of life is that men, who are so sexually hungry, cannot see how they cut themselves off from their greatest pleasure. When they disregard the feminine, they inadvertently distance their female partners. Tell your guy that!

Allow me a small digression into goddess communities. These sophisticated cultures were not taken seriously for a long time because of the people who discovered them. Archaeologists were white Christian males who arrogantly belittled findings of goddess cultures because they didn't jive with the Victorian mindset. That the then-known world prayed to a female and reproduction was deemed sacred met with swift patronizing. But around 1890, Arthur Evans found the splendid complexity of Crete's goddess culture (3500 to 1500 B.C.E.), where females officiated over religious festivities and inheritance was matrilineal.[298] Stone-paved roads, clay pipes that safely carried water and sewage,[299] buildings two or three stories high, with tiled roofs, wood walls, stone floors, and lavish décor gave evidence of an advanced culture.[300] Palaces had exterior and interior staircases, courtyards, light wells, and massive columns. Women wore multi-layered flounced skirts and allowed their breasts to be exposed, or wore strapless, tight bodices—that is, they were sexually self-assured and open.

In the early 1960s, James Mellaart excavated the goddess Turkish culture (7000 to 4000 B.C.E.), finding an absence of authority figures or military and concluding it was an egalitarian and peaceful community. In general, the remnants of goddess communities indicate a peaceful existence. Why? As Eugene Ionesco, the French dramatist, said, "Ideologies separate us. Dreams and anguish bring us together." That is, the left brain—the hemisphere where most men live—establishes dogmas, while the right brain—the hemisphere where females prefer to live— imagines and feels and supports unity and peace.

Women had developed the foundations for modern farming, constructed religious and philosophical thought, and developed trade and profitable diversification. We know women had high status because their burial plots were in preferred locations compared to men's. A well-planned 1,000-year settlement with stunning art and homes for 2,000 families in sixty-foot apartment complexes could only be trivialized by the most supercilious Victorian male.[301]

Another anomaly in our otherwise patriarchal history occurred from 500–1000 C.E. when the Age of Chivalry arose along with fair Camelot. The knights lived to provide for and protect ladies. All men, according to French policy, were to honor and serve the gentler sex. What does a woman want today, asks every male from Freud to Mel Gibson. *These knights!* Trained in martial arts, and the chivalric code, knights were to "Hold women in respect and love; this increases a young man's honor... Short his praise who betrays honest love."[302] What happens when women are honored with the gender equality that marked these 500 years? Romantic love flourished. Note, too, that during this time, Christianity changed from a male-centric dogma to a more loving inclusion of Mary. Her pictures, either holding an infant or a dying man, adorned most homes in Western Europe, while the French built 180 churches and cathedrals in Mary's honor.[303]   The Holy Grail, molded to fit Helen of Troy's breast,[304] signified both life-giving breast milk and the uterus' space, and men's hearts were given to this treasure hunt. The movie *The Mists of Avalon* portrays the changing of the guard during the age of chivalry, from the Old World Goddess culture, where the healing and spiritual powers of women were honored by men, to the barbaric Saxon culture.

Women want a knight!

Consider two cultures, one from recent times, the Victorian Era, and one from pre-historical times, the Egyptians. A well-bred woman of the Victorian Era was, ideally, sexually repressed and sexually ignorant, abstaining from carnal desires. A true lady was submissive and pure. This combination led to many hilarious yet sad writings of the time when "ladies" were *disgusted by their husband's advances, yet obliged to give in.* Her sole means of winning society's respect was to marry, be a housekeeper, and bear children as an asexual human. Talking about sex or wanting it was out of the question. Virgins were guarded by their mothers because impurity would render them damaged and unmarriageable. Men were to restrain themselves, too, but their special drives were understood and prostitution flourished. Sex was only, even between the married, for procreation. In fact, some upper middle class couples refrained from sex and bearing children, rendering them worthy to be deemed truly "refined." Sex was an awkward unmentionable of married life. The possibility of a woman climaxing was unthinkable.[305]

In sharp contrast, around 3000 B.C., the Egyptians marked their communication through a complex pictorial script based on images, requiring artistic skill. The pattern of the picture sentences had to be grasped simultaneously, drawing on the *right brain*.[306]   The female essence was represented by the vulture, for its foresight. If you, like me, hate snakes, put your biases away for a moment to understand the following. For Egyptians, the snake represented a woman's walk, dance, sexuality, and by extension, life itself. Orgasming was like the bursting forth of a coiled snake. The snake curling to make a circle represents the steady cycling of the female body. The eye of the snake was seen as the doorway to mystic understanding. Thus, the coiled cobra topped the pharaoh's headdress.[307] This feminine culture produced art, sculpture, and architecture. The highest status known to Western history was afforded to Egyptian females: women were venerated. A British naval officer and student of Egypt saw them as light-hearted, happy, and *remarkably fond of life*. Contrast this with your average American today. He also noted the sexual equality.[308]

Egyptians viewed sex not just as acceptable or exciting, but as sacred. Erotic pictures were carved on the inside walls of tombs and temples. Sex was not taboo or guilt-ridden, but an open celebration. Tales of adultery and masturbation were popular. They identified aphrodisiac potions made of radishes and honey or coriander in wine. It is suspected that the lotus was used as a sexual stimulant. The Turin papyrus includes erotic scenes that some now call shocking. Pregnancy in an unmarried girl was celebrated, probably as an entry into adulthood; there was no community shaming. All of life was imbued with sexual meaning and linked to the divine.[309]

The Egyptians were far more sexually sophisticated than Americans today. They would, no doubt, view us as practicing elementary sex, but leaving untapped its spiritual potential. The Egyptians, studying sex for thousands of years, linked it with eternal life because they found a way to harness the energy of orgasm. If one deliberately guides her or his orgasmic energy, using imagery and Mer-Ka-Ba breathing, back into the spine, it will circulate, increase, and recharge a person, leading to a higher consciousness. The process takes discipline to learn and is explained in *The Ancient Secret of the Flower of Life, Volume II*. They practiced *sixty-four* sexual modes, complex practices underlying the Tantra systems of the world. Their procedures so empowered them, the Egyptians believed their brand of orgasm led to longevity and the energy was connected to the heightened consciousness associated with the divine.[310]

Quite possibly, sex lights up the right brain in men.

Interestingly, some believe sex lights up the right brain in men, due to the effect of female pheromones. This may explain why men become more emotionally engaged and expressive after sex. Watching porn doesn't do the same thing; it seems to have to do with experiencing female energy directly. During intercourse, a man relinquishes his yang essence, says the Chinese yin–yang tradition, causing him to be, temporarily, more yin. That is, he relaxes, goes inward, and becomes more relational and nurturing. Women often like the afterglow better than the actual sex for this reason. As a male friend who works for the defense industry told me, "If men everywhere had the sex they needed, they wouldn't be inclined to wage war."

In summary, the influence of a right-brained culture brings greater gender equality, more sex, happier men, and men women are more inclined to like.

As the feminine spirit becomes more represented and felt in our culture, the self esteem of women will of course climb. This will give way to greater sexual expression, contributing more joy and health to the human experience.

Putting Limits on Romance, Woman Will Rise

Long ago, psychiatrist Carl Jung believed the only way to save western man was through restoring feminine values. Whereas male values seek to compete and rule, female values seek to collaborate and form networks. Whereas man explains himself to others as though he's superior, woman explores and understands. While he is independent, she seeks interdependence. While he is firm, she is flexible and compromising. He seeks achievements and she seeks relationships.[311] Patriarchy has devalued the heart, emotional closeness, and care of the earth in favor of profit. It is time for a balance.

Carl Jung believed the only way to save western man
was through restoring feminine values.

What Jung didn't see was that, until women became loosened from their *expectations of romantic relationships*, they would continue devoting themselves and sacrificing their own ambitions to trying to make these relationships better. But as women limit what they're willing to give to men, they are taking their energy and love into new areas. For this reason, the feminine will rise.

Endnotes

[1] Shlain, Leonard. 2003. *Sex, Time and Power*. New York: Penguin Group. 11.

[2] Brinig, Margaret; Douglas W. Allen (2000). "These Boots Are Made for Walking: Why Most Divorce Filers are Women". American Law and Economics Review 2 (1): 126—129.

[3] Hosseini, Khaled. 2007. *A Thousand Splendid Suns*, New York: Penguin Group. 119.

[4] Fisher, Helen. 2004. *Why We Love. The Nature and Chemistry of Romantic Love*. New York: Henry Holt and Company. 54.

[5] (Seligman, M.E. "Depression and Learned Helplessness." In (R.J Friedmand and M.M. Katz Eds.) *The Psychology of Depression: Contemporary Theory and Research*. Washington D.C.: V.H. Winston and Sons, 1974.

[6] Fisher, 58

[7] Brizendine, Louann. 2010. *The Male Brain*. New York: Random House. 13, 32-3, 39.

[8] Faludi, Susan. Backlash. 1991 with preface 2006. *The Undeclared War Against American Women*. New York: Three Rivers Press. 52.

[9] Saarni, Carolyn. The Development of Emotional Competence.

[10] Young, J.E. Loneliness, depression, and cognitive therapy: Theory and application. 82. In L.A. Peplaud & D. Perman (Eds.)., *Loneliness: A source book of current theory, research, and therapy*. New York: John Wiley & Sons, 1982. 379.

[11] Maccoby, Ellen. 1998. *The Two Sexes: Growing Apart, Coming Together*. Cambridge, Mass.: Harvard University Press.

[12] Lerner, Sharon. October 2009. "The Real Reason American Women Are So Unhappy." *Life* online.

[13] Gray, John. 1992. *Men are from Mars, Women are from Venus*. New York: Harper Collins.

[14] Gottman, John. 1999. *Seven Principles of Making Marriage Work*. New York: Three Rivers Press.

[15] Real, Terrence, M.S. 2008. *The New Rules of Marriage*. New York: Ballantine.

[16] Weiner-Davis, Michele, MSW. 1992. *Divorce Busting*. New York: Fireside.

[17] The National Center for Health Statistics reports that in 1975, women initiated about 72 percent of the divorces, in 1988, about 65 percent, and currently about 66%. A study reported in "These Boots Are Made

for Walking: Why Most Divorce Filers are Women," American Law and Economics Review. 2000, agrees that overall more than two-thirds of divorces are filed by women, and that throughout the 19th century; women filed 60 percent of the time. The statistic holds for women with children. Among almost all (90%) of college educated couples the wives filed, and in states with no-fault divorces, over 70% are filed by women. See the online source "Divorce Lawyer Source." The AARP's 2004 study on divorce among 40-60 year olds also reported that 66% were filed by women. AARP. May 2004. "The Divorce Experience: A Study of Divorce at Midlife and Beyond, The Full Report.

[18] National Opinion Research Center. Mismatch.

[19] Fisher, Helen. *The First Sex*. 125-6. Offers references showing that girls are more likely to complete projects, women show more patience in work settings and when investing in the stock market. The 1996 International Gallup Poll on gender and Society voted that women were the patient sex.

[20] Thomas, Susan Gregory. March 3-4, 2012. "The Gray Divorces." *The Wall Street Journal*.

[21] Pinker, Steven. 2002. *The Blank Slate: The Modern Denial of Human Nature*, Part I. New York: Penguin Group.

[22] Dabbs, James. 2000. *Heroes, Rogues, and Lovers: Testosterone and Behavior*. New York: McGraw-Hill.

[23] Stevenson, M.R., & Black, K.N. 1988. "Paternal absence and sex-role development: A meta-analysis." *Child Development*, 59, 793-814. Found in Lippa, Gender, Nature, and Nurture, p 142.

[24] Shlain, Leonard. 2004. Sex, *Time, and Power: How Women's Sexuality Shaped Human Evolution*. New York: Viking Penguin, p. 222.

[25] Maccoby, E.E. 1998. *The Two Sexes: Growing Apart, Coming Together*. Cambridge, Mass.: Harvard University Press.

[26] Berkson, D. Lindsey. *Hormonal Deception*. 2000. Lincolnwood, Illinois: Contemporary Books. XXI.

[27] Gilder, George. 1973. *Men and Marriage*. Gretna, LA: Pelican Publishing.

[28] AARP. May 2004. "The Divorce Experience: A Study of Divorce at Midlife and Beyond," Executive Summary, AARP, May 2004. Results from "The Divorce Experience: A Study of Divorce at Midlife and Beyond" are based on surveys with 1,147 men and wom

en, ages 40 to 79, who experienced a divorce in their 40s, 50s or 60s.

[29] Daly, M. and Wilson, M. 1983. *Sex, Evolution and Behavior*. Boston: Willard Grant Press.

[30] Fukuyama, Francis. May 1999. "The Great Disruption." *The Atlantic Monthly Company*. Volume 283, No. 5; pages 55-80.

[31] Synnot, Anthony, Ph.D. October 6, 2010. "Why Some People Have Issues With Men: Misandry." *Psychology Today*.

[32] Stanford, Craig B. 1999. *The Hunting Apes: Meat Eating and the Origins of Human Behavior*. Princeton: Princeton University Press. p. 40, 70.

[33] Schlain. *Sex, Time and Power*. p. 28.

[34] Baron-Cohen, Simon. 2003. *The Essential Differences: The Truth About the Male and Female Brain*. New York: Basic Books, p. 100-1.

[35] Baron-Cohen, Simon. 2003. p 33.

[36] Goleman, Daniel. 1995. *Emotional Intelligence*. New York: Banton Books. p. 138.

[37] Cross, S.E., & Madson, L. 1997. Models of the self: Self-construals and gender. *Psychological Bulletin*, 122, 5-37. As found in Lippa, Richard A. Gender, Nature, and Nurture. p. 29.

[38] Josephs, R. A., Markus, H.R., & Tafarodi, R.W. 1992. Gender and Self-Esteem. *Journal of Personality and Social Psychology*, 63, 391-402. p. 29 Gender, Nature, and Nurture by Richard A Lippa.

[39] Zak, Paul. April 25, 2010. "Five tests to Determine if your partner will cheat." *Psychology Today*.

[40] Konner, Melvin. 2002. *The Tangled Wing: Biological Constraints on the Human Spirit*. New York: Henry Holt, pp. 102-5, as referenced by Shlain, Leonard. Sex, Time and Power. p 95.

[41] Schulz, Mona Lisa, and Northrup, Christiane. 2005. *The New Feminine Brain: Developing Your Intuitive Genius*. New York: Simon and Schuster.

[42] Booth, Alan and Dabbs, James M., Jr. Dec. 1993. "Testosterone and Men's Marriages." *Social Forces*. Vol. 72, No. 2. University of North Carolina Press, pp. 463-477.

[43] Lydon et al. 2008. "If-then contingencies and the differential effects of the availability of an attractive alternative on relationship maintenance for men and women." *Journal of Personality and Social Psychology*, 95 (1): 50.

[44] Mead, Margaret. 1967. *Male and Female: A Study of the Sexes in a Changing World*. New York: William Morrow. p. 192.

[45] Zak, Paul J. April 25, 2010. "Five tests to determine if your partner will cheat." *Psychology Today*.com.

[46] Schlain, Leonard. 2006. *Finding Balance: Reconciling the Masculine/Feminine in Contemporary Art and Culture*. Austin: University of Texas.

[47] Lippa, R., Arad, S. 1999. Gender, personality, and prejudice: The Display of authoritarianism and social dominance in interviews with college men and women. *Journal of Research in Personality*, 33, 463-493. As found in Lippa, Richard A. Gender, Nature, and Nurture. p. 14.

[48] Staff. May/June 2008. *Psychology Today*. p 29.

[49] Buss, D.M. 2005. *The Murderer Next Door*. New York: Penquin Group.

[50] Fisher, Helen. 2004. *Why We Love: The Nature and Chemistry of Romantic Love*. New York: Henry, Holt, and Company. 176-8.

[51] Garner, D, "After atom bomb's shock, the real horrors began unfolding," *New York Times*, Jan 20, 2010.

[52] Ibid, p 177.

[53] Eagly, A.H., & Steffen, V.J. 1986. Gender and aggressive behavior: A meta-analytic review of the social psychological literature. Psychological Bulletin, 100, 309-330. As found in Lippa, Richard A. 2002. As found in Gender, Nature, and Nurture. New Jersey/London: Lawrence Erlbaum Associates. 13

[54] Feingold, A. 1994. Gender differences in personality: A meta-analysis. Psychological Bulletin, 116, 429-456. As found in Lippa, Richard A. 2002. Gender, Nature, and Nurture. New Jersey/London: Lawrence Erlbaum Associates. 13

[55] Gibbs, Nancy. Wednesday, Oct. 14, 2009. "What Women Want Now," *Time Magazine*.

[56] Sadker, Myra and David. 1994. *Failing at Fairness*. New York: Charles Scribner.

[57] Chapman, Anne. 1997. A great balancing act; Equitable education for girls and boys. Washington, D.C.: National Association of Independent Schools.

[58] University of Newcastle upon Tyne (2005, September 15). "Men Who Lose Social Status Much More Likely To Suffer Depression Than Women." ScienceDaily. Retrieved July 10, 2011, fr26e.

[59] Emory University. March 1, 2011. "Depressing future for men? Shift in employment balance between spouses a factor." ScienceDaily.com.

[60] Betzig, Laura. 1993. "Sex, succession, and stratification in the first six

civilizations: how powerful men reproduced, passed power on to their sons, and used power to defend their wealth, women, and children" in L. Ellis (ed.)., Social Stratification and Socioeconomic Inequality: A Comparative Biosocial Analysis, vol. 1, Westport, Conn., Praeger. As found in Baron-Cohen, Simon. The Essential Difference. 125

[61] Eichler, Alexander. 7/7/11. "Fortune Global 500 Now Richer, More International, But With Same Number Of Female CEOs." *The Huffington Post*

[62] Ogas, Ogi, & Gaddam, Sai. 2011. *A Billion Wicked Thoughts*. New York: Penguin Group.

[63] Zak, Paul. December 16, 2009. "Testosterone's Effect On Giving." Center for Neuroeconomics Studies determines Testosterone affects Generosity. Claremont Graduate School online site.

[64] Chagnon, N.A. 1979. "Is reproductive success equal in egalitarian societies?" in N.A. Chagnon, and W. Irons (eds.), Evolutionary Biology and Human social Behavior: An Anthropological Perspective, North Scituate, Mass., Duxbury Press. As found in Baron-Cohen, Simon. The Essential Difference. 124.

[65] Babiak, Paul and Hare, Robert. 2006. *Snakes in Suits: When Psychopaths Go To Work*. New York: HarperCollins.

[66] Ron, Jon. The Psychopath Test: A Journey Through the Madness Industry

[67] Gibbs, Nancy. May 30, 2011. "Men Behaving Badly: What is it about Power that Makes men Crazy?" *Time*. 26-30.

[68] Sun, Feifei. May 30, 2011. "The Misconduct Matrix." *Time*. 29.

[69] Willingham, W.W. and Cole, N.S. 1997. Gender Fair Assessment, Hillsdale, NJ, Erlbaum. 16

[70] De Waal, F. 1993 "Sex differences in Chimpanzee (and human) behavior: a matter of social values?" in M. Hechter, L. Nadel and R. E. Michod (eds.), The Origin of Values, New York, Aldine de Gruyter, pp. 285-303.

[71] Brizendine, Louan. *The Male Brain*. 2010. New York: Three Rivers Press. Xv, xvi

[72] Ibid. 32

[73] Oliver, M.D., & Hyde, J.S. 1993. Gender Differences in Sexuality: A Meta-Analysis. *Psychological Bulletin*, 114, 29-51. As found in Lippa, Richard A. Gender, Nature and Nurture, 21.

[74] Feingold, A., 1990. "Gender differences in effects of physical attractiveness on romantic attraction: A comparison across five research

paradigms. *Journal of Personality and Social Psychology*, 49. 981.93. In Lippa, Richard A. *Gender, Nature, and Nurture*. 23.

[75] Buss, D.M., & Schmitt, D.P. 1993. Sexual Strategies Theory: A Evolutionary Perspective on Human Mating. *Psychological Review*, 100. 204-232. As found in Lippa, Richard A. Gender, Nature, and Nurture. 23.

[76] Roscoe Diana, & Brooks, R. H. 1987. Early, Middle, and Late Adolescents' View of Dating and Factors Influencing Partner Selection. *Adolescence*, 22, 59-68. As found in Lippa, Richard A. Gender, Nature and Nurture. 218.

[77] Lippa, Richard A. 2002. *Gender, Nature, and Nurture*. New Jersey/London: Lawrence Erlbaum Associates. 122

[78] Schmitt, D. P., T. K. Shackelford, et al. (2001). "The desire for sexual variety as a key to understanding basic human mating strategies." *Personal Relationships*, Special Issue: Evolutionary approaches to relationships 8 (4): 283-300.

[79] Harley, Jr., Willard F. *His Needs, Her Needs*. Grand Rapids, Michigan: Fleming H. Revell. 10.

[80] Fisher, Helen. *Why we love: The nature and chemistry of romantic love*. p 201.

[81] Ibid, p 211.

[82] Ibid, p 212.

[83] Duran, J., Esnaola, R., & Iztueta, A. (2001). "Obstructive sleep apnea-hypopnea and related clinical features in a population-based sample of subjects ages 30 to 70 years." *American Journal of Respiratory and Critical Care Medicine*, 163, 685-689.

[84] Urban, Nina, Kegeles, L., Slifstein, M., Xu, X., Martinez, D. et al. (2010). "Sex difference in striatal dopamine release in young adults after an oral alcohol challenge: A positron emission tomography imaging study with raclopride." *Biological Psychiatry*, 68, 689-696.

[85] AARP. May 2004. "The Divorce Experience: A Study of Divorce at Midlife and Beyond." The Full Report.

[86] Tarter, R., Kirisci, L., Kirillova, G., Gavaler, J., Giancola, P., & Vanyukov, M. 2007. "Social dominance mediates the association of testosterone and neurobehavioral disinhibition with risk for substance use disorder." *Psychology of Addictive Behaviors*, 21, 462-468.

[87] Dabbs, J. M., Jr., & Ruback, R. (1988). Saliva testosterone and personality of male college students. *Bulletin of Psychometric Sociology*, 26, 244 — 247.

Goudriaan, A. E., Lapauw, B., Ruige, J., Feyen, E., Kaufman, J. et al. 2010. "The influence of high-normal testosterone levels on risk-taking in healthy males in a 1-week letrozole administration study." *Psychoneuroendocrinology*, 35, 1416-1421. And

Kirillova, G. P., Vanyukov, M. M., Gavaler, J., Pajer, K., Dunn, M., & Tarter, R. 2001. "Substance abuse in parents and their offspring: The role of sexual maturation and sensation seeking." *Journal of Child and Adolescent Substance Abuse*, 10, 77– 89.

[88] Caine, Janel. 1991. "The Effects of Music on the Selected Stress Behaviors, Weight, Caloric and Formula Intake, and Length of Hospital Stay of Premature and Low Birth Weight Neonates in a Newborn Intensive Care Unit," *Journal of Music Therapy*, 28: 180-91, 1991. As found in Sax, Leonard. Why Gender Matters. 16

[89] Dr Leonard Sax in an interview with Al Roker on the Today Show. 2/15/2005. See genderdifferences.org.

[90] Cone-Wesson, Barbara, & Ramirez, Glendy. 1997. "Hearing Sensitivity in Newborns Estimated from ABRs to Bone-Conducted Sounds," *Journal of the American Academy of Audiology*, 8:299-307 and Sininger, Yvonne, Cone-Wesson, Barbara, & Abdala, Carolina. 1998. "Gender Districtions and Lateral Asymmetry in the Low-Level Auditory Brainstem Response of the Human Neonate." Hearing Research. 126:58-66. Referenced by Sax, Leonard. Why Gender Matters. 17

[91] Brizendine, Louanne. 2006. *The Female Mind*. New York: Doubleday Broadway Publishing Group. 5

[92] Storey, A. E., C. J. Walsh, et al. (2000) "Hormonal correlates of paternal responsiveness in new and expectant fathers." *Evol Hum Behav* 21 (2): 79-95.

[93] Cheng, Y., Tzeng, O.J., Decety, J., & Hsieh, J.C. (2006). Gender differences in the human mirror system: a magnetoencephalography study. *NeuroReport*, 17, 1115-1119. Cheng, Y., Decety, J., Hsieh, J.C., Hung, D., & Tzeng, O.J. (2007). Gender differences in spinal excitability during observation of bipedal locomotion. *NeuroReport*, 18, 887-890. Cheng, Y., Decety, J., Yang, C.Y., Lee, S., & Chen, G. (2008). Gender differences in the Mu rhythm during empathy for pain: An electroencephalographic study. Brain Research, in press. Cheng, Y., Lee, P., Yang, C.Y., Lin, C.P., & Decety, J. (2008). Gender differences in the mu rhythm of the human mirror-neuron system. PLoS ONE, 5, e2113.

[94] Maccoby, E., and C. Jacklin. 1974. *The psychology of sex differences*. Stanford, California: Stanford University Press. Hoffman, Martin L.

19977. "Sex differences in empathy and related behaviors." Psychological Bulletin 84 (4): 712-22. Brody, Leslie R., and Judith A. Hall. 1993. "Gender and emotion." *In Handbook of Emotions*, edited by Michael Lewis and Jeannette Haviland. New York: Guilford Press. As found in Fisher, Helen, *The First Sex*. 120-1.

[95] Maccoby, E., and C. Jacklin. 1974. *The psychology of sex differences*. Stanford, California: Stanford University Press. As found in Fisher, Helen, the first sex p 121.

[96] Goleman, Daniel. 1995. *Emotional Intelligence*. New York: Bantam Dell. 132.

[97] Fitzpatrick, Laura. Friday, Sept. 25, 2009, *Time Magazine* online. 6 Pardo, J.V., P. J. Pardo, and M.E. Raichle. 1993. "Neural correlates of self-induced dysphoria." *American Journal of Psychiatry*. 150:713-9. Tucker, D.M., P. Luu, and K.H. Pribram. 1995. "Social and emotional self-regulation." In "Structure and functions of the human prefrontal cortex," edited by J. Grafman, K.

[98] J. Holyoak, and F. Boller. Annals of the New York Academy of Sciences. 769:191-211. George, M., T. A. Ketter, P. I. Parekh, P. Herscovitch, and R. M. Post. 1996. "Gender differences in regional cerebral blood flow during transient self-induced sadness or happiness." *Biological Psychiatry* 40(9): 859-71. As found in Fisher, Helen. *The First Sex*. 119.

[99] Krakovsky, Marina. Nov/Dec 2006. "Novel Delights." *Psychology Today*, 51.

[100] Eckholm, E. May 20 1998. "Homes for elderly replacing family care as China grays," *New York Times*. Found in Fisher, Helen, *The First Sex*, p 287.

[101] Ellison, Katherine, 2005. New York: Basic Books. *The Mommy Brain: How Motherhood Makes us Smarter*, 43.

[102] Ibid,, p 17. Dissecting late-pregnant rats reveals a complex "remapping of neural pathways in the hippocampus, the center for learning and memory." The brain slowly manufacturing new neurons, perhaps resulting in brain shrinkage, but the nerve cells in the hippocampus had sprouted more spines. 17

[103] Ibid, p 18.

[104] Ibid, p 18. Kinsley and Lambert found that "neural activity brought about by pregnancy and the presence of pups may literally reshape the brain, fashioning a more complex organ that can accommodate an increasingly demanding environment".

[105] Hartup, W.W., French, D.C., Laursen, B., Johnston, M.D. and Ogawa, J.R. 1993. "Conflict and friendship relations in middle childhood: behavior in a closed-field situation," *Child Development* 64, pp 445-54. As found in Baron-Cohen, Simon. Essential Differences. 50.
[106] Brizendine, Louann, M.D. *The Male Brain.*
[107] Goleman, Daniel. *Emotional Intelligence.* 133. see reference number 10
[109] Regnerus, Mark, and Uecker, Jeremy. 2011. *Premarital Sex in America: How Young Americans Meet, Mate, and Think about Marrying.* New York: Oxford University Press. 201
Ibid 122
[110] *Mismatch.* 116
[111] Wallerstein, Judith S, and Blakeslee, Sandra. 1995. *The Good Marriage.* Boston, New York: Houghton Mifflin Company.
[112] Zak, Paul J., Kurzban, Robert, Ahmadi, Sheila, Swerdloff, Ronald S, Park, Jang, Efremidze, Levan, Redwine, Karen, Morgan, Karla, and Matzner, William. December 16, 2009. "Testosterone administration decreases generosity in the ultimatum game." *PLoS One.* 4(12): e8330, online.
[113] George, M., T. A. Ketter, P.I. Parekh, P. Herscovitch, and R. M. Post. 1996. "Gender differences in regional cerebral blood flow during transient self-induced sadness or happiness." *Biological Psychiatry* 40 (9): 859-71.
[114] Schulz, Mona Lisa, and Northrup, Christiane. 2005. *The New Feminine Brain: Developing Your Intuitive Genius.* New York: Simon and Schuster, p 33.
[115] Shlain, Leonard. 2004. *Sex, Time, and Power: How Women's Sexuality Shaped Human Evolution.* New York: Viking Penguin, p. 273.
[116] Baron-Cohen, Simon, *The Essential Difference: The Truth About the Male and Female Brain.* 2003. New York: Basic Books.
[117] BBC News online. Thursday, 18 March, 2004. "Men in touch with feminine side."
[118] Lippa, Richard A. 2002. *Gender, Nature, and Nurture.* New Jersey: Lawrence Erlbaum Associates. 66
[119] Baron-Cohen, Simon *The Essential Difference.*
[120] BBC News online. Thursday, 18 March, 2004. "Men in touch with feminine side."
[121] Baron-Cohen. P 5.
[122] Baron-Cohen, Simon. August 8, 2005. "The Male Condition," *New*

York Times online

123 Brizendine, Louann. 2010. *The Male Brain*. New York: Three Rivers Press.

124 Weinberg, M. K. T., Z. Edward, J. F. Cohn, and K. L. Olson. 1999. "Gender differences in emotional expressivity and self-regulation during early infancy." *Developmental Psychology* 35 (1): 175-88. As found in The Male Brain. 11.

125 Connellan, J., Baron-Cohen, S., Wheelwright, S., B'tke, A. and Ahluwalia, J. 2001. "Sex differences in human neonatal social perception." Infant Behavior and Development 23, pp. 113-8. As found in Baron-Cohen, Simon. *The Essential Difference*. 55

126 Hoehl, S., and T. Striano. 2008. "Neural processing of eye gaze and threat-related emotional facial expressions in infancy." *Child Dev* 79 (6): 1752-60.

127 Kaplan, Ehud and Benardete, Ethan. 2001. "The Dynamics of Primate Retinal Ganglion Cells," *Progress in Grain Research*, 134:17-34.

128 Zahn-Waxler, C., M. Radke-Yarrow, E. Wagner, and M. Chapman (1992). "Development of concern for others." *Developmental Psychology* 28: 126-36.

129 Hoffman. 1977; Zahn-Waxler, Radke-Yarrow, Wagner et al. 1992. Hoffman, M. L. 1977. "Sex differences in empathy and related behaviors," *Psychological Bulletin* 84. 712-22. Zahn-Waxler, C., Radke-Yarrow, M., Wagner, E. and Chapman, M. 1992. "Development of concern for others." *Developmental Psychology* 28. 126-36. As found in Baron-Cohen, *The Essential Difference*.

130 Peltola, M.J., J.M. Leppanen, Et al. (2009). "Emergence of enhanced attention to fearful faces between 5 and 7 months of age." *Soc Cogn Affect Neurosci* 4 (2) 134-42.

131 Lutchmaya, S. and Baron-Cohen, S. 2002. "Human sex differences n social and non-social looking preferences at 12 months of age." *Infant Behavior and Development*. 25 (3) 319-25.

132 Serbin, Lisa and associates. 2001. "Gender Stereotyping in Infancy: Visual preferences for and knowledge of gender-stereotyped toys in the second year." *International Journal of Behavioral Development*. 25:7-15. As found in Sax, Leonard, *Why Gender Matters*. 27.

133 www.genderdifferences.org/playfighting.htm as found in Sax, Leonard. Why Gender Matters.

134 Meaney, Michael and Beatty, William. "Sex Dependent Effects of Amygdalar Lesions on the Social Play of Prepubertal Rats." *Physiology*

and Behavior. 26:467-72. 1981. As found in Sax, Leonard. *Why Gender Matters*.

[135] Alexander, Gerianne and Hines, Melissa. 2002. "Sex differences in response to children's toys in nonhuman primates." *Evolution & Human Behavior*. 23:467-79. As found in Sax, Leonard. *Why Gender Matters*.

[136] Collins-Stanley, Tracy; Gan, Su-lin; Hsin-Ju, Jessy; and Zillman, Dolf. 1996. "Choice of Romantic, Violent, and Scary Fairy-Tale Books by preschool girls and boys." *Child Study Journal*. 26 (4) 279-302. As found in Sax, Leonard. *Why Gender Matters*. 58-9.

[137] Maccoby 1998.

[138] Hassett, J.M., E.R. Siebert, Et al. (2008). "Sex differences in rhesus monkey toy preferences parallel those of children." *Horm Behav* 54 (3): 359:64.

[139] Collins-Stanley, Tracy; Gan, Su-lin; Hsin-Ju, Jessy; and Zillman, Dolf. 1996. "Choice of Romantic, Violent, and Scary Fairy-Tale Books by preschool girls and boys." *Child Study Journal*. 26 (4) 279-302. As found in Sax, Leonard. *Why Gender Matters*. 58-9.

[140] Maccoby. 1998.

[141] Sax, Leonard. "Girls' Friendships have distinct values and exhibit different dynamics compared with boys' friendships," *Why Gender Matters*. 84

[142] Perry, David; Perry, Louise; and Weiss, Robert. 1989. "Sex differences in the consequences that children anticipate for aggression." *Developmental Psychology*, 25 (2) 312-19. As found in *Why Gender Matters*. 59

[143] Baron-Cohen, O'Riordan, Jones et al. 1999; Bosacki. 1998. As found in Baron-Cohen, *The Essential Difference*. 31-2.
Baron-Cohen, S., Richler, J., Bisarya, D., Gurunathan, N. and Wheelwright, S. 2003. "Recognition of faux pas by normally developing children and children with Asperger Syndrome or high-functioning autism." *Journal of Autism and Developmental Disorders* 29. 407-18. Bosacki, S. (unpublished Ph.D. dissertation), "Theory of mind in preadolescents: relationships among social understanding, self-concept and social relations," University of Toronto.

[144] Hall, Judith. 1984. *Nonverbal sex differences: communication accuracy and expressive style*. Baltimore, MD: John Hopkins University Press. 142. As found in Lippa, Richard A. Gender, Nature, and Nurture. 20.

[145] Lindenfors, P., C. L. Nunn, et al. (2007). "Primate brain architecture and selection in relation to sex." *BMC Biol* 5:20. as quoted in *The Male Brain*. Dunbar, R.I. (2007). "Male and female brain evolution is subject to contrasting selection pressures in primates." *BMC Biol* 5:21. as quoted in *The Male Brain*.

[146] Cahill, L., L. Gorski, et al. (2004) "Sex-related hemispheric lateralization of amygdala function in emotionally influenced memory: An FMRI investigation." Learn Mem 11(3): 261-66.

[147] Canli, T., J.E. Desmond, et al. (2002). "Sex differences in the neural basis of emotional memories." *Proc Natl Acad Sci* U S A 99(16): 10789-94.

[148] Dindia, K., & Allen, M.. 1992. Sex differences in self-disclosure: a meta-analysis. *Psychological Bulletin*, 112, 106-124. Zeman, J., & Garber, J. 1996. Display rules for anger, sadness, and pain: It depends on who is watching. *Child Development*, 67, 957. As found in *Gender, Nature and Nurture*. 28.

[149] Zeman & Garner, 1996.

[150] Clark, M., & Reis, H. 1988. Interpersonal processes in close relationships. *Annual Review of Psychology*, 39, 609-672. As found in *Gender, Nature, and Nurture* by Richard A Lippa. 28.

[151] Van Vugt, Mark; Iredale, Wendy. 2012. "Men behaving nicely: Public goods as peacock tails. *British Journal of Psychology*, DOI: 10.111

[152] Gray, John. *What Your Mother Couldn't Tell You and Your Father Didn't Know: Advanced Relationship Skills for Better Communication and Lasting Intimacy*. p 259

[153] Sheehy, Gail. *Sex and the Seasoned Woman*.

[154] de Waal, Frans, Ph.D. February 21, 2010. "Men like power more than they admit: Men and male chimpanzees are very much into power." *Psychology Today*.

[155] Savin-Williams 1987.
Savin-Williams, Ritch. 1987. *Adolescence: An Ethological Perspective*. New York: Springer-Verlag. As found in The Essential Difference. 38

[156] Weinberg, M. K. T., Z. Edward, J. F. Cohn, and K. L. Olson. 1999. "Gender differences in emotional expressivity and self-regulation during early infancy." *Developmental Psychology* 35 (1): 175-88. As found in *The Male Brain*. 11.

[157] Maccoby, E.E., ed. (1998). *The Two Sexes and Their Social Systems*. Washington, DC: American Psychological Association.

[158] Lever, J. (1976). "Sex differences in games children play." *Social Problems* 23:478-87.

[159] Maccoby, E.E., ed. (1998). *The Two Sexes and Their Social Systems.* Washington, DC: American Psychological Association.

[160] Baron-Cohen, Simon. *The Essential Difference.* 91. See also Perry, D.G. White, A.J. and Perry, L.D. 1984 "Does early sex typing result from children's attempts to match their behavior to sex role stereotypes?" *Child Development* 55, pp 2114-21.

[161] Daly, M. and Wilson, M. 1983. *Sex, Evolution and Behavior.* Boston: Willard Grant Press. As found in The Essential Difference. 70, 93.

[162] *The Essential Difference.* 71

[163] *The Essential Difference.* 73

[164] Macoby, E.E., Snow, M.E. and Jacklin, C.N. 1984. "Children's dispositions and mother-child interaction at 12 and 18 months: a short-term longitudinal study," *Developmental Psychology* 20, pp 459-72.

[165] Brizendine, Louann. 2006. *The Female Brain.* New York: Morgan Road Books.

[166] Hughes, C. and Cutting, A. 1999. "Nature, nurture, and individual differences in early understanding of mind." *Psychological Science.* 10. pp 429-33. As found in The Essential Difference.

[167] Killgore, William, Oki, Mika, and Yugelun-Todd, Deborah. 2001. "Sex Specific Developmental Changes in Amygdala Responses to Affective Faces." *NeuroReport* 12:427-33. and Schneider, Frank, Habel, Ute, and associates. 2000. "Gender Differences in Regional Cerebral Activity During Sadness." *Human Brain Mapping.* 9:226-38. Both as found in *Why Gender Matters.* 29

[168] Symons, Donald. 219. *The Evolution of Human Sexuality.* New York: Oxford University Press.

[169] Roscoe, B., Diana, M.S., & Brooks, R. H.. 1987. Early, Middle, and late adolescents; view on dating and factors influencing partner selection. *Adolescence,* 22, 59-68. As found in *Gender, Nature, and Nurture* by Richard A Lippa 218.

[170] AARP 2004.

[171] *Mismatch* 12

[172] Hare-Mustin, Rachel T., "Sex, Lies, and Headaches," *Journal of Feminist Family Therapy* Vol. 3, Iss. 1-2, 2008.

[173] Lippa, Richard A. *Gender, Nature, and Nurture.*

[174] Lever, Janet. "Sex Differences in the Games Children Play," *Social Problems,* 23:478-87, 1976, and "Sex differences in the Complexity of

Children's Games, "American Sociological Review, 43:471-83, 1978 as found in Sax, Leonard, M.D., Ph.D., *Why Gender Matters*, 58.

175 Fowlkes, M.R. 1994. Single worlds and homosexual lifestyles: Patterns of sexuality and intimacy. In *Sexuality Across The Life Course*, ed. A. S. Rossi. Chicago: University of Chicago Press. And Tannen, D., 1994. Talking from 9 to 5. New York: William Morrow.

176 Fisher, Helen. 1999. *The First Sex: The Natural Talents of Women and How They Are Changing the World*. New York: Random House. And Travis, C. 1992. *The Mismeasure of Woman*. New York: Simon and Schuster, pp 15-25.

177 Travis, C. 1992.

178 Gore, Al and Tipper. 2003. *Joined at the Heart*. New York: Henry Holt and Company.

179 Niedenthal, P.M., Kruth-Gruber, S., & Ric, F. (2006). *Psychology and emotion. (Principles of Social Psychology series)*. ISBN 1-84169-402-9. New York: Psychology Press.

180 Sax, Leonard, M.D., Ph. D.. *Why Gender Matters*, 35.

181 Crawford, M., and D. Marsh. 1989. *The Driving Force*. London: Heinemann. 157. As found in Sex, Time and Power. 252

182 Halpern, D. F. 2000. *Sex differences in cognitive abilities*. (3rd edition). Hillsdale, NJ: Erlbaum.

183 Van Goozen, S.H. M., Cohen-Ketenis, P. T., Gooren, L. J. G., Frijda, N. H., & van De Poll, N. E. 1995. Activating effects of androgens on cognitive performance: Causal evidence in a group of female-to-male transsexuals. As found in *Gender, Nature, and Nurture* by Richard A Lippa. 111.

184 Sax, Leonard, M.D., Ph.D. *Why Gender Matters*. 29.

185 Maccoby, Ellen. 1990. "Gender and relationships: a developmental account." *American Psychologist*. 45. pp 513-20.

186 Crombie, G. and Desjardins, M.J. 1993. "Predictors of gender: the relative importance of children's play, games and personality characteristics." New Orleans, conference paper, Society for Research in Child Development (SRCD.) As found in Baron-Cohen, Simon. *The Essential Difference*.

187 Hill, Jacqueline, Wheelwright, Sally, Golan, Ofer, and Baron-Cohen, Simon. . 2003. *Mind Reading: the interactive guide to emotions*. Cambridge University.

188 Mannle, S. and Tomasello, M. 1987. "Fathers, siblings, and the bridge hypothesis" in K. A. Nelson and A van Kleek (editors),

Children's Language. Hillsdale, N. J., Erlbaum.

[189] David, Mark H., and Oathout, H. Alan. 1987. "Maintenance of Satisfaction In Romantic Relationships: Empathy and Relational Competence." *Journal of Personality and Social Psychology*. 53, 2, pp 397-410. As found in Emotional Intelligence. 132.

[190] The study of husbands' and wives' complaints: Robert J. Sternberg, "Triangulating Love," in Robert Sternberg and Michael Barnes, eds., *The Psychology of Love*. New Haven: Yale University Press, 1988. "

[191] Leaper, C. 1991. "Influence and involvement in children's discourage: age, gender, and partner effects." *Child Development*. 62. pp 797-811, and Maccoby, E.E. 1998. *The Two Sexes: Growing Apart, Coming Together*. Cambridge, Mass., Harvard University Press.

[192] Baron-Cohen, Simon. *Essential Differences*. 48

[193] Campbell, A. 1995. "A few good men: evolutionary psychology and female adolescent aggression." *Ethology and Sociobiology*. 16, pp. 99-123. As found in Baron-Cohen, Simon. *Essential Differences*.

[194] Happe, F. and Frith, U. 1996. "Theory of mind and social impairment in children with conduct disorder." *British Journal of Developmental Psychology* 14, pp 385-98. As found in Baron-Cohen, Simon. Essential Differences. 31.

[195] Hartup, W.W., French, D.C., Laursen, B., Johnston, M.D. and Ogawa, J.R. 1993. "Conflict and friendship relations I middle childhood: behavior in a closed-field situation." *Child Development*. 64. pp. 445-54.

[196] Lippa, Richard A. *Gender, Nature, and Nurture*. 28.

[197] Levenson, Robert et al. "Husbands dislike squabbles: The Influence of Age and Gender on Affect, Physiology, and Their Interrelations: A Study of Long-term Marriages," *Journal of Personality and Social Psychology* 67 (1994.)

[198] April 1, 2008. "Men are from Mars: Neuroscientists find that men and women respond differently to stress." *Science Daily*. The information was originally produced for the American Institute of Physics series Discoveries and Breakthroughs in Science by Ivanhoe Broadcast News.

[199] Zak PJ (2008) The neurobiology of trust. *Sci Am* 298: 88—95.

[200] Gottman, John. What Predicts Divorce. As found in Goleman, Daniel. Emotional Br

[201] Gottman, John. *Why Marriages Succeed or Fail*

[202] Husbands dislike squabbles: Robert Levenson et al., "The Influence of Age and Gender on Affect, Physiology, and Their Interrelations:

A Study of Long-term Marriages," *Journal of Personality and Social Psychology* 67 (1994.)

[203] Real, Terrence. *"The Awful Truth."*

[204] Baron-Cohen, Simon. *Essential Differences.* 87

[205] Baron-Cohen, Simon. *Essential Differences.* 88

[206] Real, Terrence. *The Awful Truth.*

[207] Woodman, Marion. "Conscious Femininity." A keynote speech delivered at the 3rd Annual Women and Power Conference organized by Omega Institute and V-Day. September 2004. Found at the website Feminist.com.

[208] Mlot, C. 1998. "Probing the biology of emotion." *Science* 280:1005-1007.

[209] Walsch, Donald Neale. *Conversations with God.* Book I. P 3.

[210] Andrew Hacker in *Mismatch: The Growing Gulf Between Women and Men.* (2007). 13

[211] Harrison, A.A., and L. Saeed. 1977. Let's make a deal: An analysis of revelations and stipulations in lonely hearts advertisements. *Journal of Personality and Social Psychology* 35:275-64.

[212] "American Journal of Psychological Research'" Internet Dating Ads: Sex, Ethinicity, Age-Related Differences, and Support for Evolutionary Theory; Carl A Bartling, et al.; Jan. 5, 2005 (PDF)

[213] Sprecher, S. A. Aron, E. Hatfield, A. Cortese, E. Potapove, and A. Levitskaya. 1994. Love: American style, Russian style, and Japanese style. *Personal Relationships* I:349-69.

[214] Pines, A. M. 1999. *Falling in Love: Why We Choose the Lovers We Choose.* New York: Routledge. As found in Fisher, Helen. *Why we love The nature and chemistry of romantic love.* 103

[215] Brizendine, Louann. *The Male Brain.* P 35.

[216] National Center of Education Statistics, National Council on Education 2009.

[217] Hacker, *Mismatch.*

[218] Morella, Carol and Keating, Dan. Thursday October 7, 2010. More U.S. women pull down big Bucks, *Washington Post.*

[219] Sax, Leonard, M.D.., Ph.D. 2/2/05. "Are Boys and Girls Hardwired Differently?" From the *Today Show*, MSNBC.com.

[220] Mychtwaldm, Maddy. 2010. Influence. Hyperion, New York 2010, p 7. and Luscombe, Belinda, "Woman Power: The Rise of the Sheconomy," *Time Magazine*, Monday, Nov. 22, 2010.

[221] Agostino, Raeleen. March 01, 2008. "Global Psyche: Forever

Mamma's Boy." *Psychology Today*. P 28.

222 Sax, Leonard. Friday, March 31, 2006. "What's happening to Boys? Young Women These Days are Driven—but Guys Lack Direction." *The Washington Post*.

223 Dougherty, Conor. Young Women's Pay Exceeds Male Peers. *The Walls Street Journal*, September 01, 2010.

224 Bureau of Labor Statistics. Women's earnings and employment by industry, 2009. Chart data, February 16, 2011

225 Gibbs, Nancy. Wednesday Oct. 14, 2009. "What Women Want Now." *Time Magazine*.

226 Anita, Raghavan. 4-1-2008. "Men Receiving Alimony Want a Little Respect." *The Wall Street Journal*.

227 Joanne, Lipman. 10-24-2009. "The Mismeasure of Women." *The Wall Street Journal*.

228 Huang, 1986; Lamb, Frodi, Frodi, & Huang, 1982) p 219 *Gender, Nature, and Nurture* by Richard A Lippa

229 Manohar, Rathi. July 23, 2010. "Mother's Heart in Sync With Unborn Baby's." *Research News*. Found on Med India online.

230 Baron-Cohen, Simon. *Essential Differences*. 54

231 Ibid, 54

232 Maccoby, E.E., & Mnookin, R. H. 1992. *Dividing the child: The social and legal dilemmas of custody*. Cambridge, MA: Harvard University Press.

233 Bronstein, P. 1988. Father-child interaction: Implciations for gender-role socialization. In P. Bronstein & C. P. Cowan (Eds.). *Fatherhood today: Men's changing role in the family.* (pp. 107-124). New York: Wiley.

234 Storey, A. E., C. J. Walsh, et al. (2000) "Hormonal correlates of paternal responsiveness in new and expectant fathers." *Evol Hum Behav* 21 (2): 79-95.

235 Muller, M.D., and F. W. Marlowe, et al. (2009). "Testosterone and paternal care in East African foragers and pastoralists." *Proc boil sci* 276 (1655): 347-54.

236 National Commission on Children. 1991. "Speaking of Kids: A National Survey of Children and Parents."

237 Garfinkel, Irvin. July 11, 1998. *New York Times*.

238 (Bronstein, 1988) 219 *Gender, Nature, and Nurture* by Richard A Lippa.

239 Campbell, Anne. (1995), "A few good men: evolutionary psychol

ogy and female adolescent aggression," *Ethology and Sociobiology* 16, pp. 99-123.

[240] Baron-Cohen, Simon. *Essential Differences*. 48.

[241] Yeung, W. Jean. Feb. 2001. "Children's Time with Fathers in Intact Families." *Journal of Marriage and the Family*.

[242] Stern, Daniel N. 1985. *The Interpersonal World of the Infant a View from Psychoanalysis and developmental Psychology*. New York: Basic Books.

[243] Siegel, Daniel and Hartzell, Mary. 2003. *Parenting from the Inside Out*. New York: Penguin Group.

[244] Whealin, J. & Barnett, E. (2009). U.S. Department of Veterans Affairs. Child Sexual Abuse. Retrieved from ttp://www.ptsd.va.gov/professional/pages/child_sexual_abuse.asp

[245] LaFontaine, Jean. 1990. *Child Sexual Abuse*. Polity Press.

[246] Renvoize, Jean. 1993. *Innocence Destroyed: A Study of Child Sexual Abuse*. Routledge.

[247] Fisher, Helen. *The First Sex*. 85-6.

[248] Gartrell, Nanette and Bos, Henry. Pediatrics. Using information coming from the U.S. National Longitudinal Lesbian Family Study. As found in Park, Alice. Monday, June 07, 2010. "Study: Children of Lesbians May Do Better Than Their Peers." *Time Magazine*

[249] Ventura SJ. Changing patterns of nonmarital childbearing in the United States. NCHS data brief, no 18. Hyattsville, MD: National Center for Health Statistics. 2009.

[250] European Commission. Eurostat Live births outside marriage. Accessed March 11, 2009.

[251] Furstenberg, Frank. July 11, 1998. *New York Times*. As found in Hacker, Andrew. Mismatch. 56.

[252] Johnson, Paul. The Birth of the Modern: World Society 1815-1830, 479. As found in Schlain, Leonard. *The Alphabet and the Goddess*.

[253] Hackman. *Mismatch*. 45

[254] Ibid, 47-8

[255] Baumeister, R. F., & Sommer, K.L. 1997. "What do men want? Gender differences and the two spheres of belongingness. *Psychological Bulletin*, 122, 38-44. As found in Lippa, Richard A. Gender, Nature and Nurture. 29-30.

[256] Lippa, Richard A. *Gender, Nature, and Nurture*. 30-2

[257] Baron-Cohen, Simon. *Essential Differences*. 46

[258] Lippa, *Gender, Nature, and Nurture*. 31

259 Ibid, 28

260 Ibid, 220.

261 Maccoby, 1998

262 Baron-Cohen, Simon. *Essential Differences*. 43-7.

263 Betsey Stevenson & Justin Wolfers, 2009. "The Paradox of Declining Female Happiness," *American Economic Journal*: Economic Policy, American Economic Association, vol. 1(2), pages 190-225, August.

264 Lerner, Sharon, 2010. *The War on Moms: On Life in a Family-Unfriendly Nation*. New Jersey: John Wiley & Sons.

265 "Gender Differences in Voter Turnout," Center for American Women and Politics, November 2011

266 Rubin, Gretchen. 2009. New York: HarperCollins. *The Happiness Project: Or, Why I Spent a Year Trying to Sing in the Morning, Clean My Closets, Fight Right, Read Aristotle, and Generally Have More Fun.*

267 Bailey, Ronald. February 26, 2008. "Why are People Having Fewer Kids?" *Reasononline*.

268 Schulz, Mona Lisa, M.D., Ph.D. *The New Feminine Brain.*

269 Cutrona, C. E. (1982). Transition to college: Loneliness and the process of social adjustment. In L. A. Peplau & D. Perlman (Eds.), *Loneliness: A sourcebook of current theory, research, and therapy* (pp. 291-309). New York: John Wiley & Sons.

270 Lerner, Gerda. "The Necessity of History." *Why History Matters: Life and Thought*. New York: Oxford UP, 1997. 113-128. As found in Geller, Jaclyn. "Why the History of Marriage Matters. P 37. Edited by DePaulo, Bella. 2011. *Singlism: What it is, why it matters, and how to stop it*. US: DoubleDoor Books.

271 DePaulo, Bella. 2001. "Emotional Independence." *Singlism: What it is, why it matters, and how to stop it*. US: DoubleDoor Books. 255.

272 Cayce, Edgar, *Soul Mates*, p 133.

273 *The Mother-Daughter Book Club*: How Ten busy mothers and daughters came together to talk, laugh and learn through their love of reading says it all and opens a door for fulfilling times. 44b (HarperCollins)

274 "Friendships between Women Good for Health" by Gale Berkowitz, September 2003, Sisyphe.org (online), September 28, 2003.

275 Healy, Melissa. June 15, 2005. "Science confirms that women reap health benefits from friendships." The *Seattle Times* online. Originally published in *Los Angeles Times*.

276 Healy, Melissa. May 09, 2005. "Our innate need for friendship."

Times staff writer, *Los Angeles Times*.

277 Rather, Tom. August 1, 2006. *Vital Friends: The People You Can't Afford to Live Without*. Gallup Press.

278 Hacker, Andrew. *Mismatch*. 144.

279 M. Armstrong, M. Pettigrew, S. Trow, *The Burning Times* series: *Women and spirituality* series; 2 National Film Board of Canada. Studio D. Los Angeles, Calif. : Direct Cinema Ltd., 1990. 1 video cassette (58 min.) : sd., col. ; 1/2 in. ISBN 1-55974-330-1.

280 Dworkin, *Woman Hating: A Radical Look at Sexuality* New York: Feminist Press, 1973.

281 Gladwell, Malcolm. 2005. Blink: *The Power of Thinking Without Thinking*. New York: Little, Brown, and Company, 88-91.

282 Sax, Leonard, M.D., Ph.D. *Why Gender Matters*. 46.

283 Backlash, Faludi, Susan, New York: Crown Publishers, Inc., 1991, p 91. The Newsweek Research Report on Women Who Work: A National Survey (Princeton, N.J.: Mathematica Policy Research, 1984), p. 32, and The 1990 Virginia Slims Opinion Poll, pp. 79-81.)

284 Shankar, Vedantam. Salary, Gender and the Social Cost of Haggling. *The Washington Post*, July 30, 2007. Clark-Flory, Tracy. The costs of asking for a higher salary. Salon, Jul 30, 2007. Montell, Gabriela. Damned if They Do. *The Chronicle of Higher Education*, July 31, 2007. Bowles, Hannah Riley, Linda Babcock, Lei Lai (2007). Social incentives for gender differences in the propensity to initiate negotiations: Sometimes it does hurt to ask. Organizational Behavior and Human Decision Processes, Vol. 103, pp. 84—103.

285 Weber, Tim, Business editor. "Why companies need female managers. *BBC News* website. Saturday 26 January, 2008. Interview with Helen Fisher.

286 Luscombe, Belinda. Monday, Nov. 22, 2010. "Woman Power: The Rise of the Sheconomy." *Time Magazine* US online.

287 The Oprah Winfrey Show. October 21, 2009. "Women Around the World." | Oprah.com.

288 Wagner, Sally Roesch (1999). "Iroquois Women Inspire 19th Century Feminists." *National NOW Times*. National Organization for Women. http://www.now.org/nnt/summer-99/iroquois.html.

289 Weber, Tim, Business editor. "Why companies need female managers. *BBC News* website. Saturday 26 January, 2008.

290 Schlain, Leonard. 1998. *The Alphabet and the Goddess*. New York: Penquin Group. P 432. Schlain also inspired my summaries of history

from the review of Taoism, Buddhism and Christianity to the shapers of Christianity.

[291] Schlain. *The Alphabet and the Goddess*.

[292] O'Brien, Barbara. *"Buddhism and Sexism: Can there be Buddhist Gender Equality?"* About.com Guide.

[293] Schlain. *The Alphabet and the Goddess*.

[294] Ibid.

[295] Spector IP, Carey MP. Incidence and prevalence of the sexual dysfunctions: A critical review of the empirical literature. *Arch. Sex. Behav.* 1990;19(4):389−408.

[296] Chiechi LM, Granieri M, Lobascio A, Ferreri R, Loizzi P. Sexuality in the climacterium. Clin. Exp. Obstet. *Gynecol.* 1997; 24:158−159.

[297] Bhui K, Herriot P, Dein S, Watson JP. Asians presenting to a sex and marital therapy clinic. *Int. J. Soc. Psychiatry.* 1994; 40:194−204. and Jindal UN, Dhall GI. Psychosexual problems of infertile women in India. *Int J Fertil.* 1990; 35:222−225.

[298] Mellaart, James. Excavation at Hacilar. 249. And Interview with Professor Jean-Phillippe Rigard. National Geographic. 448. Both as found in Schlain, Leonard. *The Alphabet and the Goddess*. 34-6.

[299] Patricia Rosof p.12. 1985. *Family History*. New York: Haworth Press.

[300] Biot Report #595: February 22, 2009. "Catalhoyuk: Discovery of Massive 9000-Year Old Neolithic Settlement in Anatolia." Suburban Emergency Management Project online.

[301] Ibid.

[302] Taylor, Henry Osborn. *The Medieval Mind: a History of the Development of Thought and Emotion in the Middle Ages*, Fourth Edition, Vol. 2. 8.

[303] Baring, Anne and Cashford, Jules. *The Myth of the Goddess: Evolution of an Image*. 551.

[304] Symonds, J.A. *Studies of Greek Poets*. 73.

[305] Felder, Deborah G. 2003. *A Century of Women: The Most Influential Events in Twentieth-Century Women's History*. US: Kensington Publishing Corporation.

[306] Davis, W. V. "Egyptian Hieroglyphics." Reading the Past. 81.

[307] Shlain. *The Alphabet and the Goddess*. 54.

[308] Gardner, Alan Sir. *Egypt of the Pharaohs*. Oxford: Oxford Press, 1961. 91.

[309] Seawright, Caroline. April 9, 2001. "Ancient Egyptian Sexuality."

Ancient Art and Antiquities and Ethnographica. BC Galleries online.
[310] Melchizedek, Drunvalo. 2000. *The Ancient Secret of the Flower of Life, Volume II*. Flagstaff, Arizona: Clear Light Trust. As seen in Drunvalo. "Ancient Egyptian Sexual Ankhing. The Spirit of Ma'at, Vol 1 No. 9 online. www.spiritofmatt.com/archive/apr1/prns/ankhing.htm.

[311] Chorn, Norman. "Is good leadership a feminine thing?" October 24, 2011. Blog: Future Strategy, Living Organization, Organizational Design.

[312] Applewhite, Ashton. 1997. *Cutting Loose: Why Women Who End Their Marriages Do So Well*. New York: HarperCollins.

[313] Smith, T. W., Uchino, B. N., Berg, C. A., Florsheim, P., Pearce, G., Hawkins, M., et al. (2007). 'Hostile personality traits and coronary artery calcification in middle-aged and older married couples: Different effects for self reports versus spouse ratings. *Psychosomatic Medicine*, 69, 441−448.

[314] Orth-Gomer, K., Wamala, S. P., Horsten, M., Schenck-Gustafsson, K., Schneiderman, N., & Mittleman, M. A. (2000). Marital stress worsens prognosis in women with coronary heart disease: The Stockholm Female Coronary Risk Study. JAMA, 284, 3008−3014.

[315] Laurenceau, J.-P., Barrett, L. F., & Pietromonaco, P. R. (1998). Intimacy as an interpersonal process: The importance of self-disclosure, partner disclosure, and perceived partner responsiveness in interpersonal exchanges. *Journal of Personality and Social Psychology*, 74, 1238−1251.

[316] Eaker, E. D., Sullivan, L. M., Kelly-Hayes, M., D'Agostino, R. B. Sr, & Benjamin, E. J. (2007). Marital status, marital strain, and risk of coronary heart disease or total mortality: The Framingham Offspring Study. *Psychosomatic Medicine*, 69, 509−513.

Index

hopelessness, 23
hormonal cocktail, 14, 23, 111, 147
hormones
    cortisol, 47, 147
    dopamine, 18, 19, 41, 67, 111
    estrogen, 74
  Mullerian Inhibiting Substance, 24, 41
    norepinephrine, 18, 19
    oxytocin, 18, 23, 37, 74, 86, 128–129, 133, 145–146, 196
    prolactin, 74, 170
    puberty and, 23–24
    romantic love and, 18–19
    violence and, 47
hunter-gatherer societies, 37, 66–67, 205
Huston, Ted, 144
Hysteria (film), 126

I
the Ideal Woman, 113
incest, 177
Influence (Dychtwaldm), 166
integrated stories, 175
intellectual accomplishment, 164–166
intercourse, 127
interruptions, intimacy and, 198
intimacy
    brain structures and, 123
    development of, 26–27
    interruptions and, 198
    "in-to-me-see" of, 26
    talk and, 144
intuition, 210
involved fathering, 174
Ionesco, Eugene, 218
Iroquois Indians, 209
irreconcilable differences, 184
Italy, 166
Iztueta, A., 67–68

math proficiency, 122

Mead, Margaret, 42, 204

medial preoptic area, 59

Mellaart, James, 218

men, realistic expectations of
  conflict resolution, 144–154
  fact-driven communication, 137–144
  growth differences, 154–162
  sex as motivation and source of connection, 126–137

Men are from Mars, Women are from Venus (Gray), 30–31

mental functioning, 123

Mer-Ka-Ba breathing, 220

military marriages, 169

Mills Longitudinal Study (1990), 25

mirror-neuron system, 72, 98–99, 145

The Mists of Avalon (film), 219

"mommy track," 204

money. See also finances
  autonomy and assertiveness and, 206
  social dominance and, 52–54
  testosterone and, 86

monkeys, 104. See also chimpanzees; mammals

moral masochists, 190

Morgan, Rachel, 193

mother–child bonding, 74

The Mother-Daughter Book Club, 194

Mullerian Inhibiting Substance (MIS), 24, 41

multiple mates, 60

multitasking, 70

murder, 36, 46–47

The Murderer Next Door (Buss), 46

mutual respect, 161

Myers-Briggs Type Indicator, 139

N

narcissistic personality disorder, 90–93

National Center for Education Statistics, 164

National Opinion Research Center report, 33

negative emotion, 123, 140

neocortex capacity, 107

premature ejaculation, 85
presumption, empathy and, 80–84
pride, relationships and, 130–131
primal influences, 35
procreation, sex and, 219
prolactin, 74, 170
prostitution, 60, 219
psychiatric disorder, predictors of, 104
psychological problems, 217
Psychology Today study, 73
puberty, 24, 29–30

R
race bias, 202
rape, 48, 173
Rath, Tom, 198
Real, Terrence, 31, 125
reciprocity, 182
Regnerus, M., 83
relational closeness, 181–184
relational needs, men's inability to meet, 28
relationships
    brief, 194
    effort required, 113–114
    emotional cues and, 26–27
    empathy and, 75–80
    equality in, 164–166
    gender expectations of, 34
    gender responsibilities for, 31
    high price of, 112
    language and, 37–38
    men's prioritization of, 38–40
    pride, self-respect, and, 130–131
    responsibility for, 66–67
    systemizers and, 102–103
    two-paycheck families and, 142
    work–life balance and, 186
religious teaching, 51–52, 211
    tantric yoga, 217
    Taoism, 211–212

world population decline, 186

Y
Yamaguchi, Tsutomu, 47
yin-yang tradition, 221
Young, J.E., 28

Z
Zak, Paul, 40, 45, 55, 86, 147
Zunshine, Lisa, 73

When Your Relationship Changes

A COMPANION BOOK TO
The Naked Truth About Men

By

Kathryn Foster, Ph.D.
Psychologist

*We have wound our psyches
too tightly around romantic love*

Rivercreek Publishing
Texas
2013

When Your Relationship Changes

From the days of Jane Eyre (when finding a partner was the most important thing women did,) till now, the ability of women to be self sufficient has greatly changed. With financial autonomy comes emotional independence as well, so that we enter into relationships, not because we must, but because we desire them. And if you find yourself without one, you can appreciate the solitude and seek other fulfillments in life.

Chapter I: Relationships Change

"The definition of insanity is doing the same thing over and over again and expecting different results." --Albert Einstein

"As soon as you trust yourself, you will know how to live." —Goethe

Trusting Yourself to Know What You Need

While attending a women's retreat, Suzanne, 42, wondered into the forest, and found herself coming face to face with her fears of leaving her marriage. She lived in uncertainty and hesitation, but, deep down, she knew the relationship was wrong for her. Stepping into silence, outside her daily routine, she met with both her fear and her genuine self.

Feelings provide a channel through which to know yourself. Entrenched in the male thought structure, Suzanne, a partner in a demanding law firm, felt she'd largely lost touch with her feelings, having silenced them for years. But with the possibility of a break up and the subsequent crying, she reawakened to herself and began giving clout to her intuitions again.

Jenny, 50 and married for 25 years, was at the same retreat. Hiking alone, she realized that she needed, not divorce or resolution of a particular conflict, (as though one can neatly be found,) but regular rests from her relationship. Sometimes a few hours, a day, or a week. Just a break, a reprieve. Time apart. We need rest from other things, she thought, from work, from household responsibilities, and even from a vacation.

Specifically, she needed rest from her sense of responsibility for the relationship. She's had many years to experience the difficulties of pairing with a man. She suddenly realized that her years there were an accomplishment and she could be proud of her efforts to make the relationship continue. She wanted an attitudinal rest, and to allow herself to feel a little of that self-pride men so readily access.

Women need reprieve from their relationships.

On the other hand, you may find that if you are deeply honest, you are ready to embrace a new way of life. Moving out of a relationship is often a vital part of moving forward into your evolving self. The favorable circumstances under which you began your relationship have now changed in some way. You seek to harmonize the needs of your surfacing soul-changes with your circumstances. On a deep level, you may know that a different location or life circumstance would nurture you in a way that allows new values or goals to emerge.

Moving out of a relationship is often a vital part of moving forward into your evolving self.

We have made break ups larger than life by making up myths. One myth is that a break up necessarily means ending everything that's good about the relationship (i.e., the support we give each other in morning phone calls.) Another myth is that singleness equals aloneness, or that divorce equals social judgment, or that moving on from judgmental people would be bad. Actually, a break up opens the door for other relationships. In Cutting Loose, Ashton Applewhite interviews fifty women who, after divorce, report they're flourishing. The quality of their lives vastly increased, they experienced a renewed belief in themselves, and their fears of fiscal, personal or relational devastation did not come true.

We have made breaks ups larger than life by making up myths.

How do you know when it's time to break up? You feel soul-deadened as you find it of no use to speak because you will not be heard, when your partner doesn't seek to listen or understand. When you are not known. Words are automatic, unthinking, unfeeling, and mechanical. You want to want to stay but you are saddened by who you have become. You see only obligation in the eyes of your mate. Or his eyes tell you, if you are courageous enough to see it, that the connection has died and cannot be revived.

Listen to your own voice rather than the voice of others who have no way of comprehending the subtleties of the relationship known only to you. Many people are moralistic, offering advice about staying in a marriage when it is simply not for them to say.

Your body may tell you it's time to leave. Our bodies speak to us because they're connected to our right brain and thus, to our feeling selves. Kate is a dancer and tunes into her body where she listens and finds wisdom. Through dance, she realized her relationship felt like a physical handicap, blocking her free movement. Rather than feeding her, it stole from her emotionally and spiritually.

Your body may tell you it's time to leave.

But how detrimental can a broken relationship be? Can a relationship slowly kill you?

Yes, some studies find. Among three hundred unhappily married couples who were deemed free of heart disease, the anger and opposition coming from their marriages were clearly associated with a developing coronary artery calcification severity. Among Swedish women already diagnosed with heart disease, their risk increased almost three times with marital, but not work, stress. But the real clincher comes down to this: Women tend to suppress their feelings with the less empathic, less emotional gender and women pay a very high price for emotional inhibition. Squelching results in a shut down feeling and a sense that the relationship isn't worth much. The risk of mortality for women who self-silence during marital conflicts was four times as high ten years later as women who spoke up. The problem is that many women give up on reasoning or securing understanding from their guy and just plain don't think the fight is worth it. Stifling can kill you.

Women's health is at serious risk in relationships
where they silence their concerns.

Carole reaches out to her husband, James, feeling desperate about growing older while his job is becoming less stable. For a moment, he allows her touch on his hand, but then he freezes, shuts down, and begins criticizing her—why didn't she pick up his dry cleaning yesterday, etc. His boss called this morning: they're cutting his hours again. His body language contradictorily tells her both "come near me" and "go away." She senses his deeply buried fragile side, his need for her nurturance, but then she is met with his desire to crush whoever brings out this vulnerable side in him.

At the beginning of their marriage, she was taken off guard, in fact, shocked by this pushing away. She had thought these moments of tenderness were what marriage was all about. She can't help but know she's in a bind: while he pushes her away, he also holds her responsible for not rescuing him from the torment he feels. Carole has been emotionally exhausted from the push-pull and the poverty of their relating, the thousands of unspoken words, the repressed gestures and feelings. Her natural compassion is met with protests she's never understood and he returns to his self-centered pose.

Unrecognized and squelched, she turns more and more to her girlfriends who are simply there for her. The flow of love she was so willing to offer him was damned up long ago. She hasn't divorced him because she fears he can't take it. She's used to putting him first. Routinely, she monitors her feelings, squelching them when around him. Their relationship supplies no emotional support for her. She cannot safely communicate anything even slightly negative, though they are supposedly partners in finances, home ownership and raising children, because he would experience this as a personal attack on him. He evidently imagines himself as a white knight, so her having any negativity would mean she's accusing him of not doing his job. The degree of alienation that resulted from this blocked communication is bringing on a psychic death in Carole.

Deadness of spirit. An inner kind of dying. The vibrancy of a once hot love is barely burning. Carole's feelings, soul, and even her body tell her the relationship has changed and is ready to end. She has to trust these cues.

Feeling Obliged to Stay

We've been told relationships are supposed to last forever. We don't want to be a bad role model, alienate friends, go against our faith, put ourselves in a bad position financially, or hurt our spouse. We want to be "good."

Sometimes, letting go is not loving less but fearing less.

Sessions:
Memoirs of a Psychotherapist

A novel

℘

KATHRYN FOSTER, PH.D

CHAPTER ONE

Psychotherapy is a naked event. The client is stripped, but so is the therapist. There are no machines, no papers to hide behind. Just two people sitting together. I wondered what a surgeon entering psychotherapy would look like. From my second story office, I glanced down through the trees and the huge window in the foyer below to see Michael Stern stately ascend the stairs. Most of the surgeons I knew believed they had no needs. It was 4:00 on a Friday. I had seen clients since nine and would see two more--this session and one other before my workday would end.

Actually, Dr. Stern wasn't coming for psychotherapy; he was coming to interview me, to see if I was "qualified to help him" since his "problems were unique." Yes, he'd been in therapy before; in fact, he'd had three other therapists. Over the phone, his many questions and formal manner made me feel like a schoolgirl being grilled by a strict father about her whereabouts on Friday night: I was 44 years old; my GPA in graduate school had been a 3.9; no, I didn't feel prejudiced against people who used marijuana and went to exclusive men's clubs even though I'd been a minister at one time.

As he ascended the stairs, I could see his handsomely chiseled face. His posture was too correct, as though he was made of perfectly stacked bricks. His hair, short and combed back, every strand in place, was as black as his suit and starkly opposite his white shirt. I ran my fingers through my brown hair, trying to get curls I usually didn't bother with to line up correctly. Glancing into a mirror I kept on my bookshelf, I saw my mascara was okay, but I reapplied my burgundy lipstick. *Relax.*

Paula, my matronly, overweight office manager greeted him. Though most people, nervous about entering therapy, took to her mothering ways like a thirsty flower to water, her nurturing seemed out of place with Michael. He would have felt more at home with sterile white walls and an abrupt uniform-clad receptionist than in my waiting room filled with photographs, antiques and a cozy cotton couch. I had guessed he also wouldn't appreciate Dumplin', my therapy dog, so Paula, whose own relationship with the Shitzu was tentative, had resigned herself to babysit.

After she had done her thing with insurance papers and signatures, I usually walk out to greet the client, but my legs wouldn't move me past the office door, about 30 feet from the waiting room. Stuck, I saw what I am usually too busy to notice--my diplomas and licenses hanging on the wall--six of them, each framed in gold, matted in tweed.

One proved the state had licensed me as a psychologist. One said I'd earned a Masters in Marriage and Family Therapy and the next, a Ph.D. in Psychology and Counseling. I was certified to treat drug and alcohol addictions and was in good standing with a society for hypnotists. One the psychology board required brazenly stated if you didn't like me, you could call the board and complain.

If I had it my way, I would have placed my grandmother's antique mirror on the wall and forgotten the credentials. In psychotherapy, the only proof clients really want of your expertise is what actually happens between you and them. Michael, however, had wanted to know about each piece of paper hanging on this wall. Psychotherapy, I had imagined, would be hard for him.

It's a holy encounter, meeting another person for the purpose of healing. Clients unwrap their souls and show me the part they do not yet understand. I look, trying to interpret, and, always, as I see them, I see myself. We search together for a special ointment that will heal. We explore ingredients, like an herbologist walking among a multitude of plants, choosing a few to put in her apron.

So often, I remember Dr. Endicott, my old supervisor, saying, the ingredient needed is a rare plant growing inside the client. The discovery that they are the Rainforest for their own cure teaches how powerful we humans are, even in our pain.

My own internal parent told me now to relax and just be myself with Michael. Having grounded myself, I ventured down the hall.

He was movie star good looking--sleek, perfect. His demeanor was cool, as though he had no soul. He was bathed, shaved, properly cologned and probably had no holes in his socks.   He needed holes in his socks, just so he wouldn't be confused about being part of the human race. A naughty side of me fought back the urge to mess up his shiny, black hair.

I preferred people made of warm rubber who could bend with life's troubles and not break. People who fully claimed their humanity, embracing even their worst socks. On the other hand, I had my own problems with perfectionism, and knew if we delved into his, I'd come face to face with mine.

What Women Want....Really!

By

Kathryn Foster, Ph.D.

"Most the time if I hit the bull's eye with a woman,
it's just dumb luck," one guy said.
Well, here's a precision guide.

"The greatest living experience for every
man is his adventure into the woman. The man
embraces in the woman all that is not himself,
and from that one resultant, from that embrace, c
omes every new action."
--D. H. Lawrence

Rivercreek Publishing
Texas
2014

Chapter 1: A woman is endeared to a man who asks her about her feelings.

Women like living in the right hemisphere of the brain, where approximately 412 different feelings have been identified. Women feel more strongly and more often than men do. Men tend to feel neutral, cheerful, angry, or horny. Women feel....well, that could be a very long list.

~~~~~~~~~~~~
Dialoguing is to women
as sex is to men.
~~~~~~~~~~~~

Women feel *their thinking*.

As she talks, her feelings rise. Your own feelings are probably more connected to what you **do** and to your **decisions**. Thus, the old joke. The wife of 25 years asks, "Do you love me?" The husband says, "Of course. Haven't I gone to work every day?" His comment **doesn't register** with her on any deep level: she needs words to understand if he loves her.

> Note: It's unlikely a woman would use tears to manipulate you. It's highly likely her tears flow from deep inside and are real. Women feel deeply.

A woman has *tremendous capacities* for exploring the many emotions she feels. You may feel worn out and frustrated by her emotional marathon. You want her to get to the behavior she's seeking from you. Then you can DO it! But if you irritably say, "Tell me what you want!" she will feel you **don't care enough to actually know her**. Her *real* self is found, she believes, in the expression of her feelings.

So, when she begins talking, soften and relax:

❑ release your jaw, shoulders, hands and other muscles
❑slow your breathing down (this is under your conscious control)
❑ picture that your mind is a serene lake with a smooth surface
❑ tell yourself, "She just wants me to know what she feels. It's ok—I don't have to do anything."
❑ enjoy her relational and holistic feminine mind

~~~~~~~~~~~~~~
A relationship goes dead
when a woman feels her guy
doesn't care enough to
listen to what she feels
~~~~~~~~~~~~~~

Women have special rules that men don't know about. One is that, if she asks you a question, you will ask **the same question** of her.

Women, out of politeness, accommodate men, believing men want to talk about themselves. Therefore, they ask men questions. Answer the question, but then **ask it back**, because she may be the one who really needs to talk.

✔ She says, "How was your day at work?"
✔ After answering, you say, "Tell me about your day."
✔ She says, "Do you think Kevin really meant what he said when he was talking about spying on his wife?"
✔ You say, "I'd like to hear what you think." (You don't have to go to all the work of guessing.)

If a woman asks you what you think and you give your opinion but don't ask for hers, it does not feel reciprocal and may be taken to mean that you don't respect or care to know her opinion. This can be a slight that builds and over time causes the woman to feel uncared for.

Making Disclosures of Your Own

It's believed that women don't fall in love with a man unless he reveals his need for her.

Your strength makes her initially interested, but your revealing your vulnerabilities to her will cause her to commit.

A man can use his penis as a metaphor for who he is. Sometimes he is hard, ready for action, assertive, and sometimes he is soft, vulnerable, and empty. He must embrace that he is changeable and that is okay. A woman won't be happy unless he shows her everything—the hard and the soft sides of his psyche.

~~~~~~~~~~~~
Your penis is a metaphor for life
~~~~~~~~~~~~

That said, it is unappealing when a man becomes sappy and drippy with feeling sorry for himself. If he "for the sake of honesty," uses no discernment in revealing all his emotions, it is unattractive. Constant complaining about your job, for instance, feels heavy to a woman. (She doesn't just "listen," she gets **inside** your feelings and **experiences** them.)

■ Note to the "silent type" man: stretch, and **say more than "fine,"** when a woman, seeking connection, asks about your day. Try disclosing more personal information, use more tones in your voice so you express a broader emotional range, avoiding sounding monotone. Talk about your plans or dreams, your feelings and opinions.

Made in the USA
Charleston, SC
04 February 2015